Learning to Live with Crime

Learning to Live with Crime

American Crime Narrative in the
Neoconservative Turn

Christopher P. Wilson

THE OHIO STATE UNIVERSITY PRESS / COLUMBUS

Copyright © 2010 by The Ohio State University.
All rights reserved.

Library of Congress Cataloging-in-Publication Data

Wilson, Christopher P. (Christopher Pierce), 1952–
 Learning to live with crime : American crime narrative in the neoconservative turn / Christopher P. Wilson.
   p. cm.
 Includes bibliographical references and index.
 ISBN 978-0-8142-1137-3 (cloth)—ISBN 978-0-8142-9236-5 (cd-rom)
 1. True crime stories—United States—History and criticism. 2. Crime in literature. 3. Criminal investigation in literature. 4. Crime on television. I. Title.
 PN56.C7W55 2010
 810.9'3556—dc22
                    2010012826

This book is available in the following editions:
Cloth (ISBN 978-0-8142-1137-3)
CD-ROM (ISBN 978-0-8142-9236-5)
Paper (ISBN: 978-0-8142-5764-7)
Cover design by Laurence J. Nozik
Text design by Juliet Williams
Type set in Adobe Sabon

Contents

Acknowledgments		vii
Introduction		1
Chapter 1	Getting Wise(guys): The Witness Protection Narrative	21
Chapter 2	The Box in the Box: Putting Interrogation in Prime Time	49
Chapter 3	The Time of the Crime: Cold Case Squads and Neoconservative Social Memory	77
Chapter 4	Risk Management: Frank Abagnale Jr. and the Shadowing of Pleasure	98
Chapter 5	"Doing Time": Keepers, Brothers, and the Prison Exposé	123
Epilogue	Public Secrets	153
Notes		165
Index		195

Acknowledgments

Although book projects always have many origin points, the central arguments of this one first took shape in the classroom, in an interdisciplinary course entitled "Crime Stories" that I taught from the mid-1990s to 2007. My greatest debt is to the students who have enrolled in that course over the years. Their curiosity, enthusiasm, and insight have sustained and inspired me.

Initial planning for that course, in fact, was supported by an internal teaching grant from my home institution, Boston College. In the years that followed, I also received a Boston College Faculty Fellowship (many thanks to Joe Quinn and Mary Crane); support for an undergraduate research assistantship (undertaken by the endlessly capable Nicole Wong); and then subvention going to press (thanks to Vice Provost Kevin Bedell and Dean David Quigley). At B.C., I have benefitted from the expertise and support of many colleagues. At the head of that list should go Jim Smith and Carlo Rotella, who re-righted the ship on more than one occasion with their clarity, candor, and friendship. Min Song read a draft of my Introduction in the early going; I am repeatedly amazed by Min's seriousness and range. Paul Lewis has brought his gifts of humor, emotional support, and intelligence to my cause so many times I have lost count. Laura Tanner and James Krasner offered wonderful commentary on an earlier version of chapter 2; Lad Tobin has continuously shared with me his love of literary nonfiction; Nirmal Trivedi sustained my passion for this project by adding his own. Thanks also to the extraordinary assistance of the research staff of Boston College's library system, especially

Brendan Rapple and Anne Kenny. From other friends and colleagues, I have received support, both tangible and intangible, for which I am very grateful. Thanks to James Bernauer, S.J., Patrick Byrne, Bob Chibka, Paul Doherty, Rhonda Frederick, Candace Hetzner, Robin Lydenberg, Kevin Newmark, Brendan Rapple, Jamin Rowan, Robert Stanton, Beth Wallace, Jim Wallace, Matthew Watson, Judith Wilt, and Cynthia Young.

Topics in this book have also generated discussions, no less helpful to me, from afar. Sean McCann first prompted me to think about the relationship between crime and the state; Lee Bernstein weighed in, invaluably, on an early prospectus; Tom Ferraro shared his enthusiasm for directions in my work that began, in part, by thinking about Italian Americans. I could also not have imagined more professional guidance than that which I received from the staff, and the anonymous outside readers, of The Ohio State University Press; thanks especially to Maggie Diehl and Sandy Crooms. For scholarly assistance and general good will I must also thank Christine Bold, Greg Conti, Peter Doyle, Sean Patrick Griffin, Gene Newman, Nicole Rafter, Stuart Scheingold, Christophe den Tandt, and my dear Uncle George. Like so many, I was saddened by the passing of Emory Elliott in the spring of 2009. Emory became my faculty advisor during my senior year as an undergraduate; in those days, for the first of many times, I benefited from the example of his unpretentious wisdom and scholarship. Every time I find myself climbing out on some unsupported limb, I see his eyes dancing.

The John Fitzgerald Kennedy Presidential Library and Museum at the University of Massachusetts-Boston kindly allowed me access (reflected in chapter 1) to Joseph Valachi's manuscript and to correspondence in the Library's Peter Maas Collection. I have presented portions of this book at several venues: thanks to the joint colloquium on Irish and American Studies at B.C., particularly Kevin Kenny and (again) David Quigley; to the American Studies Summer Institute at the University of Massachusetts-Boston (thank you, Judy Smith and Nina Tisch); and to the "Crime Cultures" Symposium hosted by the University of Portsmouth, in the UK. Thanks must go to Bran Nichol and his fellow organizers of that Symposium, who offered comments on a version of chapter 4 that will appear in the volume *Crime Cultures: Figuring Criminality in Literature and Film* (London and New York: Continuum), edited by Bran Nicol, Patricia Pulham, and Eugene McNulty. The following publishers and institutions have also allowed me to reprint portions of *Learning to Live with Crime* from their journals: Springer, from "'Where's Whitey?' Ethnic Criminality and the Problem of the Informant," *Crime, Law, and Social Change*

(March 2005): 175–98; Duke University Press, from "Undercover: White Ethnicity and Police Exposé in the 1970s," *American Literature* 77 (June 2005): 349–77; and the University of Albany School of Criminal Justice, from "'Let's Work out the Details:' Putting Interrogation in Prime Time," *Journal of Criminal Justice and Popular Culture* 12 (Spring 2005): 47–64. Selections from "The Time of the Crime: Cold Case Squads and American Social Memory," *Prospects: An Annual of American Cultural Studies* 28 (2004): 497–518, are reprinted with the permission of Cambridge University Press.

My wife Greer and my daughter Jesse have sustained this project in countless ways. They have also had the extra burden of learning to live with me. I hope they know they are the joys of life itself.

Introduction

> Much of our crime problem is rooted in the structure of American society and culture. However, knowing this does not provide much help in formulating a realistic crime policy. A democratic crime policy, relying as it does on the lawful use of force modified by discretion, can neither alter the social structure nor reform criminals. Most of what it *can* do well is very traditional and unexciting. It can defend social tranquility and protect citizens by deterring crime, preventing crime, and apprehending offenders. It can restrain for some time offenders who are likely to repeat their transgressions. No doubt, when these functions are not performed well, our crime problem is much worse. But criminal activity is likely to remain relatively high in the United States in the foreseeable future, regardless of the wisdom of crime policy.
> —Robert P. Rhodes, *The Insoluble Problems of Crime* (1977)

> "There is no condition one adjusts to so quickly as a state of war."
> —A character in Alice Sebold's *The Lovely Bones* (2002)

I.

This is an interdisciplinary study of the contemporary war on crime, and how that war has made its way into cultural representation and public consciousness. In particular, it is about the real-world tactics of this campaign—strategies that, surprisingly, have not often occupied much space in our cultural and literary criticism. Over the last three decades we've seen an explosion of critical interest in crime narratives of all kinds: superb examinations of sensational serial killer stories, of fictional Godfathers and real *Sopranos* watchers, of noir and neo-noir private detectives. And yet, despite these scholarly investigations, what is striking is how comparatively infrequently critical attention has been paid to representations of the less sensational dimensions of the war on crime. With our eye on the fears and phantoms of our "culture of crime," we pay relatively less attention to writing that wrestles with what is happening in our police interrogation rooms, our precinct houses, or even our prisons.

This subject is, nevertheless, a battlefield with many fronts. For example, what happens when a journalist from *New York* magazine approaches the campaign against organized crime not through the romantic depiction of Godfathers but through a low-level, workaday mechanic who informs on his mob? Why is it that interrogation scenes became central to some prime-time police melodramas in the 1990s—and what role did everyday police practices have in shaping those scenes? What is behind the recent fascination with cold case homicides—murder cases reopened years and even decades after their occurrence—to the point that such cases populate everything from American prime time to elite magazines like *The New Yorker*? And more importantly, what do these different trends have in common, and what do they tell us about the larger contours of political authority and consent in our era? About how recent changes in criminal justice and law enforcement have affected core American ideas about citizenship, criminal accountability, and state authority?

My approach to these questions is historical, and my governing argument is easily stated. By focusing largely on political rhetoric, partisan battles, and legislative action, most studies of the war on crime point to a generalized climate of fear created by a moralistic, conservative mood swing in American politics and society. I argue, however, that this emphasis has largely caused us to overlook more continuous developments in the "micropolitics" of law enforcement that often worked beneath the radar of the superheated and often polarized public debate. By referring to the "micropolitical," I mean to identify a series of subtle changes in on-the-ground law enforcement tactics and criminal justice methods—the tools police and others use in everyday crime control—that worked not to implement moral or classically conservative approaches at all. Rather, as my title suggests, these strategies reflected the desire to *accommodate* the justice system to what was assumed to be crime's pervasiveness and inevitability. On the ground, the idea was therefore not simply to fight crime, but to manage its perpetual risks to citizens, to incorporate its knowledge through intelligence gathering, and even, at its worst, to mimic crime's own operations. In this light, the familiar conservative rhetoric of moral uprightness, personal responsibility, and zero tolerance was more like a cover story, shielding more pragmatic practices that altered everyday procedures on the street, in police stations, in courtrooms, and elsewhere. In turn, recent crime narratives suggest, these tactics were often aimed at a remodeling of public consent. Time and again, citizens were directed to see crime not as accessible to broad-scale state solutions but as a risk of modern living. In a mournful phrase that has resonated throughout recent decades, citizens have been directed to "learn to live" with crime.[1]

The traces of this crucial refashioning of consent can be found in how this war entered into the realm of crime writing. Because new crime-fighting tactics fundamentally reshaped the flow of information around criminal justice, they inevitably altered the business of storytelling as well. Thus, my title *Learning to Live with Crime* also refers to a range of adjustments in those writing practices: how writers came to terms with the new prominence of criminal informants in combating organized crime; how the retooling of deception in police interrogations set the stage for TV series like *NYPD Blue*; how a revived rationale for prisons changed what exposés could or could not reveal about them. Many of the stories I discuss have certainly grabbed prime-time audiences or sensational headlines. Yet many of these same stories originated in the everyday realities of police tactics, in the smaller-scale practices through which, as Jonathan Simon has so eloquently argued, crime intersects with matters of governance.[2] It is at this level where we see that small adjustments in policing or prosecution or punishment achieve what might be called a "specific gravity," an importance out of proportion to their seemingly local or instrumental status.[3] We must turn our eye toward such institutional practices and their deceptively mundane outcomes. This is not a book, then, that travels along the more recent paths of literary and cultural criticism. It is inspired, instead, by the lamentable twist that the last forty years have put upon the old Birmingham School maxim: that much of the most fundamental work of culture and power happens at the level of the everyday and the ordinary.[4]

II.

Many readers are already familiar with the general history of the recent war on crime. Starting in the mid-1960s, the story goes, American politicians responded to public concerns about ever-expanding street and drug disorder by ratcheting up a series of measures designed to "get tough" on crime: the expansion of police powers; the increasing of crime penalties (eventually, the creation of mandatory-minimum sentences and "three-strikes" provisions); and the funding of the unprecedented growth of our prison system. Over these decades, the war on crime would become the linchpin of a broader, moralistic, conservative backlash in American politics and society. Advocates of this campaign spoke of the need for "zero tolerance"—by which they meant, variously, the need for moral rectitude from police and community leaders; the need to vigorously enforce laws and community standards against even petty crimes and antisocial behavior; and the need to eliminate or constrain judicial discretion, to allow for tougher sentencing. Most historical studies connect the ever-more fearful tone of media in this period to this general climate of conservative reaction. Conversely, images of police permeated popular culture: in crime news, in prime-time melodrama, in True Crime exposés and in new phenomena like "cop TV."

With good reason, historians, criminologists, and media critics have commonly described the war on crime as part of a broader American political disenchantment with liberal, root-cause approaches to social problems.[5] Following the civil unrest of the 1960s, as Stuart Scheingold, Frank Weed, Michael Flamm, and others have shown so well, a reaction arose against the perceived failures of the Great Society. There was a widespread public disaffection with liberal solutions, a disenchantment fueled by civil conflict, racial disorder, and police riots. Citizens came to distrust both government intrusion generally and the financial burdens its programs often entailed. Feeding off the rising causes of tax revolt, economic deregulation, and welfare reform, the call for "law and order" reshaped much of the American approach to crime. The concern over crime contributed, for instance, to the Supreme Court's loosening of controls on police conduct; to erosions in protections against preventive bail (bail too high for a defendant to possibly pay); to the expansion of legal rationales for probable cause, like the "totality of circumstances" test for police misconduct (e.g., *Illinois v. Gates*, 1983); to the emergent practice of criminal profiling, first tried in airport security in 1969, and to nab drug couriers in 1974. Meanwhile, the defunding of the safety net, along with the use of federal block grants, often channeled law-and-order money to states and to citizen's initiatives and victims' rights groups. This strategy led to several states passing victims' rights bills and to national legislation like the Reagan-sponsored Federal Victims of Crime Act (VOCA) of 1984, which established compensation funds for crime victims, partly from fees collected from criminals.[6] Neoliberals like Bill Clinton or Mario Cuomo quickly accommodated themselves to the new climate by supporting, variously, the death penalty, mandatory drug sentences, and prison expansion. By the passage of Clinton's Violent Crime Control and Law Enforcement

Act in 1994, as Samuel Walker summarizes the standard view, "for all practical purposes the traditional liberal-conservative dichotomy of criminal justice policy" had all but "disappeared."[7]

These changes were especially apparent in metropolitan police departments. The day was dominated by what was characterized as "back to basics," order-maintenance policing: the idea, made famous in James Q. Wilson and George L. Kelling's "Broken Windows" essay (1977), that police could work to restore the informal social control of neighborhoods by encouraging their cooperation and vigilance. Whereas earlier police tactics had stressed a rapid response to citizen requests, the new philosophy of "community policing" emphasized beat patrol again. It also called upon the responsibility of citizens themselves to order their neighborhoods and to tacitly accept extra-legal assertions of force by police.[8] In the 1990s, as I discuss in my second and third chapters, an aggressive crime-busting approach was reinvigorated by the arrival of computer-assisted crime analysis, often through CompStat, a management tool that used Geographic Information Systems software to chart outbreaks of crime and disorder. Police now used teams of managers and officers to literally map not only major crimes but also what became known as "quality of life" disruptions—thereby, supposedly, to better direct crime-fighting resources. Private security, meanwhile, also experienced unprecedented growth in these decades, in part *because* public officials looked for partners in policing the everyday.

To be sure, not all of these experiments or philosophies reflected an American consensus; nor did they always put U.S. law enforcement on the same page. But as "law and order" became what Malcolm Feeley rightly calls a "master theme" (125) of political debate in these decades, crime control now became described (along with national defense) as the one area of the budget where spending could not be sacrificed. By the turn of the twenty-first century, combating crime had become fully entrenched in American life. Summarizing the views of his frequent coauthor Simon, Feeley describes the new shape of the argument taking hold:

> ... as the salience of other social policies recedes, crime control takes not only a larger share of the public pie, it also takes on greater public salience ... concern with crime permeates all walks of public life. ... If crime control is a core function of government and if crime is a major social problem, it must be pursued everywhere: schools must be safe to the point that they are turned into custodial institutions; welfare must be so averse to fraud that recipients should be treated as potential criminal

> suspects; drugs are so ubiquitous and so closely connected with crime that mandatory drug tests should be expanded indefinitely; the public square must be so safe that it is relocated into the enclosed (and privately owned) shopping mall. . . . Crime policy is the one area government cannot completely cede. If there is one area where government must act, it is maintaining law and order. . . . Thus it is not surprising to find other policies defining themselves and being redefined in terms of criminal justice goals. (125)

Politicians and polemicists alike repeatedly counseled the public to accept limits on the state's authority and to understand that enduring solutions to crime's expansion were unlikely. Crime and disorder, they reasoned, were inevitable features of modern life.

And finally, media criticism on the social construction of crime generally follows suit from this story of political disenchantment and conservative backlash. As Robert Reiner has observed, this body of criticism (on both sides of the Atlantic) often tells a strikingly similar, if dismal, story. Studies have repeatedly shown that the media's representation of the crime rate, and thus public fears, accelerate far beyond crime's actual occurrence; that the media is enamored with violence and street disorder at the expense of property and white-collar crime; and that it commonly sides with innocent victims, colors its criminals with little regard to statistical accuracy, and demonizes young criminals into predatory, irrational psychopaths who are threats to middle-class security (rather than to themselves). Police, conversely, overpopulate our airwaves and are drawn up as heroic crime busters even though study after study shows police work is largely regulatory, informal, and administrative in character. Communications theorists and criminologists will debate whether "the media" should be aggregated in such a broad portrait; scholars differ as to how a citizen's everyday experience, or his or her class or race or gender, filters or selects from these images of crime, and how long-lasting their effects are; analysts disagree whether media effects should be called "agenda-setting," "priming," or the "cultivating" of attitudes toward crime.[9] But few would disagree that what once were periodic moral panics about crime now seem more like a permanent state of affairs. Even when crime rates drop or level off, the din in cultural storytelling persists. In the world of fear and moral panic, "crime pays" in prime time, or so the common lament in media studies would have it.[10]

III.

That, in my perhaps too-brutal simplification, is the historical outline concerning the recent war on crime. It is a portrait that stems from a heartfelt concern among many scholars about this war and its devastating costs to our communities. From our studies of the media and contemporary crime, we cannot help but learn how the desire for order feeds upon itself relentlessly, outpacing and sometimes contradicting actual crime rates; how (as Elayne Rapping has shown especially well) the thirst for "reality" programming only reinforces sensational, melodramatic conventions that foreground the victim's suffering at the expense of legal balance; and how the ongoing "C.S.I. effect" may rebound back upon the judgments of juries and absurd public estimates of police effectiveness.[11] Several important studies have also shown us the earlier history of our contemporary war—how it has responded to shifting political winds and how it continues to shape our cultural apprehension (in both senses of the word).[12] There is also, as Stephen Brauer has helpfully pointed out, a long line of criticism in which *Learning to Live with Crime* participates, a tradition that looks beyond describing genre formulae to how social and political attitudes are encoded in stories about crime. Because they often engage so many layers of citizen and state action, crime stories necessarily negotiate readers' ideas about the boundaries between public and private spheres, between local and federal governance, and between popular and elite authority.[13]

However, it also must be said that, despite the work above, the particulars of our recent war on crime too rarely make their way into academic criticism on crime narrative. Instead, with the notable exception of studies on organized crime, scholarship on crime narrative tends to be dominated by more sensational matters: the unpacking of the psychosocial mechanics of public fear in True Crime and serial killer narratives; the decoding of the intricate dimensions of social hierarchy around race, ethnicity, and gender in detective fiction; and resolutely (and rightly) demonstrating the literary sophistication of popular texts too long neglected by traditional critical approaches. Vitally important as these approaches are, the details of the war on crime usually appear as little more as a backdrop, while nonfictional texts—or, more broadly, texts that make a truth claim of the kind I examine in this book—necessarily take a back seat as well. Meanwhile, there is usually little interest, among literary or film critics, in the *inner* or everyday dimensions of crime's management that I focus on here.

Indeed, because of the general scholarly skepticism about the representational fidelity of many forms of crime narrative, there seems to be little interest in getting closer to these everyday matters by crossing disciplinary boundaries. For all the heralding of interdisciplinary work in literary and cultural criticism, there has actually been little consulting of some of the more recent debates in American, British, and Canadian criminology. This is, I think, a real loss. Some of our most provocative scholars—Scheingold, Simon and Feeley, Richard Ericson and Kevin Haggerty, David Garland, Richard A. Leo, Ian Loader, Gary T. Marx, Jerome Skolnick, and Elizabeth Stanko, to name but a few—work quite decisively in a narrative and cultural vein, deciphering what crime and its control asks of us.

More to the point, these scholars have developed a more particularistic and grounded account of the history we think we know. By and large, many of our histories of the war on crime have been driven by what we might call "macropolitical" concerns: by attention to the large-scale redirection of economic, social, and political resources since the mid-1960s, and the policy decisions stemming from a period of right-wing recoil and public fear. On the left, this era has often been characterized as one of structural economic and political crisis, a view shared by many of the scholars I list above.[14] But instead of focusing exclusively on these themes, the thinkers above also take up less-often-recognized topics like the rise of victims' rights, the place of private security, or the role of what are often termed the "actuarial" approaches of "risk management" policing—that is, methods that extrapolate from past crimes to predict future ones, with the aim of reducing the risk of crime rather than simply reacting to it.[15] Instead of capitulating in the face of the mythology of the state's powerlessness, these scholars look at the retooling of the state's reach at the private, local, and everyday level. Instead of thinking dichotomously about the public or private dimensions of crime control, they recognize that the signature of today's crime-control markets is the blurring of such boundaries. I would be perfectly content if the sole effect of my work was simply to make this set of scholarly approaches better known among non-specialist audiences than it apparently is at present.

The central portrait provided by this body of work has been crucial to my own rendering of what I call "the neoconservative turn": a sea change in law enforcement and criminal justice methods, extending over the past four and a half decades, that combines back-to-basics order-management with new technologies of risk and control.[16] I have retained the prefix "neo-" to remind us that, in the strategic semantics of neoconservatives like Wilson and Kelling, William Ker Muir Jr., Robert Rhodes, and others, perhaps the most fundamental claim—as reflected in my epigraph from Rhodes—was not, at first blush, ideological. Rather, it was the separation of structural or "root-cause" explanations from the supposedly practical and more urgent realm of policymaking. Such a separation did not only brush aside liberal environmentalism; it also trumpeted political-science explanation over the sociological and allowed neoconservatives to claim that even if their (old liberal) heart felt otherwise, broad-scale governmental solutions were beyond the current political will of the electorate. The neoconservative turn thus claimed at once to be democratic and yet victim-centered, fatalistically realistic about the intransigence of crime and yet vigilant about social disorder, willfully managerial about "the quality of life" and thus intent upon testable, real-world tactics.[17] To contest such assumptions, in fact, I myself have chosen to respond in kind. That is, rather than tell the familiar story of the war on crime through partisan politics or a generalized public fear, I have chosen to challenge neoconservatism on its own grounds: to start with the micropolitical tactics that this "war" has generated, with those smaller-scale points of contact where law enforcement impacts directly upon its supposed object (criminality), though the citizen is never far from its effects.

Many readers will doubtless associate the term *micropolitical* exclusively with the work of Michel Foucault and his well-known exhortation that we need to study power where it "implants itself and produces its real effects" upon specific and locatable subjects.[18] However, it is more accurate to say that I have been inspired by the broader array of scholarship to which I allude above and to the *range* of small-scale tactics it has described. Again, as Jonathan Simon has articulated especially well, an altered sense of scale has been fundamental to crime management in the waning years of the welfare state. New Deal and Great Society "programs like unemployment insurance, worker's compensation, and the like," Simon writes, "were about harnessing insurance and related technologies to balance the risks produced by industrial society with the very scale that seemed the source of much of that risk." But of late, Simon adds, "[recent] techniques reemphasize the individual as a critical manager of risk, but do so through deliberate steering mechanisms rather than the threats and exhortations of traditional liberalism. . . . The new strategies aim to hold individuals more accountable, or to 'responsibilize' them, as some observers have aptly described it." Central to *this* meaning of the micropolitical is the idea that small-scale, preemptive, and often personalized risk management tactics for fighting crime have insinuated themselves into the larger macroeconomic and political transformation, installing *practices* (instead of simply policies) that might outlive their original political justification. But as a result, these tactics have often flown under the radar of our cultural criticism. Meanwhile, whether in a police interrogation room, in a mall, in airports, or most famously, in Disneyland, they have been integrated into the everyday, designed "to minimize harmful actions (accidental or otherwise) while at the same time minimizing any appearance of coercive social control."[19] These days, as Garland has observed, it seems as if "the threat of crime has become a routine part of modern consciousness, an everyday risk to be assessed and managed in much the same way that we deal with road traffic."[20]

The list of these tactics is, of course, a long one; in the chapters that follow, I will touch briefly on techniques, like warrant squads or airport profiling or DNA testing, that doubtless deserve more extensive attention than I can offer. I have instead selected five tactics that have been especially important to the neoconservative turn: the accelerating use of *criminal informants,* notably but not exclusively in the war on organized crime; the sanctioning of *police deception* in interrogation, a trend less prominent but perhaps more telling than the sensational "third degree" or physical brutality; the arrival of *cold case homicide* squads and related changes regarding victims' rights; the expansion of private security and *personal risk management;* and finally, the neoconservative rationale of prison *incapacitation,* the idea that prison is not only punishment or retribution but a strategy of crime control itself.

To some readers, no doubt, my approach will seem too piecemeal; to others, it may be too neglectful of the ideological and political forces working at the macro level. We are understandably more accustomed to thinking in grander terms of a "prison-industrial complex" than, say, the small space of a visitor's room at a prison; more accustomed to quantifying and aggregating violent episodes on prime-time TV than examining the thresholds of one series' interrogation rooms. Yet my hope is that we gain something, as well, by taking our eye, momentarily, off ideology so as to examine material effects; by moving beyond policy debates to how policies are actually practiced; by reexamining conservative nostalgia and finding, within it, disturbing future-mindedness. I do not mean to displace more macro accounts so much as complement and complicate them. Indeed, I simply mean to follow the lead of those social theorists listed above, who suggest that citizens may actually move among differential institutional orders, though politicians and cultural commentators alike more customarily speak of a singular one.[21]

In the chapters that follow, I move across these different orders. My first, for example, begins with the history of the post-1960s campaign against organized crime as it was shaped by Robert Kennedy's Department of Justice. As I've suggested, this chapter centers on the tool of criminal informants, a tactic most famously exemplified by the recruitment of Mafia informer Joseph Valachi. Here, I argue that by deploying what became officially stamped as Witness Protection, Kennedy's campaign provided several strategic templates for the broader war on crime. I then reexamine the place of informant narratives in the journalistic representation of organized crime, a story culminating with the best-selling crime narrative by Nicholas Pileggi, *Wise Guy: Life in a Mafia Family* (1986), the basis for Martin Scorsese's *GoodFellas* (1990). In chapter 2, I examine the new centrality, in the decades since *Miranda v. Arizona* (1966), of strategic deception in police interrogations, a trend that began to be picked up by prime-time police melodramas in the 1990s. Specifically, I examine the path-breaking creative partnership behind the series *NYPD Blue,* arguing that this partnership (between writer David Milch and NYPD detective Bill Clark) provides a window into the broader post-liberal accommodation with police authority. Chapter 3 describes the recent establishment of cold case homicide squads as they intersect with two other trends of the neoconservative turn: the rising influence of victims' rights and the broadly based trend toward extending legal statutes of limitations. I examine how these squads have entered into popular representation in crime news and in one instance of creative nonfiction, a book by journalist Philip Gourevitch.

Although these first three chapters focus largely on public policing and investigation, a complementary theme emerges at this book's midpoint. In the era of supposedly diminishing resources, metropolitan policing often retooled its relationship to citizens around a public-private model. As I show in chapter 3, this model is one in which a cop, much like a wartime soldier, fulfills his duty by implementing the private will of crime victims. Reciprocally, as the state has ratcheted up its powers, citizens have turned to private security, encouraged to meld public vigilance with their consumer habits. I thus pivot, in chapter 4, to the realm of private risk management, specifically to the case of Frank W. Abagnale Jr., the infamous juvenile "Skywayman," counterfeiter, and identity fraud who became the hero of Stephen Spielberg's *Catch Me If You Can* (2002). Through examining journalist Stan Redding's original book-length depiction of Abagnale's life, I explore the suffusion of consumerist and risk logic into modern security. And my concluding fifth chapter examines the effects of the prison boom, privatization, and secrecy on a recent group of journalistic exposés, measuring how they have come to terms with the neoconservative emphasis on incapacitation and control. I then examine two nonfictional renderings of these themes: an account by undercover journalist Ted Conover, his prize-winning *Newjack* (2000), and the memoir *Brothers and Keepers* (1984), composed by John Edgar Wideman and his brother, a young man cast into prison virtually right at the high (or low) point of the political turn my book describes.

IV.

What else does this grounding in everyday, material tactics of crime control show us? For one thing, it might bring together discussions of crime and its representation in criminology, history, media criticism, and literary studies that are too often talking past each other. Employing a more materialist approach might also help us rethink the largely discursive and ideological frameworks within which so much of contemporary crime criticism works.[22] What is sorely needed, in my view, is a cultural-critical history that connects the actual conditions of fighting crime with the everyday problems of writing about it.

We might also achieve a greater sense of how different dimensions of crime fighting play off one another. No one doubts that street disorder and drugs were the central fronts in the crime war; I hope my own work in the past testifies to that. But to grasp the wider scope of the neoconservative turn, we need to pay better attention to other fronts that fed into and out of this central one. For example, we can rediscover how tactics in fighting the drug war were instituted in the war on organized crime. Or, as I suggest in chapter 3, we can learn how the idea of lengthening statutes of limitations on some crimes (such as Mafia conspiracies) might affect the approach to other crimes (for example, child abuse). We likewise need to understand more clearly the relationship of policing white-collar crimes (such as identity theft) to tactics dealing with street crime; for example, how seeing the citizen as a "consumer" of security reshaped both public policing and private security. Neoconservatives, for example, often advocated the expansion of so-called victimization surveys, an initiative of think tanks in the 1970s. Rather than relying on police departments' official crime rates, many now argued, citizens should be polled for their own memories of having been victims of crime. Not surprisingly, those surveys tended to suggest crime rates were much higher than previously thought; they also suggested there was widespread distrust of the criminal justice system. As a result, they lent themselves easily to the causes of judicial "reform," of raising crime penalties, and redesigning private security around citizen habits and perceptions.[23] In this same way, actuarial risk thinking cut across many different practices: predicting "high crime" areas, organizing police manpower with CompStat, even prison incapacitation, which was aimed at "repeat" offenders especially. Even the tactic of witness protection, emerging formally from the Racketeer Influenced and Corrupt Organizations Act of 1970, had an intuitive actuarial logic behind it. (The best source on any future crime, in other words, would ostensibly be a criminal who had already committed one.)

We also discover that, far from being solely driven by conservative ideology, these tactics could be embraced by crime fighters (and citizens) of different political persuasions. That there has been popular disenchantment with liberal programs and ideology, there can be little doubt. But it is a different matter to argue that U.S. politicians on the Right cultivated that disenchantment into a solidly "conservative" ideological platform—which is largely what Flamm and others have shown—than to say that disenchantment was "conservative" itself, either in origin or in its implementation. Rather, the deeper story of the neoconservative turn, as Scheingold has written, is that crime control came to "transcend the familiar struggle between liberal and conservative policies."[24] To put this another way, public attitudes about crime in this era necessarily came to reflect both ideological preferences and what are sometimes called "pre-political" values: cultural beliefs and attitudes about work, neighborhood, personal responsibility, and even pleasure. On the ground, meanwhile, crime strategies themselves could not so easily be given a political, much less ideological, label.[25] Indeed, the classical notion of a conservative as someone who wants to limit state authority, firm up society's moral foundations, and restore regularity to criminal justice had soon become, in my view, an inapt designation.[26] On the contrary, as writers like Sheldon Wolin argued for some time, "the complexity of the current situation lies in the paradox" that, in recent years, state power has often been *enhanced* by those who "publicly professed an abhorrence of [it]."[27] Many experiments in public-private cooperation in crime control often augment governmental authority while only seeming to supplant it. As scholars such as Stanko, Loader, and Gary T. Marx have shown, the "only you" refrain of neoconservatism often *rhetorically* reinforced the theme of state powerlessness, but in fact extended the reach of surveillance and crime control to new venues.[28]

Even the chronology of the war on crime suggests a need to revisit our impulse to fall back on the story of partisan politics. Interpreters of Robert

Kennedy's pivotal influence on criminal justice, for example, might prefer to emphasize his support of liberal programs that looked to poverty and inequality as root causes of crime, an approach carried on by figures like Ramsey Clark, the attorney general who would be pilloried by Richard Nixon in the presidential campaign of 1968. In these historical renderings, RFK is remembered through his quite pronounced antagonism to crime busters like J. Edgar Hoover.[29] Yet I mean to show that, in retrospect, it would be RFK's campaign against organized crime that proved to have more enduring aftereffects in the larger war. That campaign also installed tactics more continuous with Hoover than we often appreciate. Thus was it not quite so simple as saying that liberals were "late comers" to the crime-control party. As Feeley and Simon have shown, one key liberal institution, the Law Enforcement Assistance Administration (LEAA) of the late 1960s, had been one of the earliest to apply game theory and risk management strategies to the war on crime. It was also liberals who first applied actuarial "predictors" to procedures like administrative bail reform.[30] Likewise, studies by the RAND Corporation Habitual Criminals Program—the name itself is telling—had begun, in the 1970s, to reverse earlier skepticism about the negligible crime-control impact of prison incapacitation.[31] As Joan Didion would report, *both* major parties had, in the election of 1988, seized upon the cause of law enforcement, five years before columnist E. J. Dionne Jr. began talking about "*Kojak* liberals."[32]

Nor, in turn, should we assume out of hand that political backlash led to a restoration of "traditional" police or criminal justice methods. Rather, law enforcement in the neoconservative turn has been far more resilient and adaptive than we often recognize. New powers were created even when neoconservatives claimed to be returning to "basics." Take police interrogation. Rather famously, the *Miranda* ruling of the Warren court became a focal point of conservative ire in this period. As I suggest in chapter 2, however, this furor has often led us to overlook that *Miranda* was itself eroded in this period, and that it had far less effect on police conduct in the first place. Meanwhile, the political hubbub had led us to overlook a more subtle, yet parallel, story: the Supreme Court sanctioning of police deception in interrogation during the same era. A similar byplay between the defense of "basics" and the installation of new tactics underlies chapter 3. Like many observers, I once thought the rise of cold case police squads in the 1990s marked the return of old-style detective work. But here, too, policing has actually been reshaped by modern technological changes; by a very contemporary (I argue, post-industrial) sense of neighborhood and community; and by new legal changes (again, in statutes of limitations) to support, as it were, a policing of history. Meanwhile, the return of what might seem traditional private detective work via personal security—my central topic in chapter 4—reflects a similar contemporary context. As Clifford D. Shearing and Philip C. Stenning show, the resurgence of private security may stem not so much from the vacuum created by the economic crisis of the state as from contemporary alterations in property relationships—notably the rise of mass private properties like malls, gated communities, and the like. Risk management took hold in a new America, not the older one of conservative dreams.[33]

By focusing on themes such as the use of risk or actuarialism, of course, I might seem to be complaining simply that neoconservative theorists were too driven by utilitarian logic. If so, one can imagine a few readers replying, the real problem of the neoconservative turn was that it was not actuarial or utilitarian enough—given, say, the tremendous financial burden of prisons or the dreadful waste of social and human resources crime and its policing bears witness to. But to return to my earlier thoughts about scale and preemption, the point is, rather, that the ethos of risk and management meant that such utilitarianism could be applied quite differentially and with startling arrogance about the futures it assumed.

Take, for example, the following passage from James Q. Wilson's influential *Thinking About Crime* (1983), the book that both included the original rationale for the Broken Windows theory and placed that theory within the broader neoconservative platform of differential sentencing, judicial "speed and certainty," and prison incapacitation. Here, Wilson writes about how to best target frequent offenders for punishment:

> Whenever we are trying to discover a relationship between hard-to-measure factors that operate deep inside a complex social structure, we are well advised not to rely on any single method of analysis and particularly well advised not to rely on statistical studies using aggregate data.... Above all, we should look at what happens to individuals....
>
> Ideally, we would like to know how the probability or severity of a possible punishment will affect the behavior of persons who *might* commit a serious crime. Such persons probably constitute only a small fraction of the total population, but they are an important fraction. Most of us would not commit a serious crime because of the operation of internal controls on our behavior, reinforced by the fear of embarrassment should our misconduct be detected. A few of us may commit serious crimes with only small regard to the risks, unless those risks can be made great and immediate. For example, most men would never dream of killing their

wives, and a few men might kill them (perhaps in an alcoholic rage) unless a police officer were standing right next to them. But for a certain fraction of men, the idea of doing away with their wives is strongly conditioned by their perception of the risks. Wives, and in particular feminist organizations, concede this when they demand, as they have with increasing vigor, the strict enforcement of laws against wife-abuse. . . .

Persons who are "at risk" are those who lack strong, internalized inhibitions against misconduct, who value highly the excitement and thrills of breaking the law, who have a low stake in conformity, who are willing to take greater chances than the rest of us, and who greatly value quick access to ready cash. Such persons tend, disproportionately, to be young males.[34]

Leaving aside the other dimensions of Wilson's folkloric style—which I have discussed elsewhere[35]—one sees many consequences of his rhetorical scaling operation and his metaphorical riffs on risk. Differentiating between "us" and criminals, directly insinuating a personal analogy (dear to the heart of feminists, he claims), Wilson proposes risk management as an avenue into a perpetrator's consciousness, so that "thinking about crime" doubles as our common sense and the calculations of a potential (but actually habitual) criminal. Risk becomes a way to differentiate our own private internal control mechanisms from those individuals we assume do not have any. If this is utilitarianism, it has actually abandoned any genuinely collective (or macro) sense of a greater good in the name of positioning us, his readers, as society itself—and cordoning off the fractional remainder.

I hope that the consequences that flow from *this* illogic will be apparent in what follows. Throughout this book, I mean to cast a skeptical eye on the rhetorical forms, fables, and keywords that define "crime talk" like the passage above. But my larger point would be that the defenders of the war on crime have often been obliged to deny the very practices they have put at such a premium. Despite their claim to preserve democratic order, I also hope to show, these tactics often had drastic results for the disadvantaged, for communities of color, and for "young males" already within the system. This persistent inequality is only made all the more tragic when one considers that the supposed remedy of private security is something only a few can afford. And the plot thickens in other ways. As I have suggested, rather than representing a renewed moral certainty, much less zero tolerance, in many instances my five tactics point to the state's contradictory *emulation* of criminality, its desire to incorporate the criminal's knowledge into its own operations (or, in Foucault's formulation, to turn that knowledge "inside out").[36] These tactics often represent systematic attempts to control and infiltrate criminality, and thereby garner intelligence for a more preemptive approach to security. In this final way, the catchphrase "learning to live with crime" betrays yet another irony of the neoconservative turn: that by applying these micropractices, the post-liberal state shows that it has, in effect, often learned *from* crime—learned from it, in order to supposedly construct a more vigilant public. These are tactics that are therefore both material and ideological, connected to fashioning consent as well as implementing control.

V.

The reader will quickly see that this book also attempts to shift our critical discussion of crime narrative in the direction of exposé, literary nonfiction, and memoir. At the very least, I hope to resurrect a tradition of in-the-trenches journalistic writing that is all too often overlooked in our criticism. Especially when generated in tandem with newspapers or magazines (*New York* magazine, *The New Yorker,* the *Atlantic Monthly*), nonfiction narratives are necessarily bound by conventions and professional norms about truth telling, sourcing, and direct witnessing that open up the inner workings of power and representation in instructive ways. Unpacking those conventions and journalistic methods returns us to an awareness of the material obstacles that working crime writers confront when representing social processes that are often out of view, restricted by legal considerations, or obscured by the vexing silences that accompany policing disorder, committing a crime, or being a crime victim.

Conversely, bringing a sensitivity to narrative form to such nonfiction—to the literary archive writers consult and the interpretive effects created by the array of story styles they choose—helps us understand the power and limitations of the truth claims nonfiction makes. Through such attention to narrative form and technique, we also discover issues about crime and its representations that too often elude us in empirical studies and in the relentless counting, recounting, or debunking of "images" of disorder. Like the novels they often emulate, these nonfiction accounts invite nuance over static constructions, entangle emotions like fear with strains of hope or humor. As Wendy Lesser has so aptly put it, they also draw us into the intellectual and ethical pressure that results "the further we move away from the neatly contrived and the artificially resolvable."[37]

For example, we discover that a criminal's authentic voice is an especially elusive quarry for literary representation; that individual informants are often mistaken for representatives of entire mobs or underworlds; that the creative representation of criminality sometimes involves, out of sheer necessity, inventing forms that are collaborative and "double-voiced" in execution.[38]

However, if works of literary nonfiction are often the centerpiece of my chapters, *Learning to Live with Crime* also discusses everyday news coverage, several television series, a ghost-written autobiography—and even, in my epilogue, a Danish mystery novel. I also explore an eclectic range of issues along the way: for example, why recent crime writers have been returning to "retro" versions of older genres, blending "street" realism on TV with interior melodrama, or making con men look cool and cold cases look like hot ones. Within this range of genres and issues, however, each chapter focuses on the material contact zones between cultural representation and the conditions of its production—in this case, the conditions of contemporary crime management. I mean to ask, at every turn, how a writer's knowledge of disorder and governance is filtered and shaped by the ways that law enforcement gathers up criminality, or the methods by which our legal system judges and punishes it. Literary styles and generic codes within the gangland narrative, or the prison exposé, or the cold case narrative thus often play a pivotal role not just "in-forming" us, but in re-forming the explanation forms that organize social data in the first place.[39] Sometimes this means a writer must apprentice in the knowledge work embedded in a criminal's past or in crime management as such. Sometimes it means brokering relationships between police authorities, cooperating witnesses, and victims. Sometimes it means going undercover.

However, there is also a somewhat deeper layer of exchange at work here. It is hardly news that the process of crime management creates a material scrim through which writers of TV shows, memoirs, and exposés have often first had to pass: rules about whether you can interview an informant, watch an interrogation, or even enter a prison. But criminal justice also presents what we might call "a story scrim" writers must negotiate as well. Storytelling has often been on the crime scene long before any given writer arrives there. That is, there is an intrinsic symbolic and narrative dimension that suffuses crime's accounting in the first place: a moment when an organized crime informant is asked to tell his story; when an interrogation pivots on confession; when a crime victim's memory of pain becomes part of a criminal's future sentence, in a court of law, or in an exposé. In other words, crime-fighting tactics are not merely instrumental practices but communicative, symbolic, and meaning-making expressions from the get-go. Crime managers generate stories about the causes of crime, about a criminal's motivation, or about how the larger war has been waged; they offer constructions of violated neighborhoods, the relationships between past and present, and the remedies citizens must embrace. In many instances, then, a writer's knowledge of crime is invariably joined at the hip with law enforcement reconstruction—or, to cite John Edgar Wideman's allusion, the knowledge of brothers is necessarily bound to that of keepers. As I try to show in chapter 5, for example, prison incarceration had already been rewritten at the level of cultural understanding before Ted Conover or John Edgar Wideman arrived there (by such different routes). That is, prison had been already drafted into the key themes of the neoconservative turn: as my earlier quote from *Thinking About Crime* suggests, prisons were narrated through the language of risk assessment and a "plotting" that cut short the résumé of "young males." Writers' attempts to engage such already-existing stories, embedded even in small-scale tactics, and to re-craft those stories into longer (or, in David Milch's case, serial) narratives, is in many ways the subject of this book.

All this being said, I do not mean to suggest that in the narratives I have selected we will find the full reach and power of American social experiences with crime. Many Americans have direct experience with criminal indictments and police sweeps, with community meetings and plea bargains, with courtrooms and probation systems. Nor do I mean to suggest that media stories impact each of us in the same way, or that more empirical studies of citizen fears, neighborhood victimization, and family trauma are somehow less important than what I do here. Far from it.[40] My own work merely attempts to come to terms with narrative renderings of the dire situations such studies also attempt to grasp. But as Ian Loader has suggested, even the seemingly most empirical measurements of risk, disorder, and personal pain about crime are frequently tied up with rhetorical, symbolic, and narrative constructions that extend beyond the actual crime event itself. Such constructions often provide the frameworks through which we blend actual experience and social knowledge, direct witnessing with rumor, and common knowledge of crime with personal observation. We need to be aware of how experience with crime often comes to us already narrated, and even how those things we call facts are often rhetorically constituted at the very level of their facticity.[41]

How we tell ourselves the story of this neoconservative turn is, therefore, far more than a problem of the political labels we prefer. It is also a matter of how we describe our own accommodations with the tactics

I describe. The very fact that this turn has been marked by a redrawing of fundamental social boundaries—between public and private, criminal and civil justice, neighborhood values and personal responsibility—also suggests that this war has not been waged by tactics somehow beyond our own everyday lives. On the contrary: attending to these crime stories may help us understand how we, as readers and as citizens, have come to live with what otherwise we might find criminal.

1

Getting Wise(guys)
The Witness Protection Narrative

> No matter what anyone claims about being clever or brilliant, there is only one way organized crime can be cracked. Unless someone on the inside talks, you can investigate forever and get nowhere.
> —Sid Feder and Burton B. Turkus, *Murder, Inc.* (1951)

AT THE CLOSE of the twentieth century, few stories about American crime received the attention accorded the scandal of the Boston-based gangster James "Whitey" Bulger. The story emerged from reporting in the local *Boston Globe,* from prosecutions in U.S. District Court—and then, most sensationally, in a series of nonfiction True Crime exposés, led most of all by *Black Mass: The Irish Mob, the FBI, and a Devil's Deal* (2000), by *Globe* reporters Gerard O'Neill and Dick Lehr. *Black Mass* recounted how, starting in the mid-1970s, local FBI agents, principally John J. Connolly, Jr. and John Morris, had enlisted Bulger and his partner Stephen Flemmi in bringing down the local Italian American Mafia. In FBI jargon, Bulger had been brought in as what is called a criminal (or "confidential") informant. And yet, in order to sustain that relationship, Connolly had turned a blind eye to Bulger's role in loan sharking, drug dealing, and even murder. And as was shown in Connolly's racketeering and obstruction of justice conviction in 2002, the agent had both helped Whitey Bulger evade prosecution and given him advance warning of an impending criminal indictment in 1995.[1] This outcome sent shockwaves rolling back through older prosecutions, some of which had been central to the closing down of New England's leading crime families. New Department of Justice (DOJ) guidelines on informants (2001) have even been attributed to aftermath of the Bulger debacle.[2]

The Bulger case certainly made headlines. But it did not have the effect of bringing the history of mob activity together with that of the broader war on crime, a campaign that blossomed over virtually the same span of time as Bulger's mature mob career (1965–95). Instead, the history of organized crime is most commonly treated as a distinct subject of its own, and with its own historical markers, personalities, and legacies.[3] As a result, it is easy to forget that tactical innovations in crime control shuttled from one front to another, often under the sponsorship of some of the same players. In particular, it is clear that informant use, so celebrated in the war on the Mafia, would proliferate across the criminal justice system as the war on street disorder and drugs escalated in the 1970s and 1980s. In such a light, therefore, we can begin to see the pivotal importance of Robert F. Kennedy's earlier campaign against organized crime, notably as its methods have been recently unveiled by key lieutenants such as Ronald Goldfarb or Gerald Shur, the godfather of the Witness Protection Program (or WITSEC).[4] Reexamining RFK's legacy, moreover, can help us understand the connections between fighting the war on crime and some of the fundamental ways that, in journalistic exposés of the Mafia, it came to be represented.

That the use of informants has exploded in the last four and half decades is beyond dispute. Law enforcement representatives and the press, for instance, often presented John Connolly as a "bad apple" or said his failures resulted from his shared "Southie" (South Boston) ethos with Bulger.[5] In fact, as Ralph Ranalli has shown, Connolly's strategy was part of what was called a "top echelon" informant program approved at the highest levels of the FBI.[6] Indeed, as Clare Bond Potter has demonstrated, strategic informant use had defined J. Edgar Hoover's exploitation of the war on celebrity gangsters as far back as the 1930s.[7] Later use, however, dwarfed Hoover's initiative. The Drug Enforcement Administration (DEA), for example, established in 1963 by Richard Nixon, came to manage some 60,000 "cooperating individuals" by the late 1980s. In many federal divisions, new forfeiture and seizure statutes would make ever-greater sums of money available for paying informers. Government agencies were now allowed to share with informants up to 25 percent of seizure assets per case, beneath a cap of a mere $250,000. In a special series on informants for the *Atlanta Constitution*, Mark Curriden showed that search warrant affidavits filed in Atlanta's U.S. District Court in 1989 had used confidential informants 90 percent of the time, up from 60 percent in 1980. By the mid-1990s, the former head of the DEA's Boston and New York offices would admit that one "almost never [made] a case" without using an informant.[8] And if the federal government doubled its payments to informants between 1987 and 1989 to a whopping $63 million, local authorities handed out another $60 million on top of that.[9] In U.S. cities especially, the war on crime's reinvigoration of street policing, the use of random drug sweeps, and the broadening of administrative plea bargains would all contribute to the informant boom.[10] And so, let it be said, would the horrendous expansion of prison populations. Many of the accused or imprisoned would become informers to circumvent the new mandatory sentences imposed for drug-related offenses. A harsh prison sentence thus became the main inducement not to reform, but to inform; as prison populations expanded, so did informing.[11]

The Bulger scandal was therefore not the anomaly many claimed it was. Rather, it was all too characteristic of problems the informant system could create at many levels of the criminal justice system. On the one hand, crime warriors like Rudolph Giuliani—a pivotal figure, on many fronts, in his role as federal prosecutor of organized crime, New York City mayor, and chief sponsor of the "Broken Windows" style of policing—testified to the pivotal importance of the tactic. In 1994, Giuliani insisted that criminal informants, undercover officers, and citizen informers (even, he said, in our schools) were all made necessary in an era when we must learn to live with crime, largely because they sent an important message to the public at large. In a moment when crime permeated everyday living, he said, it was a matter of "whose values we are trying to protect."[12] On the other hand, the use of confidential and criminal sources often produced much-ballyhooed, short-lived victories followed by revelations of police misconduct and corruption. Showing the pervasiveness of the tactic, for instance, the *Boston Globe* reported that in 1988 virtually all of the warrants obtained in Dorchester, Roxbury, and West Roxbury courts by drug unit detectives cited what they called "unnamed" informants. Payments budgeted for informants in these units could run $5,000 to $10,000 for a two-week period. Yet little wonder that internal accounting safeguards had been easily circumvented and made useless.[13] Under such conditions, the Supreme Judicial Court of Massachusetts observed, with no small sarcasm, that the use of one informant—or so the Boston Police claimed in one case, for a dozen warrants for different areas of the city—"portray[ed] an informant with a remarkable—perhaps one should say incredible—range of knowledge." The Court's implication was clear: some confidential informants were little more than the police's literary inventions.[14] On the street, the use of confidential sources went hand-in-hand with a shotgun-style, no-holds-barred approach with, in two infamous Boston cases, disastrous results.[15]

My goal in this chapter is not, however, to rehearse these sorry histories. Nor am I here to debate the tactic's effectiveness in rousting criminals. Rather, I am interested in the relationship between its operational effects and those in the realm of culture. That is, I want to reexamine the institutionalization of this micropolitical tactic—micropolitical because it worked by leveraging the intelligence from individual mobsters into a mechanism of fighting crime in the aggregate—and how its use contributed to a broader narrative recasting of crime, organized and otherwise, in ways we have not fully appreciated. In the cultural moment when Mario Puzo's *The Godfather* (1972) garnered more sensational attention, the effects of the neoconservative turn to lower-ranking informants has had a subtler, but perhaps more enduring, impact. The reason being, as Giuliani's admission suggests, that the narratives stemming from this tactic were some of the first where crime was made to seem a threat to everyday experience—or what, under Robert F. Kennedy's leadership years earlier, had become known as the "American way of life."[16] In the journalistic portraiture of mob practices I discuss here, writers were compelled to scale down that threat, track its everyday footprints, and thereby address the paradox of an especially individualistic cast to criminality: "American" as we are American, corporate as we are corporate, loyal to ethnicities as we both are—and are not.

To get at these connections, I will first explore the general cast of RFK's war on mobsters as it laid the groundwork for the formal establishment of WITSEC.[17] Then, as I've suggested in my Introduction, I will turn to a tradition of in-the-trenches, journalistic depiction of organized crime. I will look closely at two of the books most directly connected to real-world battles with the Mafia: Peter Maas's *The Valachi Papers* (1968), emanating from Joseph Valachi's testimony before the McClellan Committee in 1963; and Nicholas Pileggi's *Wiseguy: Life in a Mafia Family* (1985), recounting the testimony of mobster Henry Hill under Witness Protection.[18] What these narratives would rewrite, of course, was the gangster narrative, whose story arc of "enterprise and success ending in precipitate failure" had been most famously described by film critic Robert Warshow in 1948.[19] These newer exposés hoped to deflate the heroic outlines of what Warshow cast as high tragedy: to write the history of the mob from the bottom up. In Maas's and Pileggi's narratives, an informant in the law enforcement sense of the word became more of an informant in the ethnographic sense: a low-level wise guy whose wisdom provided an inside look into the workaday culture of the mob.

My argument is also that using criminal informants was a rationale borne of pragmatism and expediency, not moral rectitude. And contrary to what we think about the "conservative" drives of the war on crime, such a tactic reflected the growth of state powers rather than their reduction. In fact, despite the public rhetoric of the war on crime—*pace* Giuliani, who knew better—there was something much more labyrinthine than moral straight shooting and a simple defense of "our" values, or ordinary life, at issue. Indeed, by coming clean, organized crime informants often insisted upon their own normalcy yet did so only to bewail the hypocrisy of a state that seemed to have extorted—in their argot, offered "protection"—for their witnessing.

I.

Along with referring to J. Edgar Hoover's campaign against gangster bandits in the mid-1930s, historians generally point to the period from the mid-1950s and 1960s as a critical turning point in the war against organized crime. Again, the tendency of some chroniclers to stress the personal animosity and turf wars between RFK and Hoover disguises the fact that when it came to fighting organized crime a more cohesive program was emerging.[20] As Lee Bernstein has reminded us, the 1957 raid on the so-called Apalachin Conference generated widespread law enforcement alarm about seemingly national alliances arising among what had been thought to be local or regionally oriented mobsters. Meanwhile, our histories commonly point to the seminal work of the so-called Kefauver and McClellan Committees in the U.S. Senate, the latter of which saw RFK working as chief counsel; the expansion of the FBI's "Top Hoodlum" program, which Kennedy would revamp as a "Criminal Intelligence" effort within the Organized Crime and Racketeering Section of the Department of Justice; and, again, the establishment of the Racketeering Influence and Corrupt Organizations provision (RICO) and WITSEC.[21] RFK's tenure as U.S. Attorney General (1961–64), brief as it was, had especially enduring consequences. Whereas Hoover used informants largely as crime-busting leverage against individual "celebrity" gangsters, the emerging tendency Kennedy first signaled was to use informants as part of the reconceptualization of organized crime as a corporate "entity" or enterprise—and one that could be attacked as such: by seizing assets, blocking income flows, and dismantling its organizational structure (including its front operations) from the inside.[22] Informants were used to map this supposedly corporate culture and then help undo it.

This approach, in part, stemmed from transformations within gangsters' groups themselves. In tracing the longer development of what we now call "organized crime" itself, historians and criminologists often begin with its so-called incubation in the neighborhood gangs of the mid- and late nineteenth century. Originally, these criminal street gangs began as local self-defense confederations that, over time, were incorporated into political machines and became more formally run.[23] In urban wards, these gangs had usually overseen vice operations, monopolized small old-world commodities, and run (through intimidation and kickbacks) the hiring and firing of local workers. These patterns persisted within some crime families well into the late twentieth century. Yet nineteenth-century gangs were not always "organized" in the way we often think. Dive into the famous book by New York Chief of Detectives Thomas Byrnes, *Professional Criminals of America* (1886), and one finds chapters ordered by criminal type, but in individual gallery shots only loosely connected to each other. To the extent that a figure like Byrnes pictured the organization of crime at all, his thinking remained noticeably artisanal, treating criminals as something like tradesmen or operatives within a criminal guild. Only the most daring crimes entailed integration of these individual talents. While there is some disagreement about how territorial local *vice* economies really were, wards generally provided the predominant setting for professional, collaborative criminality.[24]

That is, until Prohibition. As the principal trigger to organization in the modern sense, Prohibition led to both a broader metropolitan orientation and to an integrated, even national, system for these criminal enterprises. Prohibition also invited a market orientation and a corporate form. These larger enterprises required covert financing, market control of production and distribution, and legitimate front operations.[25] (Whitey Bulger's predecessor in Boston, Dan Carroll, controlled liquor distribution from a nightclub and managed local prizefighting, one of Bulger's own obsessions.) The turnabout was profound. The tendency of turn-of-the-century muckrakers, like Lincoln Steffens, to read organized crime *through* the political machine, in fact, would quickly seem dated. Before long, profits generated by crime's expansion created more autonomy and thus less dependence on political machines over time.[26]

Moving uptown also meant, as the 1920s would show, headline-grabbing gang warfare, the kind that became so central to the emerging popular image of organized crime. Figures like John Dillinger and Bonnie and Clyde, as Potter has shown, often appeared as romantic bandit heroes, their power interpreted through a folk idiom still resonant in the American countryside.²⁷ But back in the city, the young toughs played by Edward G. Robinson of *Little Caesar* (1930), or James Cagney of *The Public Enemy* (1931), recapitulated this modernizing trajectory from ward to uptown. As famously described by Warshow, "for the gangster there is only the city," a closed space upon which he must impose his will. The modern gangster narrative modeled a linear story of ethnic ward apprenticeship that began with petty thuggery and escalated into a wider corporate competition. In this classic form, the gangster epitomized a "pure sadism" for which death was the only final fate possible. Often hinging on the loss of boyhood friendships or betrayals by older-style criminal *padrones* or ward figures, these narratives oscillated, Warshow said, between moments of "irrational brutality" and startlingly "rational enterprise." They moved through an arc of high tragedy that returned to a bloody finale in the gangster's original milieu of the streets. These narratives also offered satirical parallels to the American mainstream even as they seemed to repudiate its charms. In *The Public Enemy,* Cagney's gangster is counterpointed, and not at all unfavorably, to a brother who fights *his* war in Europe instead of the streets, or to the college boys who lose their nightclub table, and their dates, when these celebrity gangsters show up. Robinson's Rico is, arguably, more loyal than the uptown chum who betrays him to the police.²⁸

Following the 1930s, key journalists would also begin to accentuate the modernizing and Americanizing sides of mob activity. They began to highlight the role of national syndicates in diminishing local, ward-based, ethnic loyalties.²⁹ Although many scholars now dispute the precision of the term, "Americanization" played a leading role in these popular accounts, as it would in Daniel Bell's famous formulation about criminal ethnic succession in the early 1950s.³⁰ Relying on testimonials from second-generation mob figures who exemplified, supposedly, their cohort's assimilation, this Americanization theme went hand in hand with what Vincenzo Ruggierio has aptly called a "Fordist" conception of organized crime.³¹ Prosecutor Burton B. Turkus and journalist Sid Feder, for instance, generated the famous *Murder, Inc.* trademark in 1951 and used their term "the syndicate" to refer to a "single National Syndicate . . . bound by a government of its own." Though they said the structure was too decentralized to be strictly like a corporation, they also said it was run just as tightly "as General Motors or the national Baseball League" (425). As we shall see, Peter Maas's principal goal, likewise, would be to chronicle the Americanization of the mob, largely through the purging of Sicilian elements beginning with the so-called Castellammarese War of the early 1930s.³² Just as Maas would try to downplay Mafia rituals and instead show how lieutenant positions were actually auctioned for cash, Gay Talese's *Honor Thy Father* (1971) would show Bill Bonanno, the son of a Mafia Don, growing up not in the wards of New York but in Tucson, going to the University of Arizona and majoring in agricultural engineering.[33]

In all, then, it might seem that this evolution from the urban ward to the corporate form was a natural, even inevitable, trajectory for representations of organized crime. However, we need to examine carefully the relationship between the tactical operations of law enforcement and this dominant rhetorical casting; otherwise, we will have little way to understand how these Americanizing and corporate themes were coordinated with their apparently opposite claim, the idea that organized crime was akin to an alien or Communist conspiracy. As Bernstein reminds us, Kennedy often preferred to liken organized crime to the Red Menace, just as Turkus before him had called organized crime "just as real as any fifth column of totalitarianism."[34] To these thinkers, organized crime needed to be approached not only for sensational crimes—Henry Hill's Lufthansa robbery, after all, was quite a heist—but because, like other political "enemies," the Mafia infiltrated the everyday. The journalistic emphasis on a corporate assimilation by mobsters was not, then, a simple reflection of the unmediated testimony that informants lent to writers and law enforcement officials alike. Rather, it was Robert Kennedy's war on the Mafia that gave this dual cultural likeness—corporate and yet infiltrating—an operational meaning.

To put this point another way, we have to recognize that the assumption that organized crime was embedded in the national life was a keystone of Kennedy's tactical approach. On the ground, Kennedy thought that organized crime's alien conspiracy was a threat precisely because it mimicked developments in the mainstream economy, especially the cornering of markets and workplaces (in the case of corrupt labor unions). (Hence, as well, the real meaning of Turkus's use of the older labor terms, "syndicate," or "national combination" [68]). To Kennedy, that is, organized crime was a form of monopolist predation and combination, a conspiracy that simultaneously threatened the American free enterprise system and poisoned politics, often at the state or city level. And its criminal integration was a sign of its corporate practices. Gambling, for example, could no longer be seen as a victimless or merely local vice crime; rather, to Kennedy, as for Thomas Dewey before him, gambling receipts bankrolled larger interstate operations or funneled money to respectable fronts, and thus had to be challenged as an asset-producing stream.[35] In other words, in an involution common to the cold war, the alien threat was both an enemy within and a conspiracy that was *too like* the system Kennedy vowed to defend. On the ground level, therefore, a nearly permanent tension was now installed between the bureaucratic, corporate, and ethnic labels attached to organized crime and the often-*dis*organized, decentralized, or even impulsive illegal activities it actually engaged in.[36] In a post-liberal path suggesting the ideological bridge between Kennedy's war and that of the neoconservatism to come, fighting crime became a way to protect the free enterprise system.

The state, however, was no sideline observer; rather, it was mobilized in the cause. The Mafia's putatively un-American activities were now addressed as if they were quintessentially national byproducts: mobs were corporate organizations whose assets could be attached, monopolistic practices broken up, and so forth. Though Kennedy and his lieutenants would, in public, scandalize secret oaths and the mob code of *omerta*— ethnic correlatives, they felt, to Communist Party pledges—in truth the Department of Justice began increasingly to solicit private bargains and, where needed, to play legal hardball with insiders. This included, as Kennedy's special prosecutor Ronald Goldfarb has recalled, more aggressive use of conspiracy and deportation laws; extending immunity provisions from obscure corners of the law, in order to leverage testimony from cooperating witnesses; and creating conditions where false statements (or, more ominously, silence) could constitute criminal acts in themselves.[37] It was as if the state had become a dispenser of *dis*loyalty oaths resulting from all sorts of financial and prosecutorial pressure.

Meanwhile, the government adopted the idea of conspiracy as much more than a metaphor. In the long run, the state made association itself within these syndicates into a crime. The key transformation to be effected by RICO, in fact, was less its focus on specific crimes; as William Geary has pointed out, prior government commissions had actually discovered few gaps in the criminal code as such. RICO helped to make membership in an organized crime cell itself the predicate for prosecution.[38] Whatever the legal legitimacy of these tactics, there is little doubt that they resuscitated a Hooveresque climate where naming names could lead to additional investigative leads; in turn, the threat of prosecution for membership in a criminal conspiracy allowed a prosecutor to leverage testimony. And, in turn, each bargain could be turned into another, generating a pattern where the criminal informant placed an ever-greater stake in the bargain he had struck, right down to the specifics of his identity. The protection of witnesses, therefore, was also not so much revived as reinvented. Criminals had long ratted on associates to cut a deal with prosecutors or police or the FBI. But under the leadership of Kennedy, and subsequently his former lieutenant Gerald Shur, the Federal Witness Protection Program—later reinforced, with absurd latitude, under RICO as "the care and protection of witnesses in whatever manner is deemed most useful"—took the state even more directly into the everyday lives of mobsters. That is, a criminal had to be considered both as a member of a conspiracy and as an employee—with a career plan, in some cases a family, and more.

Under Shur's three-decades-long tenure, well past Kennedy's personal campaign against Hoffa, WITSEC came to be used as more than the traditional carrot-and-stick device. Rather, it turned to enticing criminals with the promise of a newly constructed identity freed from their past and from possible vengeance by past associates. Ironically, the modernization of organized crime had itself underwritten this expansion: as it had itself extended beyond its ward bases, simple local guarding of witnesses could no longer be viable. (For a brief period, the use of protected witnesses had also offset the uncertain reception of wiretapping in U.S. courts and, in the case of Lyndon Johnson, presidential resistance.) In a pattern that would be repeated many times, the rapid rise in criminal applicants to this program also meant that it was often overwhelmed by the very bargains it had cut. To create new identities for its witnesses, as well, the government itself began to engage in forgery and other forms of identity fraud; before long, residences and mistresses and new businesses were being bankrolled, and career criminals were dumped unannounced into local law enforcement districts. Other forms of abuse followed.[39] In hindsight, certainly one of the most startling developments here was that the state parlayed back organized crime's own extortionate practices under the banner of protecting the American way of life.

Once again, however, the ethical or even practical considerations of this tactic are, for our purposes, less germane than what they tell us about the larger war on crime and how organized crime itself was being reconceived. After all, Kennedy, and after him Shur, had established a framework in which the capture of a mobster would be seen not simply as an arrest for a crime but (as Goldfarb remembered) a "major intelligence breakthrough."[40] Shur himself originally had larger ambitions for the device. At one point, he proposed that witness protection be integrated into a broader intelligence-gathering system that tracked criminal associations and patterns of activity. In a tactic of immense import for other fronts in the war on crime, in other words, he pressed for the strategy of rolling up criminal groups from lower ranks to higher.[41] In an even broader sense, here the informant was seen as a storyteller, a bearer of intelligence about the very culture of the mob: someone who could tell the public about its work patterns, its ways of life. Ironically, that is, criminals who had double-crossed their original pledge of criminality were now cast as the ultimate truth tellers. In these tensions—between the risk management of criminal intelligence, the desire to cast organized crime as corporate, and the actual everyday experience of these foot soldiers—much of the real drama of the new narratives would emerge.

II.

Robert Kennedy's desire to have it both ways—to represent the Mafia as an alien and yet decidedly American, corporate body—did not impose a uniform template on the journalistic narratives that followed. Genre coordinates are always malleable. To paraphrase an insight from Stephen Crane, the gangster's lair could always be a setting for comedy or tragedy.[42] Puzo's *Godfather*, after all, was still in the future; the influence of Warshow's pattern could still be felt; not every organized crime narrative would rely on a turned informant from the lower ranks.[43] Nevertheless, in the inner workings of those that did, we can often discover the shaping influence of what Albert Stone calls the "telling occasion" of transcription, the specific pressures of informing created by the emerging war on crime.[44] Nowhere more so than in the back story of Peter's Maas's *The Valachi Papers*, a book that emerged out of a pact with Kennedy's Justice Department following Valachi's Senate testimony. By comparing the Valachi that Maas reproduced with the testimony the mobster actually intended to deliver—available in typescript currently in the John F. Kennedy Presidential Library—we can see the shaping influence of the informant strategy.

On its face, the sheer comprehensiveness of Valachi's testimony seemed to legitimate the tactics Kennedy had used. In what is apparently a dictated typescript of over 1,200 pages, Valachi told his federal handlers a story about his rise from simple burglar to wheelman to contract killer for Vito Genovese, and then his initiation into "Cosa Nostra," a term Valachi effectively bequeathed to the FBI for future use.[45] As Alan Block has shown, this seemingly authentic first-person testimony also allowed many in the Senate to overlook the fact that the government recruited Valachi into testifying about a war of which, originally, he may have known very little.[46] ("That is the way I was told," Valachi told the Senate, when asked if he knew why he had been ordered to kill "All Castellammarese." "I never found out the reason. I never asked for the reason.") In the view of some historians, in fact, Valachi provided little more than TV entertainment and publicity for the feds.[47] In some instances, it can seem that Peter Maas simply enhanced certain of Valachi's memories, like that of his initiation into Cosa Nostra (305), by drawing on Valachi's Senate testimony, where such "ritual" elements had seemed so sensational.[48]

In the surviving manuscript, however, we find some important clues to the transaction between Valachi and Maas himself. The first contrast is stylistic; the second is in tone. What we find in Valachi's typescript is a rambling, often incoherent, naively literal act of remembrance without anything of Warshow's arc of tragedy: instead, it amounts to something like a lament. Valachi originally dictated a confessional, crime-by-crime, who-said-what-to-whom memoir, only rarely departing from mundane conversations about specific crimes to comment on their larger significance, and often more intent on justifying his own cooperation with law enforcement. In truth, editing this immense and often-incoherent manuscript must have been an imponderable task, even given Maas's talents.[49] However, Maas also reworked the context for Valachi's "telling occasion," in part by eliding the mobster's charges against narcotics agents, or what he called "frame artists" (616). In order to have the *Valachi Papers* published at all, that is, Maas had agreed to leave out Valachi's charges of double-dealing by the federal government itself, much to Valachi's own dismay.[50] From the start, therefore, a pivotal motivation for Valachi's narrative, one which reflected on his role as informant, dropped out of view.

Meanwhile, there were also some subtle rhetorical effects in the original manuscript that suggest how this mobster, sometimes calling himself "Joe Cago," saw himself. Valachi, for instance, had himself used a war conceit to describe his experience inside the mob (117, 333c), and did draw distinctions between "greasers" (Sicilians) and the "Americanized" gangsters like himself (61, 250–51, 315). But unlike the speaker we would see later in Maas's narrative, Valachi also imagines multiple readers for his own manuscript: certainly the general public but also his government handlers, interested politicians, and importantly his comrades inside the Cosa Nostra. As he informs on his mob, he often rationalizes having done so, often in the same sentence. The ideas simply run into each other, breathlessly:

> . . . let me explain to the reader what I mean by a tough guy, a man that joins the Cosa Nostra and after he joins he is supposed to be a man not a lob for you Vito and company where were you when we fought Joe the Boss and his mob. I know where you were, sitting back and see who will come out on top. You don't mind if I tell the reader the truth do you because they think that you earned your power. . . . (477)

> I want the soldiers to read what I am writing because . . . they don't know what this life really is . . . the Bosses like Vito Genovese work differently today. . . . Life got to be so sweet for the bosses and there is so much money involved today they don't even want to retire. . . . (333f)

> Don't get mad at me Vito when you read this it is all your fault. I'm sure you're going to read it Vito and you never guessed that I knew. You are no good Vito, you are no good you belong with the guy on Pelham Parkway, the old Mustard Gang. (418)

Just as intriguingly, Valachi himself refers not to broken "contracts" in the business sense so much as losing friendships with other men. "I rather have one friend that is half sincere," he writes, "than to have a hundred guys that are looking to go a step forward on your expense" (162). This personalizing lament, in turn, seems loosely connected to the reason Valachi accentuates his early poverty more forcefully than Maas eventually would: "I stole because I was hungry," he says (24), and because he was often on his own. This reference to his own lowly status, in turn, connected to the idea that he had been merely a common foot soldier who eventually became cannon fodder for bosses like Genovese, often with little actual knowledge of the ends of his assignments—again, a limit his handlers preferred not to reveal. But this was precisely why Mafia leader Joseph Bonnano would later complain about Valachi's testimony. In Bonnano's view, Valachi had never risen very high in the ranks and knew little of the Italian traditions he had betrayed.[51]

The remarkable thing here is that Valachi offers essentially a class-based reading of his Cosa Nostra membership. He speaks of his relationship to the mob, or his work in it, not at all as a corporate contract among equals but as being enlisted or drafted or employed, sometimes even against his full knowledge. When he calls himself a soldier, it designates his class status and lowly "rank." In retrospect, it would seem that Valachi's already-conspiratorial mind was made even more so by the fears provoked by his own informing. In addition, his colloquial use of the language of murder "contracts" for his "bosses" may have allowed others to exaggerate the formal, integrated, and corporate character to his outfit, playing directly into Kennedy's hands. Perhaps even more fundamentally, Valachi's manuscript reminds us that informants, usually less literate than they seem in popular transcription, can feel compelled to rationalize their movement *out* of the criminal association about which they have been asked to testify. And they can still have lingering grudges, debts, insults, or backward glances. Called upon to give a comprehensive and coherent inside view of their gang's culture, however, they can easily find these ambivalences marshaled into a tale of that culture's disintegration. In Valachi's original view, nevertheless, violent Mafia infighting had hardly been a simple byproduct of what Maas would cast as a corporate organization's inevitable decay. Rather, that violence was part of his upbringing, the war he was always in. Valachi tells us, for example, that he had come of age in an infamous "murder stable" (16) of 116th Street in New York, and *that* was where he learned the art of war. His antipathy to native Italians stems not only from his class and generational perspective, but (he tells us) from humiliations forced upon his own neighborhood by the Sicilian bosses of his youth.

In the end, however, many of these themes were subordinated when Valachi appeared in Maas's rendering. Instead of relying only on his unlettered voice, *The Valachi Papers* took a documentary approach, directly quoting the gangster's first-person memories (clearly cleaned up, grammatically), framed by Maas himself, whose narrative overvoice—in a device, like Maas's subsequent *Serpico* (1972), perhaps looking forward to movie adaptation—provided historical background on the mob. And in the main, *The Valachi Papers* used the sensational Fordist comparisons between the underworld and business organization that had been used by Feder and Turkus, and Walter Lippmann before them, and Lincoln Steffens before Lippmann.[52] As I have said, Maas's conscious aim was to debunk the idea that the Mafia's "feudal" inheritances (64) from Italy dominated its current American form:

> There has been a great deal of speculative nonsense written about the "ritualistic" aspects of a Cosa Nostra execution of one of its members: that no matter what the offense is, the victim must be killed suddenly and unexpectedly; that he must be wined and dined lavishly before he is disposed of; and that, adhering to an old Sicilian tradition, a shotgun must be used whenever possible. "Naturally," Valachi told me, "you don't want to let the guys know that he's going to be hit, or he might hit you. I never heard of them other things. You just try to be careful and do the best you can." (226)

Throughout, *The Valachi Papers* used this workaday voice to deflate the popular images of Mafia rituals. The code of silence or *omerta,* the mob's elaborate initiation ceremonies, its secret council meetings supposedly all had little lasting effect. In particular, any notion of ritual or honor had failed to forestall internecine war and, ultimately in Valachi's case, personal betrayal.

To make that case, however, Maas also found himself relying heavily on the form Warshow had described: set back upon trying to show the banality and greed behind everyday violence, Maas reproduced, essentially, a gangland narrative. Throughout, Maas punctuated Valachi's casual memories of murder with rapid-fire police reports of each falling body, the in-the-trenches journalist confirming Valachi's claims:

> When a soldier is given a contract, he is responsible for its success. He can, however, pick other members to help him carry it out. . . .
>
> On the night of [one] hit, Valachi had arranged to meet [a mobster named] Little Apples in the coffee shop. "Hey," he said, "let's take a walk. I hear there's a big game going on up the street."
>
> "Great! I got nothing to do." [Little Apples said.]
>
> According to Valachi, he positioned himself behind Little Apples as they were entering the tenement and suddenly wheeled away. "I heard the shots," he says, "and naturally kept walking down the street."
>
> (New York police records reveal that at about 9:20 PM on November 25, 1932, a male, white, identified as one Michael Reggione, alias Little Apples, was found in the hallway of the 340 East 110th Street. Cause of death: three gunshot wounds in the head.)
>
> Valachi went straight home. "After all," he recalls, "I was just married a couple of months, and I didn't want [my new wife] Mildred to think I was already starting to fool around." (107)

The end result, it seems, was that Maas ended up struggling to superimpose Warshow's arc of apprenticeship, recruitment, violent betrayal, and tragic abandonment over Valachi's blasé renderings, and the mobster's repeated need to justify his own informing. A counterpoint thus emerges wherein Valachi verifies mob rules that, in fact, he then tells us he ended up breaking (181, 184). On the whole, Maas argued that the Mafia was dominated by "savagery, avarice, and torturous double-dealing" that belied its "increasingly sophisticated and vaunted togetherness" (63). Yet Valachi himself, as a consequence of this counterpoint, comes off as very much the battle-fatigued Cosa Nostra soldier, weary of this infighting, repeatedly complaining about being caught in the "middle" (208, 251) between warring camps. In the end, Valachi seems a vulnerable and abandoned man—as if, despite his own manuscript attempt, he is a man *without* papers.

He comes across, as well, as caught between the poles of Kennedy's own interpretation.

In the end, even as Maas fought Kennedy's control in court, the informant occasion had clearly suffused the writer's treatment of Valachi. Along with the obvious endurance of the template Warshow had described, the prevailing (and contradictory) view of an "un-American" yet corporate enterprise clearly overrode Valachi's class-based reading of his Mafia years. It was a trumping that Kennedy's Department of Justice had put in motion and Maas's text simply followed through on. Meanwhile, the condition of informing narrowed the target audience to political ends. As I have said, unlike Valachi's manuscript, but following the traditional style of liberal exposé, *The Valachi Papers* speak to a unified, singular public both addressed by the journalist-transcriber and implicitly embodied in his voice. As obvious as this element may seem, it has significant consequences for how organized crime narratives often discount or stigmatize neighborhood or local attachments in the name of a disinterested public sphere. In an enduring contradiction, organized crime continues to look "too ethnic" and also "so American."

Again, the telling occasion of informing seemed only to complement this dominant counterpoint. Valachi shows us how the informant must represent the culture of the very organization he is betraying; speak for bosses when he is but a soldier, with full access to their plans; advert to codes of ethnic loyalty even when he has abandoned them (or they him). This is why so many organized crime narratives do *not* subordinate ethnic melodrama, though they almost always claim to have done so. The finale of *The Valachi Papers* is a case in point. Despite his own claims to debunk the Mafia's feudal image, Maas ends his book with a dire warning that despite its "businesslike" orientation (again the echo of RFK), the mob might well "revert to type" (259). And despite earlier dismissals of such ethnic "nonsense," he shows Valachi being given the kiss of death by Vito Genovese before being threatened during a game of bocce in the federal prison courtyard.[53]

III.

The gangster narrative with the most intriguing relationship to witness protection is Nicholas Pileggi's *Wiseguy*, the exposé capitalizing on the memories of gangster Henry Hill. Like *The Valachi Papers, Wiseguy* was clearly intended to deflate popular images of the Mafia, a task made all the more urgent, now, by the publication of *The Godfather*. Pileggi's book would delve into some of the most sensational crimes of the 1960s: the multimillion-dollar Lufthansa heist at Kennedy Airport, the scandalous point-shaving case involving the bribing of Boston College basketball players, at the top of the list. Meanwhile, the author said repeatedly that he wanted to present organized crime from the bottom up and to approach Hill much as if he were an anthropological informant (the approach, in turn, which attracted Martin Scorsese).[54] To accomplish that task, Pileggi would turn back to elements of films like *Little Caesar* and *Public Enemy* to which even Warshow had not been sufficiently attentive. Meanwhile, *Wiseguy*, more than perhaps any other gangster narrative, shows us the enduring consequence of seeing its source, its informant, through the smaller scale of micropolitical tactics. Henry Hill is at once a boy-gangster and petty entrepreneur, one who is able to work a con, I think, even upon prosecutors and Pileggi himself.

The genesis of Hill's relationship with Pileggi was quite complex. Perhaps because of his earlier work, mostly as a writer for *New York* magazine, Pileggi had been approached by Hill's defense team right as the gangster had been placed in the Witness Protection Program (3). Pileggi admittedly had never even heard of Hill, despite years of writing on organized crime (3). But he was attracted precisely because Hill seemed to counter the glamour developing around the Mafia. Commenting on the cultural coinages generated by Mario Puzo's popularity, Pileggi writes he already "had gotten bored with egomaniacal ravings of illiterate hoods masquerading as benevolent Godfathers" (3).[55] Nevertheless, this mixed position—hired by Hill's defense team, and yet clearly not intending to defend him—created unusual working conditions. On the one hand, advance funding from Simon & Schuster made it possible for Pileggi to fly around the country to interview Hill in undisclosed locations. On the other, Pileggi hoped to write a prosecutorial book. His dependence on Hill thus reflected the tactical ambiguity set in motion by the strategy of WITSEC itself. In a format similar to that of *The Valachi Papers*, *Wiseguy* directly quotes Hill, giving voice to its informant in seemingly unmediated ways. Yet the book keeps reminding us that its sympathies are not with its subject, but with the work of Edward McDonald, the head of the Brooklyn Organized Crime Task Force whom Pileggi had already favorably profiled two years earlier.[56] (As we'll see, McDonald also proves to be a pivotal character in the book.)

The direct transcriptions made possible by informing play a key role in this narrative. As admirers of the voiceover in *GoodFellas* also remember,

Pileggi's account makes startling, even comic, use of Hill's violently impulsive vernacular. In Hill's voice, we hear a volatile mixture of arrogance and self-deluding energy. And as prosecutor McDonald himself had observed, Hill often expressed "casual" nonchalance about his ability to corrupt so many different layers of society. Corruption was so "everyday" that normalcy seemed the exception:[57]

> Guys like Morton were front men for the wiseguys, who couldn't have their names on the liquor licenses. Front men sometimes had some of their own money in these joints and essentially had wiseguys for silent partners. . . . But he also had to pay back a certain amount every week to his partners, and they didn't care whether business was good or bad. That's the way it is with a wiseguy partner. He gets his money, no matter what. You got no business? Fuck you, pay me. You had a fire? Fuck you, pay me. The place got hit by lightning and World War Three started in the lounge? Fuck you, pay me. (48–49)

> Everybody reaches the jury. It's business and it's easy. During the jury selection, for instance, your lawyer can find out anything he wants to know about a juror—where he works, lives, family status. That sort of personal stuff. The "where he works" is what interested me mostly. Where a guy works means his job, and that always means the unions, and that's the easiest place to make the reach. (106)

> We used to get fake IDs from "Tony the Baker" in Ozone Park. He was a real baker. He had a bakery that made bread. (51)

However, as in Maas's rendering of Valachi, Hill's voice itself really only fronts for the argument Pileggi himself makes. *Wiseguy* thus mixes Hill's first-person testimony with other techniques: occasionally framing and bracketing Hill's voice with his own historical interpretation; including testimony from Hill's wife and mistress, often in dialogue with Henry; and throughout, including his own ironic deadpanning of mob rationalizations, often through parenthetical asides. When one of Hill's bosses claims he always "abhorred unnecessary violence," for example, Pileggi inserts the parenthetical "(the kind he hadn't ordered)" (9). Or, when Henry complains about being arrested, Pileggi writes: "It always struck Henry as grossly unfair" that Hill would serve his longest sentence for a "barroom brawl with a man whose sister was a typist for the FBI. It was as if he had suddenly hit the perfecta of bad luck. . . . [T]hey had literally made a federal case out of it" (155). By countermanding Hill's wisdom with his own mixture of irony, familiarity, and distancing formality, Pileggi hopes to make sure that we are, in other words, always making that federal case as we read.

Pileggi also wanted to deflate expectations of the *Godfather* template, specifically to undermine Mafia claims to mutual honor and patrician-like benevolence over their local neighborhoods. To execute his plan, Pileggi's bottom-up approach used Hill's personality and voice to create not the lament of a lost soldier but a frenetic, erratic, and even satirical portrait of what, in one interview, the writer called a "grubbier" Mafia existence. In some ways, this meant contrasting the Vario family with the man (Hill) they hired.[58] Pileggi uses the Varios's ethnicity, much as Maas does with Valachi's bosses, to reflect an older world actually being displaced by the Americanizing trends in mob organization. *Wiseguy* presents the Vario world as that of transhistorical, eighteenth-century Sicilian thievery (26), a casting that allowed Henry himself to mock the idea that they constitute a syndicate of any kind. They are antimodern in the extreme: never using a telephone, never writing anything down, avoiding the credit economy that would involve registering their identities in the contemporary world. As in some of Pileggi's other exposés, the Vario family is portrayed very much in the older vein of the mob's incubation phase: a gang tied into a machine that corrupts urban wards through local attachments and bribery.[59] But when it comes to Hill himself, the anti-modern strain could be reversed.

To effect that turnabout, *Wiseguy* turns back into conventions of juvenile narrative, specifically to the "street sparrow" orphan romances made famous in the nineteenth century, in books like Horatio Alger's *Ragged Dick; or, Street Life in New York* (1867).[60] *Wiseguy* thus actually turns to a tradition underwriting Warshow's genre category, stories of the street urchins who apprentice to crime in their urban wards. In Pileggi's opening chapters depicting Henry's initiation into the corner cab-stand world of mobster Paul (or Paulie) Vario, young Henry is seen running errands in the time-honored way, sitting on a telephone book while parking cars (14), waiting for the chance to be adopted by a patron who will take him away from his own working-class parents. Hill becomes like an apprentice to a religious order, a "cardboard wiseguy" (17) who—in a touch right out of Alger—acquires a flashy suit before it really fits him. Young Henry Hill, whose last name unwittingly invokes the railroad magnate who enraptured Scott Fitzgerald's Irish boy, James Gatz, is a mobile, independent, street-savvy kid, learning all the transactions of crime and capital at much too young an age. And thus, again, we remember Alger's attempt to describe why the boys many called "Street Arabs" were so resistant to the reform nostrums of rural farm retreats created by their middle-class betters. A street boy, Alger had written,

> . . . gets so attached to his precarious but independent mode of life, that he feels discontented in any other. He is accustomed to the noise and bustle and ever-varied life of the streets, and in the quiet scenes of the country misses the excitement in the midst of which he has always dwelt. (10)

> There is always such a throng of omnibuses, drays, carriages, and vehicles of all kinds in the neighborhood . . . that the crossing is formidable to one who is not used to it. Dick made nothing of it, dodging in and out among the horses and wagons with perfect self-possession.[61] (20)

Of course, Henry is far too frantic to be this paragon of self-possession, and his patrons are probably closer to *The Great Gatsby*'s Meyer Wolfsheim than to Ragged Dick's typically Anglo benefactors. But Pileggi pushes the middle-class parallel to extremes by giving Henry's rise all sorts of comic markers: rejoicing over his first kickback at age thirteen; having a party thrown for him when he is first put in jail; or, perhaps best of all, first learning how to read—in prison (170).

In an era thriving on more prosecutorial exposés, this would seem a risky narrative strategy; inadvertently, *Wiseguy* could endear this boy to middle-class tastes, much as comic moments in *The Sopranos* or *Analyze This* could. But by returning to Hill's boyhood, we also feel one residual effect of the micropolitical tactic of voicing the Mafia from the point of view of a single, lower-level worker in the ranks. Henry Hill allows Pileggi to shrink Mafia grandiosity down to size. Hill even called him a "miniature" mobster at one point (17), in order to get us to examine more closely the labor he does. Again signaling Pileggi's own narrative departure from the *Godfather* ethos, Henry's youthful savvy and mobility stem from the fact that he is actually an *outsider* to the strict bloodlines represented by Paul Vario's family. (Hill is half-Irish and the son of a construction company electrician and union man. The family of his Italian mother was from Vario's home region.) Henry's skills, in other words, allow him to both escape the fate of his class and recover it, by asserting his status as an indispensable operative within the mob itself. It is no coincidence that the first regular guy Henry's patrons must con is his own father, as they kidnap a postman and persuade him not to deliver truancy notices from school (25). In turn, Henry's rise is marked by events that his own relatives would have seen as signs of success (like getting a union card, this time through mob connections). Pileggi creates, in other words, a certain element of carnival and fantasy in this upending: "kids from the neighborhood who were always in trouble" (35) turn out not to have to unlearn those skills at all. And their parents are none the warier for it.

Despite Pileggi's subtitle of *Life Inside a Mafia Family*, however, one family does not really replace another. Hill becomes simply useful to the mob rather than a "made" man in the Mafia sense; never a "soldier," he is also not really inside. In turn, the gangster narrative is itself scaled down, made more labor-centered. (In one interview, Pileggi compared Hill to a "worker bee" who lets you see the whole hive.[62]) Or, to stress the Alger parallel again, Henry seems to stay self-made, albeit someone who (like any laborer) can be disposed of. Thus, just as his wife Karen is there to tell us that she *doesn't* feel like she is married to the mob (80), Hill, when put on trial, scoffs at being called a member of a "syndicate" (158) or, by implication, a surrogate family.

In a style crucial for so many portraits to follow, Pileggi thus produces, in Hill, something like a temporary worker: a picture of a low-rent, impulse-driven operative, a man who keeps open duffle bags of clothes on the floor of his bedroom, who never wakes up in his pajamas (56), and whose domestic melodramas with wife and mistress and kids are explicitly compared to "comic soap opera" (272). Pileggi's choice to include Hill's wife in his story likewise generates a seriocomic downscaling, a domestication of the genre. She comically reports her parents' anxiety over Henry not being Jewish, the lack of money she has for her kids (183), and of course complaints about Henry's mistresses. The closure produced by Witness Protection itself also contributes to this effect. Instead of going out in "fiery blasts of Cagney gangster glory" (289)—here Pileggi refers explicitly to the arc Warshow delineated—Hill is described, at the book's close, happily ensconced in a two-story neocolonial, his kids in private schools, in a vaguely homogeneous American town where his biggest complaint is that he can't get a decent Italian meal. He now has a Keogh plan (289). In many respects, it is the telling situation itself that allowed Henry Hill to *look* so tame. Though WITSEC is actually the tactical grounding of Pileggi's own exposé, the program now can be complained about as producing suburban banality. Hill is ultimately a premature retiree, or even a mock snowbird.

With the rise of *The Sopranos,* this suburbanization effect has dominated much recent discussion of the gangster narrative. But the more fundamental transformation Pileggi documents, I think, has happened in

Henry Hill's workplace as much as in his home life. In keeping with the displacement put in motion by Robert Kennedy, we do not see mob initiations or codes any more than we do in *The Valachi Papers*. Instead, Henry turns his Vario apprenticeship into the role of a fixer or, to use the term from Alger's day, a "mechanic": he makes things work, often babysitting Vario's own son, who is usually not up to the task at hand. And rather than expressing, as Valachi had, soldier-like discipline or ward-based antipathy to greedy bosses, Hill mainly runs afoul of his mob fathers because of this freelancing. In a clear countermanding of Mario Puzo's mythos, Hill describes the appeal of being a "wiseguy"—and here the vernacular means something like "smart mouth"—as being clever, or "getting over" on others (20, 191). Hill's pleasure and power comes from duping the everyday stiff (like his own father). Seeing from the bottom-up and outside-in, in other words, allows Pileggi to redefine organized crime as a series of schemes run on a small-scale, entrepreneurial model: as Herbert Gutman famously told us about Hill's nineteenth-century counterparts, Henry is essentially a laborer whose orientation is producerist, even middle-class in aspiration.[63] But now he is a man who aspires to a mock ownership of front enterprises. In *Wiseguy*, in other words, the craft of organized crime is now a microenterprise, a one-man version of the hostile takeover: the bribe, the fix, the "busting out" (40) of legitimate businesses by loaning them money and then buying up or selling everything they own. And thus it is here that the influence of Robert Kennedy's rethinking of organized crime really bears narrative fruit.

This transformation also is felt in how *Wiseguy* treats the traditional assimilationist thread of the gangster story. It might seem, at first, that Pileggi's intentions are akin to epic, following an Americanization story in its grandest outlines. Hill follows his white-ethnic community from places like Mulberry Street (32) to suburban Long Island; not coincidentally, his biggest heist will take place at JFK Airport, which had been transformed from a Long Island golf course (91). However, *Wiseguy*'s smaller-scale canvas means that Hill sees his landscape in localist, and again microeconomic, terms. Pileggi prefers to attend to the byplay between local geography and an area's vulnerability to crime: how tenement houses could shelter sweatshops; how immigrant arrivals in seaports made ripe territory for extortionists and kidnappers; how the adjacency to Long Island, during Prohibition, set the stage for overland bootlegging runs to barges and smugglers on the shoreline. On the one hand, JFK Airport is one sign of even globalizing times: some of the thefts are from servicemen's luggage, perhaps a Vietnam hint that comically slips into this narrative. But on the other, the airport itself is more characteristically seen in terms of its local vulnerabilities. To Hill's avaricious eye, the new airport is much like that beehive, a clustering, once again, of small entrepreneurial transactions: ticket counters, baggage handlers, storage lockers, all prime for the picking. Ironically, the ability of the airport to stimulate local labor markets only extends the mob's influence, again, into these interstitial transactions. The micropolitical tactic of individual informant testimony has, in other words, served to scale crime down to consumer- or employer-contact points.

Thus, in what is perhaps the clearest example of a witness protection narrative we have, crime goes forth, as Robert Kennedy had described it, as something that feeds off the mainstream economy and its affluence by a reordering of these micro transfer points. In a telling cycle of mutual backscratching, the larger economy is actually what makes organized crime possible. On one end, hijackers can steal goods that are made all the more saleable, at cut rates, because of monopolies that have overcharged in the mainstream economy; hijackers need not use guns because the drivers who are asked to step down from their trucks understand that they will not be fired (because of control over their union); the police need not be involved because insurance companies will pay for the loss and pass the cost back to the consumer again (98ff.). *Wiseguy* shows us an underground economy fully integrated into the aboveground one, in a synergistic relationship. That symbiotic tie explains why Henry Hill can look so entrepreneurial, so much the everyday schnook that witness protection, all too fittingly, makes him out to be (284). These small-scale contact points also provide places, as it were, to plant dynamite into the mob's foundations. Like Valachi, Henry Hill has been called upon to testify both to the mob's integration and, in the end, its inevitable disintegration. Hill shows us not only organized crime's ingenuity but also the ways in which its internal betrayals catch up with it.

However, even beyond these scaling effects, or the portrait of synergy with the mainstream, Hill had some final cons to play. As it turns out, it may be that Hill was not entirely captured by the plan his federal handlers, and even Pileggi himself, had imposed upon him. For instance, it should surprise no one that Hill seems just as often to shade his testimony in order to direct attention away from himself. He uses the past tense, for example, to distance himself from crimes or schemes no longer undertaken, and the passive voice to describe killings ostensibly carried out by others. In certain moments—for example, when a federal prison is made to look like a Holiday Inn, for the mobsters it holds—Hill's first-person testimony feels mostly like bragging about something impossible to either verify or contradict. One can easily feel that Pileggi overextends the limits of his carnivalesque intention. Meanwhile, *Wiseguy* also inherits a certain pitfall characteristic of the "street sparrow" narrative tradition, where the street-savvy, yet golden-hearted, hero is always counterpointed to the *really* violent, more criminal counterpart in his milieu.[64] In Henry Hill's telling, it is his sidekick Jimmy Burke who is the genuinely pathological killer.

As with Valachi, these touches may only suggest how an informant tries to build a justification for his own informing, or a justification for his own abandonment of the mob. At times, *Wiseguy* often has the feel of a story told by an escapee, much like the famously mediated example of the slave narrative. Hill sets himself up as the brake on Jimmy Burke's threatening violence, as if to make a case for his own unease with family rule and internecine warfare. (In effect, it is the Jimmys and the Paulies who become Warshow's heroes of sadistic violence.) If the journalist wants to emphasize organized crime as an enterprise, the informant is only too willing to distance himself from anything too violent, as "bad for business," as Hill frequently does. One revealing incident Hill recalls, for example, concerns a neighborhood outsider who is punished by local Mafia rule for snatching a purse, during the very time that the famous Apalachin Meeting had turned up the heat from the FBI. In the classic fable of neighborhood self-defense, this purse snatcher is thrown to his death from a rooftop. Hill recalls how he saw the guy hanging in the air, "flailing his arms like a broken helicopter, and then [coming] down hard and splattered all over the street" (40). Shortly after, however, young Henry decides to leave the Vario family by enlisting in the army: tellingly, he joins the paratroopers, a symbolic choice that suggests he is thinking ahead (and back) to his own golden parachute from Witness Protection.

Perhaps the most unsettling element in Hill's testimony, however, may not have been in Pileggi's control at all: the way that Hill speaks back against his own manipulation by McDonald's task force. The riposte Hill constructs, perhaps even "getting over" on his task force handlers, seems quite personally targeted. We soon discover that one of the central crimes to which Hill confesses—bribing Boston College ballplayers—refers to the very college that was McDonald's own alma mater, where he too played on the freshman basketball team. As if reprising Robert Kennedy's reaction to Jimmy Hoffa, the prosecutor was so incensed by Hill's confession of this particular crime that he nearly leapt across the interview table (285). But by so clearly targeting the investments of the prosecutor's own identity, Hill may have only been initiating one of the classic gambits of the confidence game, turning a handler's pride to the con man's own advantage. McDonald's own reflection certainly suggests that he took the matter quite personally: "I came to realize Henry didn't have too much school spirit. He never rooted for anything outside of a point spread in his life" (285–86).

Now, we can never really know if Hill was setting McDonald up. It is certainly intriguing that Hill gives him a crime—gambling—that was so high on Robert Kennedy's list of priorities. It was also a crime that drew attention to the basketball players as much as it did to Hill himself. As a result, one feels that what Whitey Bulger would raise to an art form, Henry Hill was adept at improvising. There are two additional, albeit circumstantial, elements that certainly point to such a possibility. First, it is clear that throughout his negotiation with McDonald, Hill sees the entire process as one in which the state has simply decided to play by *his* rules. As if delivering the informant's revenge upon his own incorporation, he casts McDonald simply as the mirror image of his own criminality: as extorting cooperation from him by hinting that Burke and others will kill him; by "blackmailing" him by threatening to prosecute Karen, and thereby leave their children unprotected (277). In the end, Hill actually says that cooperating with the feds *was* simply working another con (268). In this respect, it is certainly intriguing that, in the second place, Hill largely *under*sells the effects of his point-shaving bribery, clearly playing down a crime one would think he would have played up. In the end, he tells us that, following a blown effort to fix the Holy Cross game, the BC players actually left him high and dry, and he simply walked away, content to take his losses (200–201). In a sop perhaps intended to reassure McDonald and his alma mater, Hill says that the BC players were just too noble to make the scheme work profitably (200). But in the *Sports Illustrated* article in which he recounted the same scheme, Hill confesses—contrary to what he says in *Wiseguy*—that there was actually one more playoff game after Holy Cross. Apparently, Henry and his friends made back lots of money they had lost, and left, as he tells it to *SI*, "wearing happy faces."[65]

IV.

Given that Henry Hill would soon betray the trust his federal handlers put in him, and be expelled from Witness Protection itself, he exemplified some of the incomplete and contradictory outcomes of the war in which he played such a key part.[66] Little wonder, for instance, that some citizens, notably victims' rights advocates, felt betrayed by the publisher advances and eventually profits channeled to him by his participation in *Wiseguy*. Under what became known as "Son of Sam" laws, Pileggi would be sued (and exonerated) in a case that went all the way to the Supreme Court.[67] Amid the public furor, however, few seemed to notice that Hill's celebrity status contradicted a war on crime that had often claimed zero tolerance for the smallest of criminal infractions, or which vaunted moral vigilance as the touchstone of community order. Indeed, according to the logic of the war on organized crime itself, royalties would seem quite rightly a fruit of Hill's criminal labors for the state. What these moral complaints overlooked, in other words, was the more fundamental fact that criminals like Valachi and Hill (and eventually Whitey Bulger) had actually been incorporated into law enforcement operations and made a mechanism of the everyday administration of power. Instead, these contradictions of the neoconservative turn would typically be papered over by ever-renewed calls to straight shooting and moral vigilance—calls sometimes reinforced, albeit unwittingly, even by the war's detractors.

Efforts at the reform of informing currently seem just as liable to fall short. The 2001 Justice Department Guidelines, for example, do set up regulations for formal registration, internal review, and interagency cooperation. Yet there remain serious questions about whether any such guidelines could overcome the structural ambiguities inherent in the informant relationship. Even if we accept the odd semantics of the oxymoron "tough guidelines," such mandates often have the feeling of bureaucratic rules with all sorts of trap doors, internal winks, and less-than-candid breast-beating. From stories like Valachi's and Hill's, we acquire a glimpse of the nuances of a relationship that is, by its very nature, one of ingratiation, luring, and the subtle offering of implied incentives that are often promised but not delivered, said but not recorded.[68] Even comparatively straightforward measures like bribery or anti-fraternization guidelines therefore seem almost comically inapt to the practices they mean to regulate.[69] Try as one might, the tough love of straight dealing falls victim to processes of mutual manipulation, ingratiation, and even occasional intimidation that are intrinsic to the informant strategy, and that the recent turn has made ever-more common practice.[70]

For cultural texts about organized crime, meanwhile, the enduring issues may be as much interpretive are they are ethical. The revisions that both Maas and Pileggi tried to impose upon the gangster narrative tradition reflect back the institutional strategy that gave them birth. The tradition of describing an Americanizing arc was now given operational value, while what had long been emphasized as corporate or syndicated activity was made, especially with Henry Hill, a matter of microeconomic invasion, a parasitism of the everyday. In retrospect, the portrait of organized crime in a figure like Henry Hill would actually look situational or instrumental rather than corporate in the organizational sense; it was even cross-ethnic in some of its primary worker and client networks, an element that looks forward to the more recent attempts to move beyond the corporate paradigm Kennedy and others used. By the first decade of the next century, criminologists and police would be using not billy clubs to combat street gangs but social-networking software.[71] As a result of portraits such as *Wiseguy,* even the most mundane of gangster portraits often bring with them an implicit call for vigilance in the public and private spheres. If a mobster was, as in the mid-century formulation, an enemy within, he was now within everyday transactions, not simply vice operations on the margin. Necessarily, his integration into mainstream economies was used to legitimate, in a telling feedback loop, the self-same pragmatic law enforcement tactic of informing itself.

Pileggi's portrait of Hill, especially, is meant to show us the importance of closing the breaches in the everyday. Hill himself dutifully describes all the improvements that now make his past conning and "busting out" more difficult. In his depiction of the too-vulnerable past, Pileggi shows us that the crime of hijacking formerly had no clear delineation in the criminal code, just as he shows that judges had been too lenient, or that prisons had lacked the necessary discipline to prevent mobsters from racketeering behind bars. But mostly it is Hill himself who mentions, exhibiting a new wise knowledge—"wise" here acquiring its final meaning, that of being tipped off or made aware—that computer traps have now been put in place, that credit card limits now generate consumer notification, and so on (51, 63). In other words, defeating organized crime implicitly required not just law enforcement vigilance, but citizens' own alertness. This mixture of retrospection and updating serves to reassure the reader and reinforce Pileggi's intention to undermine the notorious Public Enemy effect of glamorizing organized crime. Moreover, Pileggi's historical narrative shows us how we have *already* been learning to live with crime.

That turnabout was central to the cultural work of these witness protection narratives. If we do remember that organized crime narratives may double as portraits of the state, then we also see the world that RICO and the Witness Protection Program ultimately helped to fashion around mobsters like Henry Hill. What is often dismissed as the inevitable disintegration of mob organizations—or worse yet, intra-ethnic squabbling—may actually point to the state's own refashioned strategy. At the end of *Wiseguy*, we can focus on Henry Hill's growing paranoia, but only if we ignore how infiltrated his world (and ours) actually was, in the end, by the very practices he helped to put into place. Ultimately, what is most ironic about the arrest of Henry Hill is not only that he is doggedly tracked down by the warriors on crime, with their phone taps and even helicopters hovering over his house—perhaps the typical ways in which we visualize this "war" (225). Instead, we should see that he is brought down, even surrounded on his final day, by a beehive of *other* informants (224, 247, 249, 265). By speaking to a journalist who addresses a unified public sphere, the erratic and violent informant can thus serve to galvanize his audience into action and show us some of its ill effects. Perhaps most fundamentally, a figure like Henry Hill called both state *and* citizens to a greater level of vigilance: he entered into the interstices of the everyday, making crime itself seem unavoidable unless met by an understanding of the skills he tutors. In the end, the informant's very existence seemed to call upon all of us: to get with the Program, to get wise.

2

The Box in the Box
Putting Interrogation in Prime Time

> "The true test is in there."
> —Detective Frank Pembleton, NBC's *Homicide*

THROUGHOUT THE YEARS of the war on crime, contemporary police melodrama on prime-time television has been largely about establishing "street cred" with increasingly cosmopolitan and crime-conscious audiences. Especially in earlier decades, police shows commonly imitated the urban, street-centered grittiness of films such as William Friedkin's *The French Connection* (1971), with its cops as defenders of a city decaying from drugs, gang warfare, and public indifference. Drawing mainly upon an even longer tradition of action-based melodrama from movies and radio, the template TV styles in these decades were to be found in the paramilitary street *verité* of Joseph Wambaugh's *Police Story* (1973–77); the urbane savvy of Abby Mann's *Kojak* (1973–78); the adrenaline rush of the maverick, undercover cops of Michael Mann's *Miami Vice* (1984–89); or the hardscrabble police polyglot of Steven Bochco's *Hill Street Blues* (1981–87).[1] To a degree, all of these shows were variants on what has been called the "police procedural," particularly the modern version developed by the coat-and-shirtsleeve ensemble casts of precinct investigators of "the naked city" from the 1940s to the 1960s. In *The Naked City* TV shows as such (1958–59, 1960–63), the procedural form had been applied to a mixture of psychological and crime-busting drama, often counterpointing a hip jazz soundtrack with the serious business of mystery-ratiocination, via an array of floor plans, medical reports, and clues.[2] In the twenty-first century, the mantle was taken up—and further glamorized—by forensic, lab-coat series like *CSI: Crime Scene Investigation* (2000–), now often called the most-watched show on the planet.[3]

A few series, however, began to combine urban, procedural case solving with a special emphasis on interrogation scenes. That is, what had long been a melodramatic setting for the "third-degree" grilling of suspects had become the site of more elaborate and more plot-pivotal performances. If, on Dick Wolf's *Law & Order* (1990–2010), interrogation rooms have worked in the traditional way—as junctures between police labor and criminal prosecution—on the spin-off *Law & Order: Criminal Intent* (2001–), they originally became a more elaborate setting for the perverse inventions and envelope pushing of chief interrogator Robert Goren (Vincent D'Onofrio). On Tom Fontaine and Barry Levinson's *Homicide* (1993–99), the NBC series drawn from David Simon's true-crime account of two years in a Baltimore homicide squad, viewers were introduced to what the series called "The Box," a sterile, rectangular interrogation room with a spare metal table, chairs, and the customary one-way mirror. "The Box" became, as viewers soon recognized, the particular pride and focal point for Detective Frank Pembleton (Andre Braugher), whose agony became an acknowledged signature of the series. By the arrival of the Showtime network's (TNT) *The Closer* (2005–), the interrogation room became not only—pun fully intended, one is sure—the device of "closure," but of dis-closure, the unveiling of a shy, compulsive, genteel Southern lady (Kyra Sedgwick) as a ruthless mistress of closing cases. Albeit in different ways, these shows all seemed to reflect how former police reporter Simon had himself interpreted the small space of interrogation. "[W]hat occurs in an interrogation room," he had written, "is indeed little more than a carefully staged drama, a choreographed performance." It was a space of "purgatory," and yet the place where the ultimate commandment of police work—to extract a confession—took place.[4]

This space, furthermore, seemed well suited to the medium of television. In some ways, the interrogation room paralleled Mark Seltzer's deft description of the "CSI" lab: a place for the serial re-observation of police work, a blackboxing of "conjectural reenactment" of murder cases in which TV viewers re-run crimes over and over again.[5] When it comes to interrogation, television's ability to focus our view on the criminal and his questioner's arts—as it were, through our own one-way mirror—often works to disempower the criminal suspect we are watching. That is, the close-cropped televising of this ritual often serves to reinforce an aura of police implacability, even inescapability. Typically the suspect is not just "faced down" or sweated out in the old-fashioned way—but surrounded, outmaneuvered, by detectives who angle in, as we angle in, while the perpetrator trips up and usually caves in. In the very moment that big government was supposed to be on the wane, one could hardly imagine a micropolitical scene that provided a more elemental spectacle of state power.⁶ And it was arguably on David Milch and Bochco's *NYPD Blue* (1993–2005) where the multiple dramatic possibilities of such scene making—and their possible political effects—became especially apparent. Milch himself had not only confirmed interrogation's centrality to the show, but said that he had learned the art from the police themselves: specifically, from his co-producer, former NYPD homicide detective Bill Clark.

To get a handle on this complicated interplay of genre norms, police history, and political ideology within this art of interrogation, this chapter will examine, in a microcosmic fashion, this creative partnership behind *NYPD Blue* itself. There are many reasons why this particular TV series demands close attention. From the 1990s forward, *NYPD Blue* became a ratings powerhouse, especially in the eighteen-to-forty-nine age demographic; it was celebrated repeatedly by the Emmys (with twenty-six nominations in its first season); and, not unimportantly, it received more than occasional praise from NYPD officers themselves as being remarkably true to their craft.⁷ The show also received broad public attention, most of it negative, for how it displayed interrogation scenes.⁸ For his part, David Milch—fully aware of the anxiety the series was creating among already-marginalized liberals—brashly confirmed that interrogation was at the center of the show's political intentions. That is, for Milch, as for Simon, the rights boundary illuminated by the landmark Supreme Court case of *Miranda v. Arizona* (1966) was little more than a hollow political symbol, a "patent delusion" foisted upon law-abiding citizens by defense lawyers and civil libertarians.⁹ Instead, Milch said, his series "tries to point to a kind of dirty secret that is at the heart of our culture. . . . What we [all] want the police to do is make sure the criminal is put away by any means necessary. . . ." But we also need the police to lie to citizens "about how the confession is obtained so [they] don't have to give up [their] illusions."¹⁰ Despite what his detractors said, *Miranda* was the true fiction, he argued—not *NYPD Blue*.¹¹

Of course, Milch's in-your-face emulation of police fatalism hardly made up for what seemed, to many, a show that lent legitimacy to physical brutality and coercion in the interrogation room. Led by the pioneering work of Elaine Scarry, Peter Brooks, Jerome Skolnick, and John Conroy, sociologists, journalists, and legal scholars alike had already long been troubled by the moral and legal dimensions of the coercive processes by which a suspect, prisoner, or detainee is forced to "own up" to what an interrogator wants.¹² Because police melodramas commonly present due process rights as technicalities hampering police work, portray officers with deeply moralistic approaches to crime, and ignore the very real problem of false confessions generated by coercive interrogation, analysts have long (and rightly) been concerned about whether television's indifference to Miranda rules undermines public respect for law.¹³ Today's police shows are therefore commonly said to be driven by the conventions of melodrama or to betray their roots in the genre of the Western, with its generally anti-institutional, extralegal, and even vigilante underpinnings. Despite their veneer of metropolitan savoir faire or realism, it is often said, cop dramas are fully resonant with the conservative, fear-driven politics of our day.¹⁴

And yet, it has often been easier to *describe* how Miranda rights are undermined on these shows than to explain how doing so is consistent with the still-liberal outlook of their creators. Prime-time producers like Bochco or Milch or Wolf, after all, present themselves as opposed to the right wing and Moral Majority on behalf of free speech and greater sexual frankness. If these series are as "conservative" as alleged, it is also hard to explain their appeal to the young, cosmopolitan, often well-educated audience they cultivate. On the contrary, as Robert Handt has argued, *NYPD Blue*'s celebrated resistance to network and affiliate censorship went a long way toward establishing the series' liberal image in the public mind. (Dick Wolf, similarly, has ardently defended his resistance to censorship and underlined his liberal credentials by citing his support for the Brady Bill.) If anything, these shows are often praised for their hip, seemingly pluralistic, ethos.¹⁵ David Milch was singled out on three different occasions in the 1990s for HUMANITAS prizes recognizing TV shows that expressed the "search for meaning . . . for freedom, for love, for human dignity, for unity with all our fellow human beings."¹⁶ It was hard to reconcile some of Milch's more vitriolic commentary with this humanistic reception.

The creative process behind *NYPD Blue* may well have been unique. But it may also have been an important internal weathervane of what the show's public reputation and its audience demographic suggested. In my view, that process models not a monochromatic conservative ideology but an emergent sensibility better called, but rarely so appropriately, "post-liberal," in which humanistic compassion has been chastened by the "Blue" fatalism about law enforcement that the neoconservative turn has sponsored. To demonstrate the groundwork of that accommodation, I will examine the history of the NYPD itself from the 1970s to the 1990s, in part by referring to Bill Clark's own experience. Then I will examine how this history made its way into the literary norms and creative processes of this series. My source for that process, primarily, will be Milch's nonfiction memoir about the series entitled *True Blue: The Real Stories Behind* NYPD Blue (1995). Although at first blush merely a behind-the-scenes book for the series' devoted fans, *True Blue* actually has a rich body of material on the intersection of legal norms, law enforcement practices, and aesthetic rationales. With Milch's voice appearing as the framing interlocutor of Clark's tutelage, the memoir claims—by occasionally referring to high Romantic aesthetics—that the show achieved a faithful (true Blue) picture of contemporary police work. Although I will mention about a dozen episodes where interrogation played a key role, I will close by analyzing one *NYPD* episode, a well-known script called "Prostrate Before the Law" from the series' fifth season (1998).

I recognize that my tighter, more literary focus flies in the face of methods that, for example, prefer to quantify constitutional violations across a broader sample of shows or compare audience perceptions with actual crime rates. In such studies, cops are normally not, to put it mildly, put in conversation with Coleridge.[17] Indeed, I am interested in Milch's work precisely because he acknowledges interrogation is central to his series, but not in the ways we commonly assume. Despite public perceptions, I will argue, *NYPD Blue*'s interrogation scenes tell us less about coercion or physical brutality than the often-neglected tactic of police *deception* that has flourished in the post-*Miranda* era. Examining the creative contact zone between Milch and Clark also allows us to move away from assumptions about the ideological commonality of such collaborations. We can examine, instead, pre-political cultural attitudes and unforeseen parallels in the interaction across class, ethnic, and personal boundaries. In this instance, the interaction is between an Emmy Award–winning television writer—as it happens, a Jewish, highly educated, former Yale English writing teacher and devotee of Robert Penn Warren—and a white ethnic, working-class cop who prides himself on his interrogation skills.[18] What this smaller-scale examination may bear witness to, in other words, is a crucible of a post-liberal accommodation in *both* directions. Ultimately, the lessons of the "Box" may bear witness to an important recalibration of state powers central to contemporary order-maintenance policing. In these ways, the smaller space of "The Box" connects to a much broader domain of consent, becoming the performance stage (to use Milch's phrase) for a "dirty secret" that is publicly aired.

I.

If the 1970s marked a turning point in the criminal justice approach to organized crime, it was also a decade of shifting resources at the street level, as the de-industrial blues set in. Though *NYPD Blue* itself would debut in 1992, the sheer look, feel, and sound of the series seemed to look back over its shoulder. (Several of the cases Bill Clark passed on to the series are from the early 1980s.) To a degree, of course, the seriocomic, polyglot narrative donnée of the mid-century police procedural—of "eight million stories" in the modern city—had always lent itself to serial, episodic, and downbeat melodrama. Consciously or not, Bochco and Milch's work (as in *Hill Street Blues*) only modified the style of shows like *The Naked City*, which regularly contrasted the high life of artists, the rich, and the criminal with its coat-and-tie police force assigned the thankless labor of keeping order.[19] Bochco and Milch's cramped offices and jagged, rundown cityscapes merely took that older template and gave it a more "bluesy" feel. In the 1970s and 1980s, we implicitly learn, cities now faced more than they could handle, with fewer resources coming to, and fewer pleasures coming from, police work.

Historically speaking, these decades certainly seemed a long way from the early 1960s, when rookies like Frank Serpico or Robert Leuci had entered the NYPD academy. Before the downturn of the 1970s, the department had stressed centrally coordinated, professional crime busting. In an approach much romanticized in American popular culture, cops were conceived as men of action, sent to the crime scene by a central radio dispatcher. Largely inspired by the federal government, police managers in the 1960s had put their stock in professionalization and, especially in cities like Los Angeles, paramilitarization; they turned to supposedly measurable standards of efficiency such as the Uniform Crime Reports (where citizens reported crimes to the police), the keeping of clearance rates (how many cases a department closed), and gauging how rapid their response was to citizen calls or alarms (that is, through that dispatch-automobile system). The FBI's own "straight-shooting" public image, fantastically out of step with J. Edgar Hoover's real practice as it was, inspired much local emulation. Indeed, mid-century police melodramas like *The Naked City* had reflected back a style of dapper, coat-and-tie (and often clean-cut) morality that expressed itself, in crisis moments, through swift, tactical automobility. The film of *The Naked City* (1948) had itself put the telephone dispatch system in its foreground and a chase at its climax; in uniform or in dinner jacket, the police detective would arrive in force, a bearer of investigative deduction, legal authority, and physical skill. (Despite his fame as an undercover cop, Serpico was himself a fan of "High Noon" and "Crime Busters" radio shows.[20]) Though these attempts at professionalization had little impact on rising crime rates, they did raise public expectations about law enforcement and, in turn, probably contributed to rises in police pay.[21] Base pay for patrolmen in New York City, for example, would rise to the highest in the nation in the early 1970s.[22] In such a climate, police departments had not been liable to lend their imprimatur to anything that suggested crimes were solved by "sweating" suspects, a practice previously scandalized by police reformers and, not unimportantly, film noir.[23]

But then, police departments had been rocked by corruption scandals, the urban fiscal crisis loomed, and—so the familiar story goes—the war on crime returned to "basics" like foot patrol, community meetings, and aggressive drug policing. Elite detective work, though it retained much of its status inside the police force, was often deemed too expensive, especially when—as I shall discuss in my next chapter—"meaningless" or motiveless homicides seemed to drag down clearance rates and, with them, public confidence. The need to support the imperatives in the drug war or the federal assault on organized crime (which was, we often forget, in fact the real crime front in *Serpico* and *Prince of the City*) put a heavy burden on department resources and autonomy. In New York, for instance, the overall cost of police operations had outpaced the above-mentioned pay hike by a factor of five. In retrospect, it would be clear that the rising political power of the NYPD, fueled largely by its Police Benevolent Association, had only reflected the broader expansion of service sector costs in the post-industrial city, largely among middle-class whites (and, at the time, too often blamed on the needs for such services by nonwhites).[24] Indeed, *NYPD Blue* itself is clearly shaped by a sensibility in the department that, despite a slow response to change in the population it patrolled, remained remarkably white, European, and largely Catholic in composition and tenor. At its base, *NYPD Blue* can be said to reassert, in Clark's presence and in the character of Sipowicz, the long tradition of white-ethnic "minorityism" in police lore, wherein the police come to represent (to stand in for) the diminished power of the white ethnic political machine. Still symbolically invested as the city's "force," they are also often cast as disconnected from meaningful power.[25]

In *NYPD Blue*, therefore, the mood is decidedly different. As it were, we are in not only a post-industrial moment, but a post–Knapp Commission (1971) one, both of which clearly affect the series' entire take on the Miranda ritual. It is not that the earlier professional aura has been diminished; rather, it seems held in reserve. In contrast to earlier series, that is, the detective's authority now seems like a gold shield never flashed, worn under the lapels, his power held back until that moment when the coat comes off and a perpetrator is interrogated. If the cop now seems to represent a grimmer view of crime in the streets, he also expresses a new pragmatism that goes "in house" so as to remove itself from public scrutiny and, as so many have rightly complained, the Constitution. In that regard, therefore, we need to notice how variously the famous recitation of Miranda rights on the show is used: as a threat, as a signal of narrative closure, and perhaps most unsettlingly of all, as a lament. That is, it becomes a device that signals the dismal reality of "the job" that many police officers, watching this series, seemed to echo[26]—a lament that keeps reminding us that the war on crime has been waged within a specific historical transformation in U.S. cities.

And yet, while this tale of retrenchment has often been told, the subtler story was one of internal reorganization. The public impression left by the Knapp Commission reforms was that of a broad-scale "cleaning house." Indeed, that image was assisted by the publicity around films like Sidney Lumet's adaptation (1973) of Peter Maas's *Serpico*, the book Maas wrote, in part, to offset the picture of Italian American criminality portrayed in *The Valachi Papers*. In fact, the Knapp Report elicited a much more modest rethinking of police resources. On the one hand, the report certainly declared that beat officers were the "heart of the [corruption] problem" (4) in the million-dollar payoff system originally exposed by David Burnham in the *New York Times*. In a pragmatic spirit reflective of the growing influence of risk management, the report actually looked to decriminalize activities like gambling and prostitution because they so often led to police graft. And in a gesture so far removed from our own moment, the Knapp Report even held out hope for finding other ways to deal with drug addicts than by criminalizing them (19). But on the other hand, the report focused just as much on the lax management that had produced such demoralization within the rank and file.[27] As a result, the report pulled back against formerly autonomous "special" squads and, to a degree, "crime busting" itself—and attacked the precinct code of silence by making Frank Serpico and Robert Leuci (and others) into informants. Indeed, the spate of corruption in "special" units (Serpico was in the plainclothes division; Leuci in a special investigative unit) had only reinforced the temporary backlash against detective work more generally.[28] Like many police managers in the neoconservative turn, New York Commissioner Patrick Murphy (1970–73) pointed to studies emerging from think tanks like the RAND

Corporation—in many respects, as Jonathan Simon suggests, a private-sector counterpart of the Law Enforcement Assistance Administration (LEAA)—which argued that detective work was rarely an efficient means of solving serious crimes.[29] As a former budget director rephrased it in a collegial interview with Murphy, "the basic issue is accountability. It's not just honesty, but performance across the board" (97).[30]

This rethinking did reflect a diminishing of resources. By the early 1980s, this new attitude, when combined with the larger deterioration in New York's economic base, led to cuts of nearly 30 percent in the overall police force. Though sporadic efforts at reinforcements and aggressive crime busting would be attempted under Mayor David Dinkins and Commissioner Benjamin Ward (1984–89), the political winds seemed to be blowing in the other direction. Detective work could easily seem a luxury, especially when community policing, hailing the importance of returning to "basics" of beat control and community "responsiblilization," began to dominate the headlines.[31]

But again, this proved to be more of a short-term change than we have recognized. The more long-lasting consequences were in *how* detective work would be deployed. As police analyst Albert Niederhoffer had observed at the end of the 1960s: "The freedom of the detective division to form and utilize contacts with the criminal world underlines the particularly open structure of this segment of the police force. With its easygoing approach to interpersonal relations, its lack of concern for the formal regulations that hamstring the rest of the department, and its informal discipline, the division forms what might be called a mock bureaucracy."[32] In the long term, what observations like this one suggested was that retrenchment would only temporarily mean diminished assets. More fundamentally, it highlighted the need to break down the autonomy of special detective squads and subject them to more direct managerial oversight. In the aftermath of the Knapp Commission, in fact, central division cops had been promoted over more entrenched officers, and then placed back in precincts as part of the strategy of combating corruption on site (*True Blue* 57). Going "in-house" was intended to correct past policies that had given special-unit investigators too much autonomy.

In other words, re-thinking detective work actually meant subjecting it to tighter managerial oversight—not, as *NYPD Blue*'s ethos would suggest, a simple diminishing of resources. Commissioner Murphy actually had already begun to experiment with detectives being placed back under the precinct commander for tighter accountability on site.[33] Murphy had even begun to experiment with the corporate-style "crime analysis" methods of pin maps and computer evaluation that would later mark William Bratton's tenure (1994–96). During Rudolph Giuliani's mayoral term, Bratton would actually contribute to a doubling of investigative resources in both the NYPD's Detective and Organized Crime bureaus. (Giuliani had been one of the lead prosecutors of organized crime, notably in Leuci's case, following upon the tactics I have described in chapter 1.[34]) Before long, NYPD observers could find Bratton boning up on corporate motivation, gathering a cadre of younger commanders to war room meetings, to pore over computer-generated comparative statistics (so-called CompStat findings) on precinct maps with push pins and crime reduction objectives. CompStat was terribly evocative of the contradictions of the larger war on crime: aimed at mapping (through Geographic Information Systems software) not only crimes and arrests but "quality of life" violations, the practice showed how "Broken Windows" thinking had actually been melded to aggressive tactical implementation and managerial control of neighborhoods. Logging the larger array of "violations" only enhanced the feeling of a public under siege, while it rationalized head busting on the public's behalf (and pressuring lower-ranking officers to "produce"). This was the climate that allowed Bratton to worry publicly over the apparent instances of physical coercion that often marked *NYPD Blue,* even though he had put in practice street-level methods that often amounted to the same thing.[35]

That is, the 1980s lament that "nothing works," so common in the ranks of police and neoconservative criminologists, had actually legitimated, in the long run, more aggressive approaches to crime busting: the use of decoys, informants (again), and mobile "warrant squads" conducting rapid shakedowns of suspects' residences, even when relatives claimed they were not at home. The arrival of more elaborate computerization, and with it the use of "no knock" warrants—warrants that did not require police to announce their presence before a bust—had accentuated the drive toward folding "quality of life" concerns into the larger assault-tactics regimen. In addition, police departments emphasized ways to speed up the interval between an undercover drug buy and the issuing of a warrant by using such minor violations as pretexts. As one cop who joined the force in 1995 put it, the essence of the new approach was that "stopping someone for smoking a joint allowed you to search them [sic] for weapons and run them for warrants."[36]

The legitimate concerns about civil and human rights violations in Bratton and Giuliani's tenure need not be rehearsed here. And as I've suggested, *NYPD Blue,* with its drastically interiorized and traditional precinct setting, cramped and undersized police desks, and desk phones, would seem mostly to conceal the modernizing dimensions of the in-house reforms above. Because *NYPD Blue* did adapt the "bluesy" (and Blue) ethos of disempowerment and retrenchment, especially among former "princes of city" from those special bureaus, the series' ethos seemed "Blue" collar, returning us to the fundamental precinct-procedural argot of "The Job," itself something of an anachronism. The very language of the show mythologizes its historical transformation through a retro cover story. And yet, it turns out that the interiority of *NYPD Blue,* particularly its emphasis on interrogation, also reveals key elements of its historical backdrop. If, as I've said in chapter 1, informant use reflected the neoconservative emphasis on crime fighting through "intelligence gathering," then interrogation rooms became a pivotal location for the application of that method. Seeing police work as "intelligence gathering" laid the groundwork for the notion that a suspect was, if not the particular perpetrator you wanted, a source of information (and probably guilty of something else). As Scarry observes, the most extreme form of interrogation, physical torture, inverts the process of a trial: now, punishment is used to extract evidence.[37]

Even more to the point, the protections provided by *Miranda* had actually been circumvented by police routines and by U.S. court decisions for some time.[38] The fact was that in everyday police practice nearly 80 percent of suspects waived their *Miranda* rights after having them recited or distributed to them. Indeed, as Deborah Young has argued, by establishing an easily ritualized and soon-circumvented boundary (the "bright line"), the *Miranda* decision may have actually forestalled the development of more effective due process protections. A limit that has allowed both state courts and the police themselves to freelance—or, in *NYPD Blue*'s terms, to improvise—a range of new tricks and ruses devised to secure confessions, broker plea agreements, or produce informants. If anything, the more subtly resilient court test of the "totality of circumstances," often applied in adjudicating the fruits of police *deception,* had only accelerated this practice's use—for example, tactics such as minimizing *Miranda* itself; telling perpetrators they want to hear "their" side of the story; sympathizing with suspects and offering to get them professional help; telling them they're "off the record." Likewise, whatever the impact of the "CSI" effect on TV, the everyday impact of scientific wizardry in evidence-gathering may well be only that it allows an interrogator to threaten suspects with (mythical) certain guilt unless they open up—that is, even when the evidence will not produce the certainty the interrogator says it will.[39]

By all this I don't mean to minimize the importance of coercion as a legal, constitutional, or moral issue—or to ignore the important issue of false confessions. Nor is there is a clear boundary between psychological intimidation and physical torture; the point is that each bleeds into the other, and deception can certainly generate coercive interrogations. Rather, I merely mean to suggest that focusing too narrowly on the *Miranda* threshold may have caused us to underestimate the broader narrative dimensions of interrogation, and thus the stories about criminality we receive from it. As Richard J. Ofshe and Richard A. Leo have pointed out, a confession is not solely an admission of guilt (the "I did it") that signals the crossing of a legal threshold. Rather, a confession is the fuller narrative that takes ownership of and explains a crime, a retrospective tale that can be shaped by cues and deceptions generated, to use David Simon's term again, interrogation's "choreography." Moreover, by opening up interrogation's secrets on prime time, Milch and his peers did much to reestablish the basis on which even those liberals who supported *Miranda* might be liable to give ground, reacquaint themselves with a secret admiration for police managers *above* the ranks of the now-thinner, thin Blue line. As I've said, Bratton did indeed voice concerns about *Miranda* to anyone who would listen. But we also know that Bratton would, less publicly, proudly parade *NYPD Blue*'s Jimmy Smits, a practitioner of a rather different art, before the ranks of his department.[40]

II.

An often gossipy, occasionally even petty, memoir, *True Blue* was marketed as a "tell-all" book for fans on the heels of series star David Caruso's abrupt departure from *NYPD Blue* after only one season. Packaged much like a fan's scrapbook, the hardcover edition featured a dust jacket offering a Blue-black collage of snapshots from the series, actual news photos of NYPD busts, and stills of Bill Clark's own face, all arranged around a dominating NYPD gold shield. Inside, Caruso is anything but delicately cropped from the book's illustrations. Conversely, as the dominant voice of his collaboration, David Milch courts a mixture of liberal bravado and commercial savvy that at times borders on cynicism. He admits, for example, that he always needs to build an episode of *NYPD Blue* around four climactic events to accommodate commercial interruptions (140), and that Caruso's departure forced him into fast thinking about a new partner for Andy Sipowicz—at this juncture, the character of Bobby Simone (played by Jimmy Smits). Milch seems content to talk at tedious length about his race horses or his battles to include partial nudity and street-level vulgarity when a group called the American Family Association started a boycott against the series (67–77). Oblivious to the obvious question of whether Bill Clark's own sex life was as glamorous as that of his TV counterparts, Milch's confessions of past criminality or literary pretensions only seem to draw him farther apart from the police culture he would claim to capture on TV. And one could go on: a "good case" to Clark, for instance, means a cleared crime, not (as apparently to Milch) a "story" value intrinsically conducive to good melodrama.

However, considering the broader fields of culture and power in the mid-1990s helps us start to see that Milch and Clark's partnership wasn't as idiosyncratic as it might seem. The notion that writers like Milch merely resort to formula and to predetermined ideological norms can only partially account for the fluid, improvisational, and quite politically complex exchange that actually takes place. As Pierre Bourdieu might have it, the relationship of TV (cultural production) to power (police authority) is not mechanistic; rather, as in Bourdieu's formulation, it is more like a box within a box. That is, we feel the shaping influences of certain "posts" or professional obligations—sponsors or networks on the one hand, commanders or crime victims on the other—because each partner thinks about his profession as a field not only of rewards, certification, or institutional capital, but internalized duties and satisfactions. Conversely, we feel both the weight of a given professional habit and the often-silent nuances of deportment, gesture, and demeanor in each collaborator. Any given fund of knowledge (say, of interrogation) from a radically different field (like policing) is not simply mined as raw material (as, for screenwriting). Rather, composing involves an exchange of dispositions and cultural authority.[41]

Nor are these dispositions quite as static as we might suppose. Clark, on the one hand, turns out to have been migrating to cultural work well before meeting Milch. A longtime homicide investigator and Vietnam veteran, Clark himself had moved "in house" following the Knapp Commission hearings as part of the department's reorganization. After leaving briefly to try more lucrative work in private security—a sign, perhaps, of declining job satisfaction—Clark returned to his original calling with the help of fellow reservist Ray Kelly, who would soon become (from 1992 to 1993, and again in 2002) New York's Commissioner of Police (*True Blue* 166). At the same time, Clark was no raw newcomer to media work when he joined Milch's series. On the contrary, he was already a law enforcement celebrity in New York City, having been a subject of Jimmy Breslin's columns over the years, having met the journalist while working the Son of Sam murders. Another New York tabloid journalist, Michael Daly, had actually recommended Clark to Milch in the first place (2).[42] And David Milch, on the other hand, was to be also shaped by his day in intriguing ways. We might reconsider, for instance, his disputes with ABC about profanity and partial nudity on the show. As we shall soon see, it shouldn't surprise us that Milch frames his cause in Romantic terms: as a resistance to censorship both from network executives and from those who represent or placate the Moral Majority. And yet, as even Milch admits in passing (65), one of the reasons the network finally surrenders to his demands is that broadcast television was losing older viewers to adult-oriented cable. In other words, what looks like Milch's claim to professional integrity actually supports the network in securing a bigger market share of that eighteen-to-forty-nine (largely male) demographic—bringing culturally liberal viewers into the urban world now overseen by police commissioners like William Bratton himself.

Intriguingly, the cause of resisting network censorship also provides a segue to the developing relationship with Clark. Their very first meeting takes place when Milch has returned to New York to escape network squabbles over the nudity question; he meets Clark in a diner. We learn that two episodes for the series have already been written; Clark, it would seem, is only being consulted for detail (81). But it turns out that Milch's network battle authorizes his claim to professional integrity, and through that, *True Blue* tells us, a tie to Clark's sense of duty is forged. Milch cements that bond further by calling up memories of his own father. The inner story becomes partly about class and partly about family secrets, for Milch's father had been, like Bill Clark, a silent, hardworking, and often tortured man of immigrant roots: a Buffalo surgeon of Jewish descent. On top of that, Milch's father was part of a family closely tied to organized crime—specifically, tied to Meyer Lansky during the mob boss's rise in the years following Prohibition (153). Suddenly, the very topics in *True Blue* that seem at first so tangential—Milch's family memories of pool halls, nightclubs, and most of all race tracks, all of which speak so evocatively of Lansky's own strategy of economic diversification—acquire new import, because together, as the interrogation scenes will show, Milch and Clark lay claim to a shared understanding of criminality.[43]

But they connect to this secret in unpredictable ways. Milch's father, we learn, had been saved from a life in organized crime by uncles who convinced him to pursue a college education and medical career. A friend who continued to tempt Milch's father with vice had been summarily thrown out the window of one of those pool halls (153). Thus, though that father was, like the screenwriter himself, a drug abuser (149, 157) and a lover of racehorses, Milch's memoir reveres him as an example of personal salvation through good work. We hear—just as we do on Clark's behalf—several accolades from clients about the elder Milch's professional dedication, all of which serve to erase the taint of criminality. A kind of balance is achieved, a counterpoint: to Milch, it seems completely logical to buy a racehorse with his HUMANITAS prize money (19). Just as he feels pride when Dennis Franz wins an Emmy, because Andy Sipowicz, who struggles with his own demons, is modeled on both Milch's own father and Bill Clark (159).

Of course, for the son as for that surgeon, hard work led to upward mobility. In the Milch family, one's profession reflects college training, the Blue that is Yale Blue. And yet, even Yale's teachings turn out to build a bridge to Clark. We discover, for instance, that Milch's decision to only gradually reveal the interior life of Sipowicz is neither a result of actor problems nor a naïve attempt to mirror Clark's own reticence. Rather, Milch refers to his mentor Robert Penn Warren, and to New Critical teachings about the inevitable narrative tension between a character's resistance to change and the passage of time (144). Milch's decidedly fatalistic pop consciousness is in fact reinforced by several high cultural references to Warren and to George Santayana (144) in *True Blue*: specifically, to the way (Milch says) gaps or wounds in experience, or the messy aspects of life, are healed by the work of the imagination. As Warren had himself written, "the high function of technique" is "a growth in integrity, literally a unifying of the self, of the random or discrepant possibilities and temptations of experience." This is, we gather, the philosophy the HUMANITAS prize recognized: a philosophy of ethical self-cultivation and personal wholeness, as we know, with a long tradition in Romantic aesthetics.[44]

At first, it might seem that by reverting to the decidedly individualist, Romantic rhetoric of the poet-critic, Milch effectively short-circuits *True Blue*'s claim to collaborative authorship.[45] But for his part, the Bill Clark in *True Blue* offers a telling narrative of working-class dedication that parallels Milch's philosophy. That is, as Clark migrates into television work, ultimately leaving the NYPD itself, he begins to share class secrets from police labor: the knowledge, for instance, that if you grew up in a neighborhood not wanting to run with its gangs, you'd spend time on the roofs of buildings (144). There is more here, however, than a simple sharing of stories for episode plots. More to the point, Clark's disposition makes itself felt in bodily demeanor, deportment, and gestures that Milch picks up. *True Blue* works to replicate the deeply private, reticent awkwardness of Clark's personality, a mixture of Irish taciturnity, cop mistrust of outsiders, and a supposed working-class propensity for roundabout comparison. "With nothing like the two years available we'd spent imagining [Caruso's character of] John Kelly," Milch now writes, ". . . we tried to conceive of a [new] character who would only permit himself to be known slowly and after shared experience had generated trust . . . whose life experience had left him emotionally foreclosed and inaccessible" (141).

Appropriate to Milch's many talents in this area, *True Blue* represents this temperament mainly through oblique, free-associational dialogue. Indeed, he actually credits several of the reciprocal comparisons between cop labor and TV writing to Clark's own improvisations. For example, when Milch describes his problems with network affiliates, Clark—without ever making the comparison explicitly—talks about "bosses" he has found hard to work for, on "the job" (19). When Caruso creates the aforementioned "actor problems," Clark talks about frictions between detective partners and the nuances of taking credit for a bust or not intruding on someone else's case (49). Some comparisons are more oblique and more dangerous. For instance, when Milch treats Clark to a very successful day at a Vegas racetrack, Clark tells a grim story about a sodomy-murder and a child's body he has been forced to see. The victim's parents had been irredeemably bereaved; of the horse's victory, Clark can only say, "Yeah, well, I hope it works out for you" (25). In contrast to these subtle fraternity-building moments, Caruso's lack of interaction with Clark is taken as an implicit failure. Caruso, by contrast, is a man who can't even recognize his best work on the show (137). That the actor is named David, a foil to Milch's own persona, itself carries improvisational significance.

These free-associational bonds, creative crossover in process, also take place in language, diction, and inside jokes. An NYPD word like "skel," for instance—derived from *skellum* or skeleton, to signify the bony body of a low-life perpetrator—might seem simply to transpose street argot to the show. But many other terms and phrases—again, "the job," "boss," or "like him for" (a phrase for suspecting someone of a crime)—work instead to create class parallels about autonomy, bureaucratic authority, or male friendship. For example, the term for a cop party or retirement roasting, "a racket," puns both on boisterousness or even sly law breaking and on organized crime, as well as referring to speeches that break the Blue code of reticence described earlier (85). On a markedly masculine show notorious not just for its taciturn men but for its exposure of bodies—and, notoriously, for its inability to retain actresses—Caruso terms a weak scene as being forced to put on a "dress" (71). More important for what I will argue in the next section, slang from the field of policing, much of which emanates from interrogation, resonates with familiar attitudes toward legal process. Perhaps the most celebrated phrase on the series, "lawyering up" (asking for your lawyer), connotes not only the intrusive presence of law but an unwelcome intrusion of white-collar expertise and snobbery. Moreover, "lawyering up" signals what is most to be avoided not just in interrogation itself but in police drama: it will effectively end the central drama both because it sidelines the cop stars and because it potentially signals a change in the genre—to, of all things, a lawyer show.

These improvisations between Milch and Clark, again, might seem merely a matter of their idiosyncratic personalities. And yet everything described above reflects a rather decisive political and legal subtext and the role of entertainment within it: the box within the box. The fatalism that Clark expresses about how things "work out," notably, is quite reflective of police work institutionally, particularly in the de-industrial moment, not only where one is exposed to human depravity but also where finishing the job often means speaking for a silenced victim, or believing one knows a criminal's guilt without being able to prove it. Again, to a cop, a case is "cleared" (solved) when he convinces his boss it is, not when the legal system says so. This sense of the "job" also speaks to the post-Vietnam ethos that Clark embodies and to so much of the institutional self-definition of metropolitan police in recent decades. Much as contemporary police managers speak of restoring the cop to the community in the aftermath of a Vietnam-style militarization of the streets, Clark's saddest memory of combat, *True Blue* tells us, is that of fellow soldiers defacing the bodies of slain Vietcong. Pivoting off what is virtually a mythic insignia of U.S. troop malfeasance, Clark himself, we are told, gave the bodies a decent burial. "I found one guy's wallet and he had pictures of his family and so forth same as I would, and a library card," Clark says (59). This is not a policeman, we believe, who will deface bodies, but who will restore them, and rebuild the community.[46] Here the self-appointed task of police melodrama, as so often in earlier eras, is to "un-alienate" cop labor, to clear cases that are not so in real life and restore the police's public's estimate.[47] Milch's contact with Clark involves, in other words, a desire to "humanize" the police, a word that reverberates, as we have seen, with Milch's own New Critical premiums and the HUMANITAS reception. As an artist, as we shall see, Milch most of all emulates the narrative ingenuity of Clark in performing interrogations.

Of course, the meeting between Milch and Clark has a few uneven, unpredictable dimensions. But by learning of the pre-political subtexts about the dignity of labor, and about erasing the taint of criminality, we can begin to see something more complex at work than a screenwriter looking to a cop for "color" or, in particular, realism. Rather pointedly, Milch actually describes a few instances where fidelity to fact is not the operative rule, and humanizing his cops is—that is, humanizing by closing up a wound of police or victim experience. In one episode involving a case of a child who was kidnapped and murdered, Milch admits that he brought her back from the dead in a later episode, partly to evince Sipowicz and Clark's relentless devotion to such families (120, 179). It is telling, I think, how this breaking of the realist code is legitimated: by turning once again to high cultural wisdom, in this instance quoting Henry James. When confronted with a similar charge that Fleda Vetch's actions in *The Spoils of Poynton* were too virtuous to seem real, Milch reminds us that James had famously retorted, "So much the worse for Real Life" (122). Never has James sounded so much like a fatalist Irish American cop, more Blue than true.

III.

When he first meets Bill Clark in that diner, Milch already senses that the cop is an intensely devoted, private, even obsessive man, bringing what we later learn is a subtle threat of violence to his work (149–50). They begin by discussing the murder of one Kathleen Farley, a woman brutally attacked by an addict and his brother in her own home. Clark soon initiates Milch into interrogation tactics by admitting that he withheld information about Farley's medical condition so as to convince the brothers, separately, that she would still be able to testify. Clark began his interrogation, in fact, with another deception, by allowing the brothers to claim that this was "essentially a burglary that went wrong," and all the while "minimizing the seriousness of what these guys were looking at" (8–9). Here, Clark's use of the *NYPD Blue* phrase "looking at" speaks not only to the perpetrators' legal prospects but also to his own choreography, and what he is therefore allowing them to "look at." In short, the phrase signals Clark's quite adroit control of information in order to draft a confession.

It is not that Miranda warnings or coercion are irrelevant to this opening gambit. On the contrary, staging his liberal concern as a rookie about such tactics, Milch confronts Clark with news reports that the brothers' defense team had tried to exclude the confession from the trial on the grounds it had been coerced. The screenwriter and cop subsequently have a testy exchange about whether, generally or in this instance, a cop would use force. Clark says:

> "They did it [they were the killers]. Now, has it ever happened a cop laid hands on a guy to get him on record telling the truth? Where a guy is guilty and the cop knows it—he's got witnesses like this skel's brother who've told him what happened but who might not stand up in court or even be around, and the cop knows a confession is the only evidence that doesn't go away, or that some smart-ass lawyer can't turn upside down—has it ever happened a cop laid hands on a guy to get him to tell the truth? Yeah, that's happened."
>
> "Did I beat Richard Kolomick?" Bill looked me in the eye. "No," he said. "I didn't beat him." (10–11)

Clark confesses to the general practice while claiming that no use of force took place in *this* case. Or does he? Here is where *True Blue*'s re-education actually begins. At first, it seems as if Clark is really just drawing a preliminary boundary with Milch, testing the screenwriter while being roundabout in the extreme. Milch will later restage precisely such an initiation between cop partners Sipowicz and Simone on *NYPD Blue* itself in the episode "Simone Says" in 1994. Of course, the threat of force is always present, and sometimes used. But *focusing* on physical force alone is precisely what Milch must unlearn.

Discussing another case, Clark continues the re-education by describing an interrogation where he locked the door and said to the suspect that if he didn't confess, "I'm going to beat you till you beg to die." This certainly was coercion, and Clark concludes by saying that "with that, eventually the guy went." Milch, understandably, seizes upon "eventually," and points out to us that this was precisely "the subject that had stopped our conversation earlier." But now, Milch tells us, "Bill and I knew each other better." And so Clark explains more fully:

> "Understand something [Clark says] . . . a lot of these guys have stood beatings their whole lives. Your only goal is making the guy understand you're serious with what you're saying, and you're going to accomplish your purpose. . . .
>
> [There's] a crucial time for the interview, when you're coming to the truth. The five other robberies had no violence, so my guess was it actually

was the driver's trying to protect himself that had moved this guy to kill him, the driver's grabbing for the weapon and so forth. So that's the point in the room the guy may come to feel, if he gives up what actually happened, for the first time since the interview started he won't need to be figuring angles anymore, plus getting to say he isn't a bad guy, he hadn't gone out that night to kill this driver. At that point you'd really want to reestablish in the guy's mind that's the way he should go. You reestablish your seriousness, with getting his attention, and emphasizing he should tell the truth."

"You might hit him then." [Milch says]

"Something, again, to bring home your position, your willingness to keep on with this lousy-feeling environment [Clark responds]. Raising your voice might be enough."

In this confession (83–84), the substance of which was written into the episode titled "Tempest in a C-Cup" in 1993, Clark now rather amorally considers beatings only in terms of their efficacy: they establish the basic parameters of a coercive environment a guilty man would want to escape (and, as many critics have legitimately pointed out, also an innocent one).

Within this overall approach, deception is a key tool in acquiring leverage over the person in the Box, as we often see on the show. In Episode 109 (1998), entitled "Seminal Thinking," Detective Greg Medavoy (Gordon Clapp), disgusted over a senseless rape of a homeless woman, constructs an elaborate set of lies about DNA evidence that forces a pimp to confess. At the same time, Sipowicz and Simone coach a hopelessly digressive witness to narrow his testimony to their needs and eliminate his obviously self-protective lies. Interrogation deception often moves in several directions at once. In Episode 133 from 2000 (titled "Loogie Nights"), the detectives demonstratively usher a beat cop up the precinct stairwell, to create the illusion he is about to testify against his partner regarding an alley beating. But in this interrogation tactic, having him on the stairwell also lets him hear the witness who will supposedly implicate his partner. It might well be argued here that *Miranda* protections actually work to make the *threat* of a beating into a deception itself (and a dramatic tension). Conversely, deception is made to seem a necessary recourse, since beating is "theoretically" prohibited.

Nevertheless, there is an additional dimension here that Clark wants to emphasize beyond simply using the threat of violence for leverage. Initially, that is, we might think that force or physical coercion is the primary weapon in Clark's interrogation arsenal. As I have shown, Milch stages this more classically liberal anxiety for us in his first meetings with Clark. In the long passage above, however, it is not only that Clark *actually* says that raising his voice might just as easily do the trick. Moreover, it is Clark's argument that the threat of force is more like an option or even a premise of the performance, something that can be used, among other things, to demonstrate the interrogator's own implacability. The general thrust of the threat, he tells us, is *to supplement the deception:* the opening created by reassuring the suspect that "he isn't a bad guy," that the shooting was accidental, and that agreeing with the cop would be nearly tantamount to telling the truth, whether it would or wouldn't. The principle of deception is actually what controls the outcome (the confession narrative). In the Farley interrogation, Clark does get one brother to implicate the other in these ways. In the second case cited above, Clark hides the fact that he's a homicide officer and then builds up a link to the shooting through retracing a series of robberies. He feigns confusion over different stories about a crime; he lies about his own thinking; he creates imaginary legal outs for his suspect. He tells one suspect who has flunked a polygraph that "he'd better get in front" and go with the "robbery-went-wrong" story and say he "never meant the violence to happen." As Clark puts it so bluntly, but so deceptively, "I went with remorse" (178–79). But perhaps the most misleading method, which Milch says he used in the thirty-first episode of *NYPD Blue* (1995), is Clark's playing the role of the "thick-headed" white ethnic cop (138, 178). This is the exact opposite, of course, of what he is. Through *True Blue,* we learn that he has actually been replacing his only-apparent reticence with very adroit storytelling.

IV.

To give a fuller sense of how this ethos is transposed to the show, I want to focus more closely on the screenplay by Milch and Clark for the episode "Prostrate Before the Law" in 1998. (I have selected this episode because it offers the fullest range of the interrogation deceptions the series routinely displayed.) In this episode, a badly burned male body with a bullet wound is found in a van on a parking garage roof. Four friends of the victim, a group of ex-marines who have been seen on that roof by a reluctant eyewitness, are all brought into the stationhouse. There, the *NYPD Blue* squad splits the four up into one-on-one interrogations, or what the show prefers to call "interviews." Suspects are then paired with a detective according to a preliminary scan of their own intolerance and personal weaknesses: the flirt with a female detective, an apparent racist with a nonwhite cop. The interviews quickly generate only smart-aleck rejoinders by each suspect, and we start to see that the group is actually an extremist cadre of some kind. That fact proves important to the foiling of the interrogation scenes, since the group soon spouts the Second and Fourth amendments back at detectives. One even resists making any statement by citing the protections of *Miranda*. One says "yeah, right" to a cop's recitation of "it's a free country" when he says the suspect has the right to leave. When Sipowicz's partner Simone fails on his first pass to get at the truth, a suspect mocks him about his "Puerto Rico" background, saying, "That was a hell of a beating you handed out"—as if he is not much of a man. "The day is young," Simone replies, asserting his premise.

Soon, however, the squad marshals a full battery of interrogation deceptions: trapping the suspects in a lie, pressuring them with threats of acquiring police records the squad has actually already seen, letting the suspects huddle up and write statements only so that the squad can acquire incriminating handwriting samples. But one ploy finally breaks the suspects' resistance:

> SIMONE: I'm absolutely ready [if] this turns out some gang of black or Puerto Rican kids went up on you guys on the roof. Everybody runs but Neil [the victim]. And you guys leaving your friend to get killed, well that all fits the facts. But until we hear it coming from you, well we got to treat you guys like possible perpetrators.
>
> SUSPECT #1: Yeah, that's it . . . that's how it happened. . . . Detective here worked out all the rest in his head.
>
> SUSPECT #2: That's eerie, man, chapter and verse.
>
> SIMONE: Let's work out the details.

In truth, this *isn't* what they have done, which had been to abandon a man they had already killed and disfigured. So, once the suspects' individual statements do not converge, the NYPD squad rousts their hotel room, confirming suspicions that they are actually a white supremacist group that has executed a comrade as a security risk. The squad then gradually convinces individual suspects to inform on one other (one, by being misleadingly promised mitigating circumstances though he had pulled the trigger).

Again, the collaborative, cross-ethnic partnership of the police precinct is foiled to the cadre who has abandoned one of its own, several times over.[48]

Interrogation, then, really is the linchpin of a quite complex performance within the precinct's larger fraternity. To be sure, this performance can create a farcical rendering of selfsame liberal objections we might voice to the show's scandalizing of *Miranda*. On *NYPD Blue*, the interrogator sometimes sarcastically mimics a liberal defense lawyer who has actually been excluded from the interrogation scene, thus offering a defense that, well, isn't really a defense. Or the interrogator plays the role of a friend who covers for you, or knows you've been betrayed, or takes your side. (In Episode 27, "Simone Says" [1994], one detective tells a child abuser he, too, is a "family man," in order to make it seem, erroneously, as if the entire matter can be referred to counseling and not to the courts.) And perhaps most tellingly, like a mock therapist or social worker, the cop sometimes allows the suspect to say he's been pressured by his upbringing into a life of crime. In one double homicide, Clark deceptively sympathizes with a perpetrator who says he only had a gun because of how dangerous his neighborhood was. ("I said I understood that," Clark intones [173]). Repeatedly, the cop (like his screenwriter partner in *True Blue*) gets to project himself into, and then perform, the lax conscience or rationalizations of the suspect himself, the permissive framework that supposedly told the criminal that what he did wasn't so bad.

The dominant effect here may seem as if the function of interrogation is to supplant or replace the perpetrator's voice. But the ritual on *NYPD Blue* is really not a silencing one. Instead, the pre-juridical process, much like the creative one, is intent on *drafting* the criminal rationale itself through improvisational by-play between cop and his criminal antagonist. Including the very cases where Milch isolates on physical coercion, Clark runs a number of cons, in the sense of eliciting a "belief" that the perpetrators don't initially recognize, and yet come to adopt as their own.[49] Meanwhile, rather than working from an assumed political position to begin with, interrogation often produces a wide array of such beliefs. Because it is improvisational, that is, the interrogator's routine often ricochets out to *any* available target, and the dramatic results are not always so predictable in simple ideological terms. For example, the interrogator does often serve up a morally conservative solution for the suspect (often "being a real man"), offering it as the suspect's only potential saving grace. But the point is that it often proves to be the very thing that traps him, just as racism and selfishness trap the cadre on "Prostrate." At other moments, meanwhile, the Box becomes a stage for an improvisational routine for ethnic and class crossover, allowing a working-class citizen, through verbal adroitness, to "get over" on criminals and lawyers alike. At times, however, the sheer claustrophobia of the interrogation room reverberates back upon the investigators, who find themselves uncomfortably present to human despair, the pain of crime victims, wounds they are powerless to heal by their long day on the job. These are the "Blues" of police work, a fatalism about how things "work out" in the fraternity of falsehoods into which the "perp" is only temporarily enlisted.

Ultimately, this many-layered mockery works both to reaffirm the legitimacy of the working-class cop's world and to stigmatize the "perp." But this effect is driven less by the needs of melodrama than by a prior understanding the show seeks to reconfirm. That is, the ritual performance works to confirm the cop's administrative street realism, his prior knowledge of who is guilty and who is not.[50] The spatial geography of the interrogation landscape on *NYPD Blue* underscores this point. Customarily, various interrogation "boxes" appear within the stationhouse in oddly displaced locations, given numbers ("the perp is in 1"), sometimes directly adjacent to an in-house lock-up (the external one called "the system"). These boxes are thus given a spatial coding that puts them not only adjacent to, but really in place of, the legal system. It is not only that we are in a space before formal charging or "lawyering up," in that the suspect is usually without counsel. Rather, the sheer proliferation of these boxes on the set made it seem as if Bratton's managerial ethos had made interrogation itself a "back to basics" practice, a reaffirmation of what cops had always known. So much, *pace* Milch's claims, for an illusion being displaced. Rather it is almost as if the interrogation room is, for Milch and Clark, politically prelapsarian—taking us back not only before "lawyering up" via *Miranda* but to a mythical, manly freedom prior to a liberal state that no longer holds sway.

V.

Given the various ways its "choreography" can be played, interrogation need not always have the nostalgic ethos, above, in charge. Yet as I will suggest in my Epilogue, our debates about police power will be shortsighted if they do not recognize that techniques so controversial in the superheated post-9/11 security climate—interrogation deception, the mushrooming use of criminal informants and of undercover agents,

CompStat profiling, to name but a few—had already been accentuated by the law enforcement turn I have described. In "Prostrate Before the Law," in fact, when we roust those ex-marines' hotel room, we discover the reason this supremacist cadre has executed their comrade. They have been hatching a terrorist bomb plot.

This threat, naturally, has multiple resonances. As I have tried to suggest, the framing of these ex-marines as defacing and abandoning a comrade's body is a rather pointed contrast to Bill Clark's own experiences in Vietnam; as in many recent media spectacles, un-writing Vietnam sometimes drives the cultural redrafting of police power as well.[51] The choice of a white supremacist cell also provides, or so it seems, a sharp contrast to the ethnically diverse lot that conducts the police interrogation. Indeed, as Larry Landrum has observed, the procedural genre is often used to assemble a cross-ethnic "city within the city" that counters the threat of an anarchic outside world.[52] As in many Bochco productions, *NYPD Blue*'s homicide division is itself considerably more pluralistic than its counterparts in real life.[53] In showing viewers how a cross-ethnic, egalitarian squad can defeat a militaristic white-supremacist cadre from outside the city, the interrogation box confirms a more liberal political subtext, one quite reassuring to *NYPD Blue*'s audience demographic. In the implicit connection to Bill Clark's own experiences with comrades mutilating bodies, the series works to un-write Vietnam, using (in the precinct itself) what film historians call the "foxhole pluralism" of war movies. Thus, when Bobby Simone throws his own "third world" and "mongrel" Puerto Rican identity in the face of white supremacist paranoia, an episode like "Prostrate Before the Law" claims pluralism not just as an incidental feature of *NYPD Blue* but as its central ethos. And yet, it is for this very reason—because the police interrogators are meant to model a more democratic egalitarianism under siege by threats at home and abroad—that the controversy surrounding Milch's second HUMANITAS prize, recounted in *True Blue*'s final pages, also bears examining.

To be brief, a dispute arose from remarks Milch made in accepting his second award in 1994. On that occasion, he had observed that while many police shows portrayed "black characters in position of authority" so as to acquire the "credentials of liberalism," he himself felt less "imaginative authority" in doing so on *NYPD Blue*. Since he had less lived experience on which to draw, Milch reasoned, he could not create the requisite interiority of black characters. Conversely, Milch reflected, this might be why black writers faced such difficulties writing for a mainstream (white) audience (184–85). Needless to say, this impromptu attempt to acknowledge his own limitations did not go down well in all quarters. Along with being attacked in the mainstream press as a racist, Milch found himself challenged by *NYPD Blue*'s own James McDaniel, who at the time played the African American precinct captain Arthur Fancy. McDaniel said Milch had essentially conceded to thinking "he [McDaniel] was a kind of second-class citizen, not only on the show," but in Milch's own imagination (*True Blue* 191).[54] Stung by the accusation—and thus still, after all, seeing himself as a liberal—Milch began to sponsor a seminar explicitly designed to introduce minority writers to television writing (189), and hired one of his chief critics, African American writer David Mills. On top of that, Milch wrote an episode for *NYPD Blue* in which Arthur Fancy takes Sipowicz to an all-black restaurant and makes him experience minority status. The scene is pasted into *True Blue* itself, arguably as its narrative climax.

Of course—although whether or not any of this controversy over Fancy's character was expressive of personal racism on Milch's part is not my concern here—the series' claims to pluralism had many limits. Before *The Closer*, women were rarely if ever granted the interrogator's powers I have sketched above; even now, they can do so only by edging their way into the masculine bravado relished by Milch and Clark's mutual initiation. More to the point, Milch's reaction exposed some troubling dimensions of his linking of post-*Miranda* liberalism to his aesthetic practice of making interrogation the centerpiece of prime-time viewing. To begin with, the interrogators on *NYPD Blue* exhibit few of the reservations about social empathy that Milch expressed in his comments on racial understanding and the creative process. Instead, in the series' trademark gambit, neither the cop nor the screenwriter expresses any hesitation about projecting himself into the perpetrator's experience. Instead, as "Prostrate Before the Law" suggests, the cop pitches a series of drafts not unlike a screenwriter, as if oblivious to the fact that—as each show tells us—he is in the presence of the original "author" of the crime.[55] (Hence again, the implicit claim to have a secret knowledge of criminality.) In a contradiction crucial to his claim to have transcended *old* liberal illusions, Milch can pull off his account of the omniscience of interrogation only by maintaining a silence or race blindness about the races of the cop or the perpetrator to begin with.[56]

Perhaps most disturbing, in other words, is the way the fraternal silence between Milch and Clark about their own whiteness translates its "pluralism" into to an exclusionary rhetoric about race that so often inhabits both the fields of policing and mass culture. Even the models of creative contact *True Blue* exhibits may cause us to neglect the deepest forms of in-difference in modern society: how differently racialized subjects can occupy virtually the same position in a professional field and yet have a radically different experience of the inequalities there. And, as McDaniel's retort suggested, such indifference doubles back, reinforcing that inequality in both the real terrain (policing) and the imaginary (mass culture). Thus when Milch was asked about how his own experiences in petty lawbreaking or drug abuse suited him for writing police melodrama, he responded, oblivious to the contradiction, by saying empathy was no problem on that score. The cops and criminals had a mutual understanding that, he said, transcended the "bullshit" lawyers introduced into the confession process. "A cop knows where the crime began," Milch said. "He knows what was in the guy's mind."[57] Here, the interrogator is revealed to be hardly a "thickheaded" agent of coercion, but a figure of considerable imagination.

Not surprisingly, then, Milch once again placed interrogation fully within his understanding of Robert Penn Warren. On the new episode about Fancy's challenge to Sipowicz's racism, he wrote, "My point was that a commitment to craft had allowed me to overcome any deficit of emotional commitment I might have to Fancy's character. I described how, as I was writing the scene, I began to feel Fancy come alive in my imagination, to speak with the same sort of specificity and out of the same depth of passion as Sipowicz and other characters to whom I came more easily. . . . I said that the opportunity to enlarge our spirits through pursuit of our craft was one of the blessings of our profession" (197). Having once claimed that his lack of experience had limited him when it came to race, he now said the craft of imagination could overcome that limit. Writing itself, he said, allowed "your spirit to grow. It's your bridge to humanity." It is thus hard not to think of the name "Fancy" as self-reflexive, signifying the transcendence of simple illusion by the infusion of true imagination.[58] Passions reflected upon in imaginative tranquility, in other words, become a bridge to wholeness and, supposedly, the transcendence of racial difference. In sum, Milch's claim underscores David Lloyd and Paul Thomas's point (70–71) that Romantic aesthetics has always been about cultivating an ideal of citizenship. For Coleridge as for Warren or for Milch, creative expression itself became a story about how errors of social "misrecognition"—the wounds that we now see Milch is exposing in his HUMANITAS confession—are supposedly subject to rereading and revision, thereby fashioning a claim to disinterested political judgment.

In all, therefore, before we too quickly attach the convenient label "conservative" to these ideological effects, we might do well to consider what William Ian Miller has suggested in a related context: that some aspects of retributive justice imagined in popular forms are actually enacted in the name of the state, not in opposition to it.[59] Here, echoing the accommodation Milch himself has learned, the state (the cop) is hardly an agent of brute force or simple moral rectitude; nor does the Box dramatize a receding state. On the contrary, as if it has learned from the liberalism that conservatives so often scandalize, the state is conceived as an intrusive force. One is tempted to say it is a Jamesian conception, an entity upon whom nothing is lost, able to see into criminality, mimic its rationalizations, and then enlist those self-deceptions in the criminal's own capture. Albeit feinting to the left through his melodramatic counterpoint to the right-wing extremism, the prime-time interrogator more often exhibits his real political antithesis in the perpetrator trapped in the box of old-style liberal rationalization, ready to sell out partners in crime. Even hardened criminals' confessions seem but a second-hand reflection of their own dependence on the illusions with which police mock them. As if confined to our own one-way mirror, our TV screens, rarely do we as viewers actually get to profile the demographic makeup of the subjects most often in the interrogator's chair; rather, from night to night, as Elaine Scarry might say, the Box in the box is a place where this body has no voice *as* a body.[60] To Milch and Clark, in fact, their own bond of empathy around "understanding" criminality assumes a prior knowledge of what a perp is liable to say. In other words, recalling James Q. Wilson's meditation on habitual criminality, interrogation becomes a form of risk management, a projection into a criminal mind one thinks one already knows.

Milch or Clark's anticipation of the anxieties of our current crime and security climate can be overdrawn. In "Prostrate Before the Law," they may have meant merely to throw in a taste of relevance drawn from the headlines of Oklahoma City or the World Trade Center bombing of 1993. Yet as I will suggest in my Epilogue, in its fatalism about power and justice, in its relish in "getting over" on criminality and lawyers alike, and in its turning of the Box into dramatic domestic entertainment, Milch and Clark's partnership might ultimately be quite true to our Blue moment. At the very least, Milch's confession offers up a post-liberal politics that seems not to have been coerced.

3

The Time of the Crime
Cold Case Squads and Neoconservative Social Memory

IN "A CROWN OF FEATHERS" (1972), Isaac Bashevis Singer tells the story of an orphan named Akhsa Holishitzer, doted upon by Polish grandparents who manage the estate of a local gentile Prince inside the Pale. Akhsa grows into a young woman so attached to her grandparents that she cannot settle upon a mate, and thereby suffers a crisis of faith when they die. Longing for their return from the dead, haunted by conflicting dreams of their life plan for her, in her misery she finds herself drawn to the prohibited book of Job, and from there to the New Testament stories of Jesus' resurrection. She converts to Christianity and gentile luxury, thereby launching herself on a life-long pilgrimage of ostracism, exile, and return to her own community. She begins her journey of self-doubt, however, by inaugurating a Black Mass that conjures up the very figure of Satan himself. Right to her deathbed, in fact, she will be haunted by words Satan tells her while she agonizes over the truths about death and the afterlife she is seeking. "The truth," Satan tells her, "is that there is no truth."

Singer's tale is a characteristically deft meditation on faith and the "intricate and hidden" ways of temptation, suffering, and redemption.[1] But what is more startling is the allusion to Satan's lines in the twenty-first-century nonfiction crime narrative *A Cold Case* (2001), which tells the story of a twenty-seven-year-old homicide file reopened by the New York Police Department. That *A Cold Case*'s author, *New Yorker* author and chronicler of the Rwandan genocide, Philip Gourevitch, places Satan's aphorism in the mouth of a dubious, slick, and rather mordantly romantic defense lawyer turns out to be very much to the point. For countering the lawyer's self-serving relativism is the patient industry, tireless labor, and moral certainty of the Jewish New York homicide detective who has devoted himself to the case of a barstool argument gone bad, and to tracking down a crook who has vanished from New York City. In fact, this shoe-leather hero—a detective named Andy Rosenzweig, originally from the victim's own neighborhood—thinks of cold case investigations as holding vigil for victims' families, warding off their despair over life's chaos and meaninglessness. "As a rule," a cop from *A Cold Case* says ruefully, "nobody speaks for the dead, unless we do."[2]

Criminal investigators who speak for (and sometimes to) the dead have been quite prominent in American mass culture of late. "Cold case" proved to be the catchphrase not only of Gourevitch's reportage, but of three other mysteries available in the same year (including a juvenile cyberspace novel promoted under Tom Clancy's signature), and soon dozens of mystery imitators.[3] Cold case melodrama soon made its way to TV, in some instances supplanting the "cop TV" craze of the late 1980s and early 1990s with a new procedural, forensic, and—David Milch would approve—startlingly confessional format. Such a formula became part of CBS's prime-time lineup in the crime series generated by Meredith Stiehm, a veteran of the *NYPD Blue* writing staff, as well as in A&E's true-crime show called *Cold Case Files*. Before either series, in fact, this style of investigation also inspired one of the first interactive reality-based television programs, the crime-stoppers show *Cold Case,* which began to run periodically on cable in April 1997.[4] On that show, viewers used the Internet to view (and to download) actual case materials: police files, crime scene photos, autopsy reports, transcripts of 911 calls, witness statements, and even detectives' notebooks.[5] But beyond eliciting agonizing confessions of deeply held secrets by witnesses, perpetrators, or family members, cold case melodrama expanded the domain of the crime in one other important way. Especially as the Internet or 800 numbers came into play, friends, family, and the police could not only work together in such investigations, but effectively create "virtual," Web-based shrines to victims. Cold case work, in other words, claimed to bring the police and the community together, to create what is often called the "victim circle" of a crime. Through merging the cop's dogged labor and the moral or emotional dimensions of a victim's status, the secrets of this circle now became publicly shared.[6]

To be sure, the resurrection of buried or forgotten crimes had long been prominent in writers such as Victor Hugo, Charles Dickens, and Nathaniel Hawthorne. And the cold case method was one way for police to capture the public imagination and restore public confidence in the ever-present war on crime. Cold case work was partly a response to what I have described in chapter 2 as the backlash against traditional detective work in the emerging ethos of risk management. Yet the cold case mobilization of victim experience and, above all, of what is sometimes called collective or social memory, was evidence of much more subtle transformations in the neoconservative turn. In the broadest sense, the cold case phenomenon expressed the rising power of victim-centered, retributive justice and the pre-political values and mythologies in which the strategies were often wrapped. As I have said, the cold case strategy contributed to an ethos in which the police investigator seemed no longer a simple representative of the state; rather, he came to act as a small-scale surrogate for the grieving victim, or even his or her community. Quite appropriately, then, the genre Gourevitch himself readapts to explore these dimensions is, once again, the post–World War II police procedural. If David Milch resurrected the "blues" of a multiethnic police precinct, many cold case writers drew instead upon the genre's well-known capacity for celebrating an "average" police officer who both serves his community and doubles as its representative, doing his job much as a soldier must.[7] Gourevitch's *A Cold Case,* in particular, explores the spare, deadpan, and obsessively detail-oriented procedures of a cop who becomes a neighborhood hero—in short, a mobile and humanized political symbol representing, in microcosmic fashion, governance through crime control.

Within the cold case police strategy, therefore, came two collateral refashionings of state authority—or, as it were, a tactical and micropolitical rearrangement of the relationships among cops, criminals, and victims. First, collateral to the celebration of the police as a neighborhood guy, private concerns of citizens were made a public matter, particularly as the victim's pain was "brought to" the punishment of the criminal. And second, criminal justice was increasingly likened to civil redress, specifically by implementing a more retributive, victim-centered justice by recalibrating what one might call the social clock on crime itself.[8] (Once again, Jonathan Simon's comment on "steering mechanisms" and small-scale tactics in the war on crime is quite germane.)[9] Under the cold case imperative, customary legal protections about the speediness of a trial, or conversely about the statute of limitations, were reset, lengthened, or abolished; meanwhile, just as in the prosecution of organized crime, the time measurements around crime itself were redesigned. A statute of limitation might be reattached, for instance, not to the moment of a crime's commission but to the discovery of evidence, or to the subsequent acts of a conspiracy that may have taken place for years following the crime. (Here again, the policing of organized crime as a corporate entity provided a key template.)

Meanwhile, at the other end of the process—after a criminal's indictment—the effect of victims' rights advocacy was not only to expand the scope of state cooperation with victims (on its face, a reasonable reform). More to the point, it began to cede to those victims the idea that the time of their *suffering* was something of which the state should take cognizance. Once a matter of secrecy that the state's authority shielded by superseding a citizen's role in punishment, that time of suffering now became akin to a cultural "right," entitled to redress by state power. Thus the law might take to measuring not just the results of the crime per se but its extended consequences. Though we often see this as simply the result of "zero tolerance," an element of risk management—of the double kind I discuss in regard to James Q. Wilson in my Introduction—also can be detected.[10] That is, victims' rights arguments often began to say that criminals themselves should have foreseen the time of the pain their crime might entail. In short, the punishment of the crime became linked to temporal assessment, to "foreseeable harm," as the phrase went. And here is why cultural storytelling proved so revelatory. As cold case narratives took it upon themselves to portray the suffering of the victim or victim circle—often "eternal" in its feel, seeking closure but never really finding it—of course, these stories also were forced to negotiate the reciprocal desire for compensation for that suffering.[11]

Especially in the way that cold case narratives seemed to benefit from scientific advances in DNA testing, the computerized "aging" of mug shots, or a supposed precision in firearm identification, it might seem that the main effect of cold case investigations would be to install a rationalistic approach to crime. On shows like *CSI* and many others, the effect is to highlight technological wizardry, and thereby produce an irrefutable certainty—much as the interrogation confession was supposed to. And this, along with the "speed and certainty" neoconservatives lobbied for in the criminal justice system—that is, the removal of judicial discretion, or the use of determinate sentences—such an appeal to rationality (mythical though it was) would indeed often be at the heart of the cold case genre's more extravagant claims.[12] And yet, the core of its cultural storytelling proves to be not so rationalistic, after all. The humanizing of the cop often meant the collateral emphasis on his emotional connection to victims, and his long memory about crime's disruptive effects. By hearkening back to an ostensibly more communitarian past, many cold case crime narratives also built a temporal bridge, a mythological enfolding of personal memory, neighborhood disintegration, and modern malaise about urban crime. In these ways, a book like Gourevitch's taps into the culturally vexed issues surrounding law enforcement—and the broader contours of American social memory the turn in crime control reshaped.

I.

In their earliest manifestations, cold case investigations drew the most public attention, it seemed, only toward the most sensational of crimes: the trial of Michael Skakel, the Kennedy cousin convicted in 2002 of the 1975 Greenwich, Connecticut, murder of Martha Moxley; the case of Kathleen Soliah, the former Patty Hearst kidnapper and bank robber who was discovered in 1999 living as Sara Jane Olson, a suburban wife, churchgoer, and soccer mom in the Midwest; and the conviction of Byron De La Beckwith in 1994 for the 1963 murder of civil rights activist Medgar Evers.[13] A long-unsolved case also became the basis of one of the most celebrated crime narratives of the 1990s: noir chronicler James Ellroy's *My Dark Places* (1996), a resurrection of his own mother's unsolved murder case from 1958.[14] Less commonly remarked upon, amidst these headlines, was a more mundane truth. Cold case divisions had already been installed in police departments across the nation: in the District of Columbia, Miami, New York, Boston, Cleveland, and soon many other smaller localities. In the context of what I have described in chapter 2, at first this seemed to represent a considerable reversal of priorities. Not only had elaborate homicide investigation quite recently been deemed both ineffective and costly; it had also been thought particularly inapplicable to the drug wars. Inside police squads, cold case work could easily look like second-guessing of comrades' work, a quality anathema to department culture. Suddenly, however, cold case squads were said to give fellow officers' cases a new set of eyes.[15]

Even at face value, cold case squads reversed a fundamental rule of traditional homicide investigation: to move quickly. Studies commonly show that rapidly taking a suspect into custody, as quickly as twenty-four hours after the crime, is an excellent predictor of potential success; after forty-eight, chances deteriorate markedly.[16] Yet at the turn of the twenty-first century, technological advances seemed to have altered the rules of the game. Particularly enhancing law enforcement's ability to reach back in time was DNA matching, processed in the 1990s through the Combined

DNA Index System, funded by the FBI. Police also benefited not only from better criminal record-keeping but from the overall integration of the common citizenry's birth dates, drivers' licenses, credit cards, and more. Other computerized systems have also played a role—more modest than on TV, to be sure—in tracking down suspects who have fled a locality, or in cross-referencing seemingly unrelated crimes: the Automated Fingerprint Identification System, the Integrated Ballistics Identification System, or the program called Drugfire, an FBI-developed system that computerizes the markings on cartridge shell casings, around which the Maryland sniper case of 2002 swirled.[17] In *A Cold Case* itself, we see an FBI computer animation program applied to hypothetically aging a criminal suspect's facial profile over decades (87).

Since many of these systems were and are federally sponsored or coordinated, the trend toward metropolitan cold case squads is often attributed to FBI interventions following the surge in urban homicides during the late 1980s and 1990s. Plummeting clearance rates, for instance, had led the FBI to assign agents to the Washington, DC, Metropolitan Police Department in the summer of 1992, to form its Cold Case Homicide Squad. The *FBI Bulletin* would later claim this was the first such alliance. Miami-Dade, meanwhile, was reputed to have established its own Cold Case Squad in 1983; the Massachusetts State Police formed a squad in the winter of 1996–97, and the Boston Police just a few years earlier.[18] The neoconservative genealogy of the NYPD's Cold Case Squad, founded in 1995, was evident in its sponsorship by Jack Maple, formerly William Bratton's chief subordinate from the Transit Authority; department members saw the new squad simply as an extension of the CompStat system Bratton had installed.[19] Because of sponsorship by the FBI, the precise timing of (and credit for) such innovations is often a matter of mythologizing and dispute—since, again, such squads often came with local suspicions about federal intrusion, efficiency measurements, and "internal affairs" review. Many local divisions were actually patterned after older "unsolved case" squads in urban departments, and emerged independently of FBI initiatives; in some instances, it was only when homicide rates *slackened*, in the mid-1990s, that metropolitan squads had the time to shift resources.[20] Boston's cold case unit, for instance, was patterned after earlier experiments and had notable success. In one case, a criminal was located through tracing his request for a tax form from an employer.[21] In 1994, the Boston squad tracked down a murder suspect who had been on the run for nearly twenty-seven years.[22]

Surrounded by the aura of technological wizardry, cold case squads were soon subject to various forms of popular mythologizing. In the mass media, investigators were called "time travelers," heirs of Sherlock Holmes, or "high tech" sleuths.[23] Many different storytelling traditions came into play. A&E's *Cold Case Files,* for instance, was produced very much like a true-crime procedural, with storylines re-narrated by police detectives, witnesses, and victim circle members. The series used a tough-sounding, retro voiceover that spoke of hiring "muscle" and wearing a "wire." Again, the series posted case file material on the Web; on TV, such material was presented with a typewriter-font "data line" used as a subtitle or caption. Meanwhile, personal photos and mug shots, reams of evidence, and "on site" re-creations allowed the series to blend investigative doggedness with the pain of victim circle members. Those circle members usually stand in for the dead—for instance, we might see a daughter sitting next to her father's photograph, saying she never gave up on finding his murderer. Enabled by audio- and videotape that allowed viewers to re-witness interrogation rooms, the show's documentary feel took on, as a result, a confessional aura that obviously competed with CBS's top-rated fictionalized series of the same name. That show was in fact inspired by the Martha Moxley case. Its creator, CBS's Stiehm, had traveled back to her college town of Philadelphia and interviewed a local cold case cop ("from the neighborhood," he said) named Timothy Bass; Bass then became a consultant to the show. In interviews, Stiehm has said that she has intentionally given her series a "washed-out, cold look" through sepia flashbacks and a bluish tint, even when filming the present day. Stiehm's gothic and gaunt, and at times hollow-eyed, lead investigator, Lily Rush (played by Kathryn Morris), is very much the figure of a haunted past, a figure drained by the emotions she carries. She is designed, as Stiehm put it, less to emphasize "a simple science test" but to talk to people "when they wouldn't talk before" and "psychologically get people to open up" about their secrets.[24]

Meanwhile, the romancing of cold cases in newspapers also went well beyond technological romance. Journalists across the country emphasized how cops solved old or forgotten mysteries, demonstrating their long memories, and thus how they had used a case to forge a renewed connection to their communities.[25] Media outlets would often emphasize how a case had never left the thoughts of the detective. Less overtly, the cold case was also said to provide detectives with freedom they never had when taking on a politically "hot" one. In this sense, a case could express a chance for professional independence. In police stations with a strong tradition of legal pragmatism and longings for occupational autonomy, this chance carried a great deal of weight.[26] Most of all, detectives who never gave up were cast as honoring the victim and his or her family; professional dedication was translated into communal heroism and identification with victim experience.[27]

A few local examples of media coverage may illustrate how this joint enterprise was portrayed. For instance, in my own metropolitan area in 1992, *Boston Globe* columnist Mike Barnicle wrote about a seemingly meaningless crime inflicted upon an Irish immigrant. The man, described by his family as a "nice quiet guy just struggling to make a living for himself," was initially only "Incident No. 02007787" in the impersonal police case files. He had been murdered in 1990, the police said, by someone looking "to score crack money." But as Barnicle tells it, the case was reexamined a year later by the cold case unit, which pored over files, reconducted interviews, and got its man—fittingly—on St. Patrick's Day. A detective is quoted: "You don't have to know the victim or see the victim dead to work hard at it. . . . Someone's got to care. It's like Peter O'Malley [another homicide detective] says: 'We speak for the dead.'" In Barnicle's boilerplate rendering, cold case work redeems the immigrant dream from the violence of drug-invested streets—honored, no less, than by a cop named O'Malley.[28]

At times, the wound so healed could have originally been of the police's own making. Covering another cold case solved in 1992, for instance, the *Globe* interviewed a local man who had, years before, appeared on television to complain about the ransacking of his Mission Hill neighborhood during one of the Boston Police Department's sorriest episodes: the Charles Stuart case of 1989. In that infamous instance, police officers had followed the false leads provided by a murderous husband, and terrified this neighborhood while searching for a black assailant who proved to be Stuart's own invention—thereby heightening racial tension in a city already notorious for it. But for one resident, after the Cold Case Squad later solved the murder of his sister, a change of heart was in order—and, apparently, a shuffling of time as well. In the distant past—that is, in the pre-Stuart years—he said he could have counted on his community to assist in solving the crime. "There was a time when Mission Hill policed itself," this man said. "I still had some hope that somebody might come forth, if not to the police, to me and whisper in my ear. But that never happened." And so, now, having seen the police do what the community no longer did, the man apologized for his earlier complaints. He even now said the cops were usually just "doing their jobs."[29]

Perhaps the most telling profiling of cold case work in the *Globe*, however, was left to contributor Steven Levingston in the Sunday *Magazine* in

1996. Introduced to the story of a murder following a dispute over petty cash in 1967, we begin to see how resetting the clock in a longer format could expand the possibilities of political allegory. For instance, in Levingston's piece, we read about *The Graduate* on a theatre marquee, area residents purchasing fondue sets, and then local cops already overwhelmed by a crime wave that we, sitting in the 1990s, know is coming their way.[30] Echoing Attorney General Elliot Richardson's sentiments from thirty years ago, Levingston then—with little evidence—makes the single crime representative of a larger social trend. "Poorly equipped, underpaid, and understaffed police," we are told, "were losing a battle against the swelling ranks of burglars, rapists, and murderers." By this particular reversal of hindsight, the journalist is able to make the rhetoric of "law and order" look positively prophetic—rather than, say, inflammatory or politically strategic—and thus return the political clock back to the original clarion call in the war on crime. And so, when we turn to the cold case policemen at work in 1991, going through "dusty files," we see history's own mistakes being redressed. Working from "a feeling, an instinct, a sixth sense," the cops can now turn to the latest technology and investigate across state lines partly by intuiting where a suspect who liked to "live large" would probably have escaped to. (Like the 1960s, the criminal here—one thinks of Michael Skakel, for example—is a figure of impulsiveness.) Time also figures in his reckoning with justice. In the aftermath of the conviction, the victim's widow testifies about the emptiness that greets her every Christmas. The successful cop, reciprocally, "liked to say the Cold Case Squad exists for the victim's families. . . . 'We just got the guy,' he was able to tell [her,] 'who caused you to be a widow all these years and raise three kids alone.'" Importantly, then, a crime is not merely solved; rather, a debt measured by the victim circle's experience of time is repaid. A seemingly "meaningless" crime is made, or so it seems, meaningful again. And the war on crime is itself renewed.[31]

Of course, these cases expressed real trauma in their communities and a legitimate desire for personal closure. The latter is actually all too rare in the experience of victims or their families. In truth, the cultural resonance of cold case narratives may be in the way they reconcile, symbolically, tensions resulting from competing poles in the victims' rights movement: (1) the impulse embodied in post-Nixon law-and-order federalism, of the kind Levingston invokes so nostalgically; and (2) the grassroots advocacy for giving victims a voice in the criminal justice system. As an icon of speaking for the dead and victims' families as well as representing the vigilance of the state, the cold case investigator brings together these sometimes-competing agendas within the neoconservative turn.[32] The figure of the cop with a long memory is particularly well attuned to consciousness of the victim circle. As studies of victimization surveys suggest, people affected by crime tend to "reverse telescope" their sense of time, bringing the episode closer to the present; collaterally, as the victims' avenger, the investigator always carries the crime with him.[33]

In narratives like Levingston's and Barnicle's, therefore, cold case work was made, through hindsight, to dramatize the prior (liberal) inadequacy of the system. But more covertly, the same work offered the satisfaction that criminals could now be made to "pay" by a more vigilant state.[34] Thus it was not only that the victim circle achieves retribution for the crime as such. Beyond just solving the crime, the resulting narrative also reinforces the idea of the state's particular affinity with the "rights" of victims, often by blurring civil and criminal conceptions of law. That is, the victim circle may desire an essentially contractual, or at least compensatory, version of criminal justice that looks to exact "payment" for its own suffering on top of the state's remedy of punishment for the crime as such. (Neoconservatives like Robert H. Rhodes, as I show in chapter 4, explicitly advocated for victimization surveys because he felt that quantifiable compensation was a way to measure state expenditure on crime.) Such thinking expressed an ancillary or covert belief in one's life trajectory as a personal property or right; the crime has shattered, in this line of thinking, one's personal worth and well-being.[35] Moreover, this differentiation was made necessary, once again, by recognizing that criminals did not assess the "risks" their actions posed. Paul Gewirtz, for example, would argue on behalf of victim-impact statements in sentencing hearings, on the grounds that "[t]he account of the suffering of the victim's survivors in individual cases is a particularization of a generally foreseeable harm." Such particularity, Gewirtz argued, invites the emotional weight, and the narrative complexity, that the more rationalistic justice system often excludes.[36]

I will address the issue of "foreseeable" effects briefly in my conclusion to this chapter. For now, however, one would simply note how compatible creating a victim's right would seem with the neoconservative argument for differentiating citizen vigilance from criminal recklessness. And in that regard, it should be said that the public mythologizing of cold case work often obscured some of the more mundane ways cases were and are actually broken.[37] For example, the particular imprinting of cold case squads not just on unsolved crimes but on the seemingly "meaningless murder" speaks volumes about the blending of public relations and pragmatism these squads represent. In law enforcement circles, the code phrase "meaningless murder" often refers specifically to the street and drug-related homicides that plagued metropolitan policing, not coincidentally, in all the localities where cold case work first arose. FBI-sponsored cold case work in the early 1990s, for example, had itself been especially focused on drug-related murders because *these* kinds had created a drastically downward pull on clearance rates and local police morale. Murders of this kind were also described as "exceedingly more time-consuming" to investigate.[38] But even more fundamentally, these murders had fundamentally disrupted traditional investigative techniques: they were, as the *FBI Bulletin* put it, "seemingly minor disputes in which participants chose to resolve their conflicts with violence or stemmed from unprovoked, random attacks in which the killer had no previous relationship with or knowledge of the victim." In short, the traditional approach "focusing on motive" was said now to provide few leads. (In David Simon's *Homicide: A Year on the Killing Streets,* the Baltimore homicide squad refers to this, prosaically, as "fuck the why.")[39]

Instead, one could turn what had traditionally been seen as a negative—the passage of time—into an investigative asset.[40] In particular, a cold case meant turning back to a crime scene that had, itself, been cooled out by time. That is, it allowed investigators to revisit a community that had previously been seen as hostile or fearful of reprisal. Now, the passage of time could mean that witnesses no longer feared payback; a killer might have moved out of a neighborhood; a falling out among criminal collaborators might have taken place. In addition, as one Long Island detective put it, the passing of time might lead the murderer to "have a false sense of security and believing [*sic*] that nobody is looking for him anymore."[41] When detectives now said that they looked for an opening, therefore, they indeed meant, at times, that they now had a forensic clue that could be subjected to new science or that the case's original investigators had missed.[42] But just as often, a new "opening" meant a change in (1) the community around the crime and (2) the constituency the criminal could still call his own. As the *FBI Bulletin* put it:

> . . . With time, relationships change. Former friends of the subject might become adversaries. Initial fear shown by witnesses might subside enough to allow them to consider some type of witness protection or relocation in exchange for testimony. Or, a particular witness now might need some sort of help within the criminal justice system and be willing to provide information to get it. . . .

> In addition, time provides killers with the opportunity to brag about their actions . . . [Thus] people then become new witnesses in an old case.

In other words, it may well have been that the original investigation confronted (or simply assumed) community distrust—as the *Bulletin* put it, "the practical difficulties of locating witnesses, overcoming their hostility, obtaining their confidence, ensuring their safety, securing their testimony." But the new assumption was that of community dispersal and reorganization over time. It was not, as the more romantic cold case narratives had said, that such communities had simply returned to their senses. Rather, such communities were implicitly understood as still under the threat of criminality, with relationships often still in conflict—and thus open to leverage.

It also isn't difficult, therefore, to see what was implied by the references above to witness protection and criminal informants. As I have suggested in chapter 1, investigators were reminded to continue to cultivate informants and cooperative witnesses as the crucial linchpins of investigation. Indeed, for all the heralding of technological wizardry, "resolution of *nearly all CCS cases*," the *Bulletin* acknowledged, "still comes from eyewitness identification."[43] Cold case work thus feeds off the same pressures that have led to an exponential rise in informants: draconian or fixed sentencing laws, RICO-style prosecutions, confiscation payments to informants, and perhaps most of all, plea-bargaining with an expanding prison population. Criminal conspiracy rulings, often stemming from the reasoning in organized crime prosecutions, also pressure informants to demonstrate affirmative assistance in helping to capture their former associates.[44] Cold case work, therefore, does not remake the current system so much as implement the central tactics of the neoconservative turn. And thus, not unlike the forms of citizen-centered victim advocacy that have often distorted the war on drugs, these investigations might easily reproduce the class and racial imbalances already in the criminal justice system.[45]

Whatever their ultimate social consequences, these political realities also provide a rather unbalanced template from which an author like Gourevitch would work. As I've suggested, the more romantic of cold case narratives can easily turn the criminal perpetrator into the lone desperado on the run (as Gourevitch puts it, less a whodunit than a "where'd he go" [18]). As both the *FBI Bulletin* and David Simon's squad admit, motive now seemed less a driving interpretive principle. And yet, conversely, the victim can actually be symbolically re-embodied in a cold case narrative, as if brought back from the dead: his or her potential life trajectory represented not only in the retelling of a forgotten crime, but implicitly in the suffering of those he or she left behind. In an equation starting with the doubling of cop and victim community and then including claims from the larger victim circle, the criminal perpetrator can easily be made to pay and pay again.

II.

As if contravening the extravagance of so much of contemporary True Crime—and the context I have just outlined—Gourevitch's *A Cold Case* is a minimalist text, spanning three decades in just over 180 pages. It is decidedly a "case"—an instance, and an argument—isolating its cop's personal devotion. With a cover like a criminal "jacket" whose red seal we reopen, and black-and-white photos we leaf through, the book even echoes the grim deadpan of the autopsy itself; we are told investigation "knows no shame" (52), like its medical prologue.[46] Rarely has the withholding, third-person reticence typical of the *New Yorker*, where the book first appeared, seemed so apt. It renders the case abstract, its drama a purified instance of dedication.

The book's neoclassical form works to make the meeting of cop and killer a spare drama of symmetrical antagonism. The text is split into two precisely equal sections, pivoting on the point of arrest: "Dead or Alive," documenting the double homicide by and capture of one Frankie Koehler; and "Reckonings," a meditation on Koehler's confession, trial, and sentencing. Part 1 opens with a crisp, deadpan chronology of Koehler's criminal career, a dull litany of violence. Before seven pages have gone by, we are in the murders of Pete McGinn and Richie Glennon, the result—there is no other interpretive option allowed us—of the aftermath of a barroom argument. From Koehler's disappearance after the crime, we shift forward twenty-seven years. Andy Rosenzweig's own memories of the crime, and of his police career leading up to it, are triggered by driving past the murder scene. In the subsequent investigation, we walk in the procedural's footsteps, re-interviewing witnesses, following known associates, spinning off possible aliases and family members. Though part 2 features a videotaped confession the book calls "sensational" (100), even "classic" (98), it can seem anticlimactic, leading only to an unsatisfying plea bargain of manslaughter. The book then drifts toward Rosenzweig's retirement to a book shop he names, with full allusive intent—and perhaps an ironic counterpointing to romantic closure in fiction—"Book 'Em" (173). Koehler, meanwhile, remains a remorseless impulse killer still enamored of his power over others, his sociopathic egotism reflected in his mimicry of infamous media-constructed gangsters—notably Jimmy Cagney (140, 158).

As the ironic allusion to Singer suggests, however, Gourevitch turns this capturing of a public enemy into a tale of its Jewish cop's moral vigilance. Contrary to Akhsa Holishitzer, Rosenzweig is a believer who never lost faith. A New Yorker to the core, he is called a boyhood friend of "his murdered pal" (12) from shared days at a community swimming pool. Brought into the NYPD by an Irish Catholic cop named Danny Lynch in the 1960s, Rosenzweig became an "active cop" (20) by resisting the petty bribery and the cooping (sleeping on duty) that would be exposed by the Knapp Commission a decade later. He eventually rises to Chief of Investigation for the Manhattan District Attorney. And Rosenzweig's lifelong motto is explicit: "Everything we do, there's a victim attached" (34).

In many ways, Rosenzweig is a figure of ethnic succession, the promise of an older New York. The vocation of speaking for the dead is itself inculcated by older Irish cops; we are even given paired stories where Lynch (15), and then Rosenzweig (59), face down a criminal at close range in nearly identical fashion. This provides a good instance where the Hemingway-inspired writing degree zero, so characteristic of the *New Yorker,* collapses differences in time: "Still, Rosenzweig considered himself justified in shooting the man once they were on the floor and the knife was out, just as Tom Hallinan had felt justified in shooting the man who stabbed him in the face and Danny Lynch had been justified when the gangster Michael Sudia put a gun to his head and Lynch killed him" (60). Gourevitch wants to differentiate this experience from that of Rosenzweig's mentors, but the style works to make the now seem like the then. Rosenzweig's entire history is thus given a strong nostalgic aura. Andy, we are told, looks like Humphrey Bogart (20); his favorite movie, again like Frank Serpico's, is *High Noon* (62).[47] Richie Glennon, meanwhile, is called a "shylock" (17), "a colorful character, high energy, a talker, glib, Runyonesque—you know, a tough guy" (14). Like the reverse-telescoping effects mentioned earlier, these echoes of the 1940s contribute to the way Rosenzweig's quest seems oblivious to the passage of time.

This cultural framing also humanizes what is an internalized state mission, again not unlike the wartime ethos upon which procedural heroes of narratives like those of *The Naked City* were first fashioned.[48] In contrast to what an assistant D.A. in the book calls a "glamour grudge" (74), Andy's *High Noon* heroism is called lonely and even "existential." It is even compared, in a departure from *New Yorker*-style understatement, to the defense of "civilization" against "barbarism" (63): not to be a matter of vocation but really no choice at all (63–64). We hear, for example, that when faced with his colleagues' corruption or indifference, "doing things right amounted to little more than refusing to do things wrong" (35)—a practically perfect equation of the state and his personality. He is called, in another moment, a "servant" (38) of his own suspicion. He has seemingly taken his duty into his own body. Thus, the common police slang for "catching a case"—which actually means the intentionally impersonal bureaucratic process where a case lands in your lap—is compared, in a long conceit, to catching a cold (43). Even after he retires, we will see Rosenzweig writing down license plate numbers (182).

In this new front of the war on crime, therefore, the importance of community vigilance, even prior to 9/11, serves to resurrect a wartime ethos, as if it means an identification with the state. And yet, *A Cold Case* also encounters contradictions in attempting to readapt this older vocabulary. It turns out that when the book shifts to Rosenzweig's apprenticeship as a beat cop, we discover his populist dedication was undermined by the very New York he had pledged to serve. The story begins in its dominant nostalgic register. "Policing in New York in the late 1960s," Gourevitch tells us, "was still intimate work, conducted largely on foot, by eye, and by ear, and Rosenzweig believed that was how it should be" (33). In the old days—as if echoing our earlier testimonial from Boston's Mission Hill district—the book claims, there was more tolerance for police mistakes; now, the public wants you to bang heads but not too forcefully (81–82). Rosenzweig elaborates on these feelings upon expressing relief that his son decides not to be a cop:

> You're given this position of authority, [Rosenzweig says,] you're supposed to enforce the laws, you're supposed to protect the public, and now you're in this situation where you have to arrest someone because you have probable cause to believe they committed a crime. They don't want to be arrested, and now they resist you. How much force can you use? Is a punch in the mouth OK? Can you hit him on the head with a nightstick? Can you just jab him in the belly? . . . Do you have to use so little force that he gets the best of you, and gets your gun away from you and kills you?
>
> . . . I'm not talking about Abner Louima, or the Rodney King case—gratuitous violence against people. I'm talking about people who have to do their jobs. It's not a pleasant thing. (67–68)

This lament about public indifference is familiar to anyone studying police culture; it explains, for one thing, his admiration for *High Noon*.[49] Yet now, a detective's cold case work subtly alters its import. Here, a detective's office work—the parallel to David Milch or Meredith Stiehm's sense of interrogation's privacy is striking—is clearly preferable to beat patrol because it avoids these explicit, street-centered, public demonstrations of state authority. The coldness of old cases, in other words, deflects the immediate risk of public confrontation and downplays New York's present passions and frictions.

Yet even the terrain of the past is not so secure. When Rosenzweig actually details his beat apprenticeship, we discover that he had been sent out into the "long hot summer" of the mid-sixties, where he had actually felt alone and distrusted (64). He was so out of sorts that he had actually neglected his duty until he was upbraided by an older cop named Dave Cody (66). As *Gatsby*-esque as the text wants to tell us Rosenzweig's subsequent rise actually was, after this upbraiding—and I mean quite explicitly, here, how a rote wisdom helps to remake a new identity, as with James Gatz—this contradiction in Rosenzweig's memory undermines much of the book's historical framework.[50] In particular, it exposes the way *A Cold Case*'s tapping into mythic memory blots out the contemporary context that the very mention of Louima or Rodney King threatens to open up. When references to matters "black and white" do appear in *A Cold Case*, they are used, again, only to evoke mid-century nostalgia.[51] The phrase comes up, for instance, in the ruminations of Koehler's lawyer, who pauses to reflect that his client is so old-fashioned he's "black and white" (129). ("Today," the lawyer said, "the pictures are in color, but the color is actually colorless, just like the criminals" [129].) By this, apparently, the lawyer means that Koehler is so full of passion, so surely judged by our sense of what is right and wrong, that he seems to have arisen out of a mid-century crime melodrama; the TV version of *The Naked City* is in fact cited at the same moment. But this is not so much nostalgia as what memory analysts call cryptomnesia, the substitution of a media experience for social or personal memory.[52]

This effect also suffuses the representation of Koehler's criminality. As I've said, Gourevitch would have us believe that Koehler's egotism is reflected primarily in his mimicry of media gangsterism. Gourevitch's own rendering of Koehler often seems, itself, retrofitted to conform to the cinematic aura of the gangster biopic. Once again, a reverse telescoping effect seems to dominate. If, for instance, victim Glennon is called a "pure New York character" (14) and yet a "method actor" (179), Koehler—who, we are told, hangs out with the prototypes for *GoodFellas* (144–45), based on Henry Hill's career—seems fully folded into his gangster role. Yet even his voice is keyed to a pre-racialized New York existing only in myth or the movies. His accent, the book tells us, was "so pure that it now sounds foreign in the very city it came from. For Koehler is a refugee of some sorts from the white, hoodlum milieu of another time and from a city that no longer really exists." He is, we are told, a "period piece" (99). When he conducts one robbery, this is what he is reputed to have said: "All right, lady, this is a heist. . . . Don't move or I'll plug you" (5). One would certainly never know from these descriptions when the murders at issue took place—that is, in 1970.

Conversely, a similar set of "retro" effects reinforces Rosenzweig's representation as the morally sound keeper of old New York's flame. The role is visible, for example, in *A Cold Case*'s illustrations. The book begins with black-and-white news photos, crime scene shots, and a police academy snapshot of Rosenzweig. But then it offers a stylized retro-noir photograph by Gilles Peress of the cop himself, in the late 1990s, sitting in the Skylight Diner, with a neon "24 hours" sign above his head. It is almost as if the FBI animation program has been reversed and the clock turned back. Like the "cold" prose discussed earlier, the overall effect is to eclipse the passage of time, and fashion a collective memory by substituting an eternally recurring or mythic past. And setting collaborates with this contrast of honoring New York: by entering that Skylight Diner, the cop literally locates himself in Koehler's former New York haunts. Like the neon sign says, the cop is always on duty, 24 hours a day.

This vigil across time also weaves together the cop and the victim circle. When Richie Glennon's daughter speaks at the sentencing hearing, she too collapses time into a mythic emblem of pain. Her statement speaks of the way her father is missed "because of everything he was and everything he was meant to be" (154). She pleads that Koehler be punished for "every hug, for every morning, for every time the sun shown on his face, for every time he celebrated," and more (155). In contrast, Koehler arrogantly says the murder was the best thing that happened to him because it gave him a chance to start a new life (147). Koehler's lack of impulse control here is also set in stark relief to the restraint and bureaucratic loyalty of Rosenzweig. The cold-case understatement of the *New Yorker* serves, itself, to cool out our response to Koehler's arrogance, making the desires of the law and the victim seem a result of rational reckoning.

As I've suggested, however, such neoclassical symmetry may bring with it certain simplifications. As Lauren Berlant has observed, one potential risk of a victim-centered populism is that it pits the certainty of the innocent in a pose of moral irrefutability, all the more worrisome when the state emulates that pose.[53] This is why it is troubling that Gourevitch's allusion to Isaac Singer's tale likens a defense lawyer to Satan. The lawyer is a kind of figure of intellectual temptation, warning all intruders away from questioning the cop's labor. Gourevitch calls the lawyer a figure for "interpretation" (132)—a warning to us all, perhaps, about moral relativism when it comes to murder. The lawyer believes, for instance, with devious ease that "[t]he past doesn't exist, there's only how we remember it" (132); Rosenzweig, however, can't believe the present Koehler is any different from the past one (109). If New York is frozen in pleasurable nostalgia—the contradiction is evident in the retro-sepia past of Stiehm's *Cold Case* as well—crime, by contrast, has to be held in its abstract, ahistorical impulsiveness, as putatively an unimpeachable fact. Gourevitch, of course, feels Koehler is not entitled to any credit for time unserved. This, however, only makes the prosecutors' decision that the passage of time has worsened their case, even with Koehler's cold confession, seem all the more tragic. We learn that Koehler's lawyer (unambiguously named Richman) has bargained for a prison term that makes his client eligible for parole by 2003 (156). And thus ultimately, for all Rosenzweig's playing out of procedural routine, all his tracing of clues, all our own reopening of those case files, we are haunted by the fact that none of it has mattered much, because we've always known *who* did the crime. But not the time.

III.

Gourevitch's *A Cold Case* is not, of course, the only literary meditation possible on this recent turn in law enforcement; the choice of narrative form is no more inevitable than its associated political stance. For James Ellroy, cold case work on his mother's death becomes a hyperkinetic confessional and exploration of the LAPD's own mythos that ends without closure—but rather, an 800 number; for journalist Dennis McAuliffe Jr. solving the murder of his Osage grandmother becomes a journey of personal re-identification and liberal redress of crimes against Native Americans.[54] Yet whatever the political inflection or aesthetic template chosen, cold case cultural narrative often restages the lingering consequences of a crime, even a kind of fixation on its ever-present status, something we all live with. Crime is thus seen, culturally, as an event not just *in* a particular moment but across time: a crime becomes linked, for good or ill, to its consequences. And because its ramifications are often especially heartfelt within the victim circle, a cold case gives us a way to reexamine the "foreseeable harm" for which Gewirtz (among others) argued.[55]

Yet the fact is that cold cases may also suggest such foresight isn't always what it seems. Paradoxically, the long passage of time may only make us *think* we see the consequences of the original crime more clearly, while raising the question about when the clock on such "harm" should stop running. And whatever it may mean for trials themselves, the remobilization of the past in these cultural narratives—for instance, Levingston's turning of Nixonian rhetoric into social prophecy, or Gourevitch's own cryptomnesia—is hardly a politically innocent strategy. The palpable nostalgia in cold case mythologies for a lost "law and order" vigilance, not unlike the wartime ethos of the recuperated 1940s, only reminds us of several troubling elements in the neoconservative turn. For example, memory of a "black and white" era prior to that of civil rights—itself a telling confounding of racial and moral vocabularies—offers a drastically telescoped history that can be too often reinforced by the police's own institutionalized racism. Even in Rosenzweig's social memory, the mutual distrust between police and New York's communities of color is presumed, erroneously, to be a recent event, supposedly caused by civil rights activism.

By its emphasis on "meaningless" crime, the cold case movement also, not coincidentally, seems focused on the criminal's lack of impulse control—a quality that is so often offered, in neoconservative thought, as contradicting liberalism's preferences for a "root cause" explanation for crime. In the media, such a criminal is more often profiled through the tracks left in criminal records, rendered in the law enforcement bureaucratese of "known whereabouts" or repeated crimes. (Here, perhaps, is another limitation of Gourevitch's choice of such a figure of motiveless malignity on which to pin his "case.") The contradiction is clear: even in prosecutions themselves, the standard of "foreseeable harm" may only suggest what remarkable foresight the criminal is asked to possess when, in virtually the same breath—as in the portrait of the blasé, media-entranced Frank Koehler—we often define the pathology of such criminality by its having so little foresight. For all the claimed connection to the emotional experience of victims, we may actually be presuming a rational criminal actor who must anticipate all future consequences—look into the future, not unlike the FBI's animation program in Gourevitch's tale, itself expressing in visual form the cultural fantasy of elongating the time of the crime.[56]

It might be argued that this popular mythology does not suggest a cultural shift; after all, the refrain has always said, there is no statute of limitations on murder. At most, cold case squads might be a product of understandable social outrage over the high incidence of homicides in the early 1990s—and the way the war on crime never seems to be won. But the realignment of time, social memory, and authority unveiled in cold murder cases is now visible in other crime categories as well. Reform or abandonment of statutes of limitations, for example, is occurring nationally, around childhood abuse (due to issues raised by repressed memory), around rape, and around organized crime prosecutions. On this broader social front, as Tyler T. Ochoa and Andrew J. Wistrich suggest, traditional assumptions about society's repose and the defendant's right to a speedy trial have been challenged by a desire to keep the crime alive. The constitutionality of these reforms, of course, is perhaps best left to the courts and to legal scholars.[57] But it is not only that these trends show us how victims can actually reproduce themselves as evidence of crime's consequences. Moreover, as J. Anthony Chavez has suggested, they show us a broader social longing to extend the temporal frame of the crime itself, so that even its aftereffects become construed as *part* of the crime. The same can be said of "Son of Sam" laws, which often divert proceeds from criminal narratives, written later in time, to crime victims and their circle.[58]

Meanwhile, despite its obvious romancing in the media, the rewriting of history in cold case work can actually provide a subtle but ultimately problematic exchange of sentiments between the cop and the community. In some cases, as in Andy Rosenzweig's, digging up the past only allows the cop to re-experience his own chronic alienation from the local community he serves, his subordination to federal (FBI) authority, his heroic but often futile desire to settle accounts with citizens. In the broader sense of political authority, *A Cold Case* gives us something far less than "closure" even its investigative phase. Instead, these days, the classic elements of investigation have actually been displaced—as I have tried to suggest in my first and second chapters—by the more mundane business of surveillance, monitoring known criminals and informants, and leveraging information from them by threats of further punishment. And in *A Cold Case*, this is precisely what happens: Frank Koehler's California habitat is heated up by police pressure and by following two nephews in and out of jail (77). And it is not exactly that the local community has healed its own wounds. For all the dedication that Rosenzweig exhibits, the case of Frankie Koehler is actually broken by a cooperating FBI agent who lets the NYPD know the crook is arriving back at Penn Station (83) after his years on the run. ("It should have been me catching this guy," Rosenzweig says ruefully, "if it was a true-crime novel" [88].)

This ambiguous claim, seeming to de-sacralize state authority while also heroicizing it, has been central to the neoconservative turn, often passing vigilance on to the responsibility of private hands. Yet if anything, the cop's identification with the victim circle may have only allowed this public servant, the representative of the state, to inherit the aura of an aggrieved and neglected party. And ultimately, the outcome of the Koehler case may illustrate the difficulties in closing the history—for "booking" the interpretive ambiguities that *A Cold Case* itself wants to set aside through its neoclassical and neo-noir style. In point of fact, the plea bargain Koehler received isn't so atypical in such circumstances.[59] Though Gourevitch would have us see Rosenzweig as the cop/victim who never forgets—an emblem of the old, pluralistic, mid-century New York—he might just as well be seen as the contradictory icon of a newer, more dispersed, post-industrial public, nursing never-forgotten social injuries, and fantasizing about a past of supposedly more communitarian social vigilance from its now-privatized and isolated spaces. Supposedly a "period piece" of old New York, Frankie Koehler in fact escapes to California; Rosenzweig, the defender of that city, himself ultimately retires to Rhode Island, where he can be seen still jotting down those license plate numbers. As Isaac Singer might say, when you long to speak for the dead, another meaning of "vigil" descends upon you—that is, the "watch" undertaken while others sleep. And if such vigilance becomes a widely celebrated cultural reflex, inevitably it may be the living who cannot rest.[60]

4
Risk Management
Frank Abagnale Jr. and the Shadowing of Pleasure

> I guess I thought in loopholes.
> —Frank Abagnale Jr., *The Art of the Steal* (2001)

IT WAS A PARTICULARLY TELLING MOMENT in the neoconservative turn when, in the early 1990s, a public-private collaborative of Philadelphia investigators, psychologists, and forensic sculptors began to reopen cold homicide cases from around the country. They called themselves the Vidocq Society, after the famous nineteenth-century French detective Eugène François Vidocq.[1] As Michel Foucault tells us, Vidocq can be an especially intriguing historical reference point. A former criminal, prisoner, and informant-turned-Sûreté founder and, eventually, fee-for-service detective, Vidocq was a man who suggested the often-fluid collaborations that take place between the needs of social order, the organization of criminality, and the evolving tactics of fighting crime.[2] And thus the changing historical terrain for what, in something of a misnomer, we continue to call "private detective" work.

Invoke the phrase "war on crime," and the never-dead metaphor still does transformative interpretive work. Under the sway of this phrase, we often implicitly compare crime control to the ethos of a ground war, even though wars can involve guerilla tactics, the use of individual spies, and intelligence gathering on the home front. The trope of war also invokes state-centered thinking, even though we know wars can involve the use of private security forces, mercenaries, or filibusters.[3] Indeed, as I have tried to show, the neoconservative turn has often used the ethos of "war" to mobilize citizens, or to generate a belief in the cop as a neighborhood defender and emblem of private redress. Meanwhile, in our time, the rethinking of public policing has often overlapped with an ongoing boom in the private security and security-consulting industries.

Over the last few decades, private security firms of all kinds have emerged to complement the war on crime, many of them staffed by former police officers, military personnel, or intelligence officers. This remarkable growth, much of it taking hold well before 9/11, has stemmed from several causes. Due to the globalization and deregulation of corporate power, the explosion in information and Internet technology, and the rise of terrorism, security consulting has achieved an international profile. ("All of this uncertainty," the president of industry giant Kroll has glumly observed, "is a natural driver for us.") In 1980, there were about 70,000 private security firms in the United States; by 1997, there were about 160,000.[4] The American Society for Industrial Security now numbers over 36,000 members worldwide, a development that should certainly challenge our traditional image of the gumshoe detective who keeps a small office, refuses divorce work, and operates by his own moral code.[5] In studies of crime narrative, however, the contemporary confluence of public and private security has largely remained out of view. Although there have been a flurry of historical studies detailing the older, corporate roots of private detection—for example, showing that the famed Pinkertons of the late nineteenth century, though posing as public servants, largely worked at the behest of local elites, large landowners, and businesses—the Sam Spade icon endures. And no split remains so sacrosanct in studies of crime narrative as the one between public and private spheres.[6]

Recently, however, one popular narrative began to tell a different story. It appeared in the book "coauthored"—I guess you can say coauthored—by Frank W. Abagnale Jr., entitled *Catch Me If You Can* (1980), recently reissued in paperback to accompany the commercially successful Steven Spielberg film of 2002.[7] (Though presented in the first person, *Catch Me* was actually ghostwritten by the now-deceased *Houston Chronicle* reporter Stan Redding, after interviewing Abagnale for only four days.)[8] *Catch Me* tells the story of how, in the early 1960s, the young Frank Abagnale—while still only a teenager—had become a criminal imposter. Before his mid-twenties, Abagnale had posed as a Pan Am pilot, a Louisiana lawyer, a Florida doctor, a Utah sociology professor, and more, all the while carrying out counterfeiting schemes and white-collar frauds. After being caught by French authorities, he served time in prison in Europe and the United States before turning his life around. Today, Frank Abagnale has become a security consultant, a man who now advises Staples, Disney, Bank of America, Discover Financial Services—indeed, by his own account, over half of today's Fortune 500 corporations. Abagnale may therefore be, by all rights, the best-known American personal and corporate security entrepreneur of our day.[9] And yet for our purposes, what is especially telling is that Abagnale's memoir and Spielberg's film attribute this transformation to the affection that developed between the con man and his FBI pursuer. Especially as Spielberg's film adaptation would have it, Abagnale (played by Leonardo DiCaprio) was reformed under the caring eye of a dogged, shoe-leather FBI investigator named Carl Hanratty (Tom Hanks), a composite figure originally dubbed "O'Riley" in the book. From the start sympathetic to and even envious of the boy, O'Riley eventually adopts Abagnale into the FBI fold.[10] In other words, Abagnale's imaginary memoir enacts a developing partnership between private security and the state: indeed, a state so hot upon Abagnale's paper trail that it hopes to learn to "live with [the] crime" that he has mastered.

In this chapter, I want to show how a close examination of Abagnale's work—his literal work as a security consultant, and his performance in the cultural fantasy of *Catch Me If You Can*—might help us rethink the way we continue to cast the "war on crime" in exclusively public terms. As earlier, I want to strike a counterpoint to the commonplace assumption in political histories, and much media analysis, that the neoconservative turn was generated exclusively by a state response to public fear and moral outrage. While there is little denying the centrality of these elements (the state, public fear, moral outrage) to the neoconservative crime formula, they each turn out to have a curious *in*applicability to the white-collar crimes in which Abagnale, as con man and security analyst, came to specialize. In truth, when analysis is directed at this particular crime sector, the more frequent complaint is that the cultural representations of such criminality are not fearful *enough*. The con man is depicted as unthreatening or even slightly appealing, and thus out of step with the tenor of much media representation of, for instance, street crime and violence. Or, to put it another way, analysts often complain that such portraits minimize the seriousness of white-collar crime. Rather than being greeted with moral opprobrium, con men are said to be treated as amiable rogues, and the transgressions of white-collar crooks suffused with the "infotainment" that celebrates "inside dope" and even insider trading.[11] In the decade featuring the scandals of Enron and ImClone—and for a film version packaged as a Christmas release—this reading is certainly understandable.[12] But I would actually call it a half-reading, in the way that it both obscures Abagnale's current occupation and perpetuates a split in our understanding of private and public approaches to crime. Even though, as I have said, a story like Abagnale's seems to enact a more reciprocal process: the adoption, as it were, of the former realm into the latter.

To change our approach, I want to explore the affiliation of *Catch Me*

If You Can not only with traditional con man stories, but with what I will call "shadow" narratives, the stories of private undercover operatives who emerged in the industrial era primarily to monitor white-collar crimes and migratory tramps. Specifically, I will explore its affinity with romances of the tramp-detective Josiah Flynt (Willard), who himself had gone on the road as a con man while still in his teens. To tie this together with themes from my first three chapters, I will suggest Flynt and Abagnale's resonance with Michel Foucault's idea of the delinquent-turned-informant, the mobile observatory and recorder of supposedly habitual criminality. Then, I will turn to the actual security services that Abagnale offers, and how they represent a downsizing, or once again a micropolitical set of tactics, that work within the interstices of state, corporate, and consumer activity. To conclude, I will return to the uses of pleasure and nostalgia in the popular narrative of *Catch Me*. I will suggest that Abagnale does not simply embody a nostalgic return to the days of personal responsibility; rather, he offers a future in which the private sphere incorporates the state's premium on an actuarial assessment of crime's risks. Cold case investigations, under the banner of a populist identification with the victim circle, offered a strategy of supplementing state authority while seeming to "de-sacralize" it. Collaterally, private security often extends the state's domain while offering empowerment to the individual consumer or corporation.[13]

And, finally, to pick up a thread I have suggested earlier, Abagnale's style of personal risk management also marks the state's recent willingness to recruit or emulate criminal intelligence to refine its own operations. The exploits of *Catch Me* thus might well be read—as I will suggest, much like Eugène François Vidocq's—as the "inside-out" stories of a man who made his criminal past into a more secure future. Or, of a man who preemptively tested security gaps so that they could be improved upon by public and private parties alike.[14] As some historians of private security have phrased it, public policing does "catch up" with the private sphere's more preventive, future-oriented approach—and hires Frank Abagnale on. The con man rushes into the security breach so as ultimately to close it. And there is pleasure in the securing.[15]

I.

An urbane mixture of guile, juvenile charm, and ingenuity, the hero of Frank Abagnale's imaginary (as told to) memoir seems to embody the style of the criminal we call an imposter or con man. As social scientists, historians, and literary critics tell us, the con man masters a kind of thievery that constructs a "confidence," often by building up a shared fellowship that draws upon the victim's own taste for chicanery. As Gary Lindberg puts it, the confidence man not only constructs a shared belief; he embodies the wishes of his victim. As such, his game or grift leads to a voluntary surrender of goods, often without violence or even its threat.[16]

Conning, however, is a malleable art. In the eighteenth century, for example, the con man was variously a rogue imposter, *faux* gentleman, picaro, or escape artist. In darker Victorian imaginings, his arts were associated with urban seduction and contamination of the young, the rural, and the innocent. As social and geographical mobility increasingly marked the industrial-capitalist order, the con man came to manipulate the elusive boundaries between fraud, everyday white-collar business speculation, and contract relations. As if the dark twin of sanctioned capitalist heroes, he was a man for whom class origin was not fate. Rather, he was man who could, like the strugglers of Victorian self-help, miraculously make something out of nothing. In so doing, the rogue imposter often demonstrated how easily occupations like teaching, doctoring, or the law could be mastered without any official training.[17] *Catch Me*'s partly comic story thus often seems akin to that of *The Great Imposter* (1959), the tale of the famous con man Ferdinand Demara, the son of a movie projectionist whose imposture of a Navy surgeon, prison warden, psychology professor, and even Trappist monk was made into a movie starring Tony Curtis in 1961. Recalling Hollywood's love affair with con artists who sell cures to River City, Abagnale himself became a movie projectionist in prison, compared himself to Walter Mitty (234), and titled one of his personal security handbooks, in a play on Donald Trump's best-seller, *The Art of the Steal* (2001).[18]

The explicit emulation of American dreamers, meanwhile, was often accompanied by a public service side to the con man. From Victorian advice literature to the modern procedural mystery, he often played a covert tutorial role, plying his schemes only to demonstrate how to avoid them.[19] As for Horatio Alger's Ragged Dick, training in the urban arts of deception sometimes made one a less easy mark and, like Henry Hill, thereby valuable to law enforcement. If we adopt this inside-out perspective, *Catch Me If You Can* becomes more reminiscent of the so-called "shadow" narratives of nineteenth-century detectives who inhabited the border world of fraud and private policing—and farther back than that, to the stories of master "thief takers" like Jonathan Wild. Abagnale's closest nineteenth-century antecedent, in fact, may be Josiah Flynt, the Chicago-born tramp expert who began, in his own teens, as a roving hobo and confidence man, and then reformed himself into a private detective, memoirist, and muckraker who would publish essays in the *Century, Forum,* and *Atlantic Monthly.* Flynt had become famous by recounting his journeys as a railroad and urban tramp nicknamed Cigarette, specializing in begging, petty confidence games, and scavenging on the road. Flynt was best known, however, for crafting a more "professional" image of the con man, principally by displacing armchair criminology's preference for skull measurements and prison confessions with the direct witnessing his undercover work offered. However, Flynt's authority stemmed not just from immersion into criminality as such, but from shadowing his own past and using (as Rolf Lindner has suggested) his memories to realign his own class loyalties.[20]

In books such as *Tramping with Tramps* (1899), *Notes of an Itinerant Policeman* (1900), and *My Life* (1908), Flynt became famous by inverting his own past as a Victorian lost boy, specifically by retooling youthful skills derived from tramping and con games into undercover surveillance for railroads and, eventually, those middle-class magazines. His first eight-month trip as a tramp—and for Abagnale the parallel would be an exact one—followed his escape from a reform school. Flynt's memoirs remind us that he was originally something of a rogue child in the classical late-Victorian mold: a boy slight of stature, blessed with a mobile facial expression, who even as an adult retained a prankish sense of the mystery he could sustain about his whereabouts and his past (*ML* 352–56). For Flynt, acting was the most alluring boy's game; yet, as for Tom Sawyer, acting was also being himself, in all his permanent boyishness. As his closest associate (one Alfred Hodder) remarked, if Flynt struck friends as a "finished actor," in a house "he was not at home; when he put on the uniform he must wear at dinner, he put off his memory . . . he was to the end a boy; he was shy; and except on his own stage he was shy to the point of silence or stammering" (Hodder, as quoted in *ML* 344–45).

More broadly, Flynt's refashioning of this sheepish private self depended upon two fundamental Victorian bourgeois mythologies: repudiating domesticity and setting out on the road. Initially, like the "good bad boys" of nineteenth-century popular romance, Flynt claimed to have rebelled against the discipline of middle-class domesticity, including its elaboration into the "cottage plan" for wayward children so favored by his own famous aunt, Frances Willard. He called this rebellion "kicking against the good" (*ML* 100). As Steven Mailloux has told us, "heading out" on the road meant not just evading domestic or female authority, but avoiding the archipelago of institutions—including prisons and juvenile homes—that targeted the orphaned, the young, and the criminal.[21] As an adult, however, Flynt would recuperate the ideology he once seemed to flout. Though he would continue to romanticize his own past, over time he would reaffirm the road as a requisite proving ground for a young man seeking his opportunities. Ultimately, he cast the road as a boyhood vice that was, like other failings, a necessary step on the way to manhood: to amount to anything, he later wrote, a young man must work his way "into a profession, and then on up the ladder until" he could return to his "people" and show them he had made good (*ML* 109). As an adult, he assured his readers that his early "kicking" now seemed "unprofitable and unmanly" (*ML* 100).

In one sense, of course, Flynt's "art" did begin as tramping in the literal sense of itinerancy or travel. Initially it was also an itinerancy very much created by its historical moment: his portrait of a tramp underworld was enabled by the railroad and by its national reach. It was not, moreover, simply personal initiative that eventually led Flynt to police the uninvited tramps who had, he said, created a mobile form of "camp life" (*TWT* 302) on railroad lines following the Civil War. Rather, he was often recruited for the task (*ML* 272ff.). Specifically, railroad executives and other business leaders hired out his services as an informant, imposter, and spy. In time, that is, he became a private detective who, like many others, patrolled the fringes of the industrial marketplace, circulating in realms left to them by local police, untouched by formal law, or deemed to need privacy by largely corporate clients. Commonly called "shadow men" (though women also worked in this role), these operatives watched over the tramps who latched onto railroads, the beggars or con men who moved from city to city to find new marks, and the embezzlers who simply left town and adopted new identities, only to start over as con men. As these specializations suggest, private detective work had arisen at a historical moment when both criminality and private capital became too geographically dispersed to rely on local, public policing alone. In the nineteenth century, as Flynt's own usage suggests, "police" was in fact a term applied both to public and private detective work.[22]

Meanwhile, much as Flynt would, the emerging private detective agencies refined their techniques by mimicking the confidence men they pursued. Listen to how, for instance, industry giant Allan Pinkerton describes the public misunderstanding of the term *shadowing* itself, which he said was at the center of the detective's art:

> Most people may suppose that nearly any one [sic] can perform the duties of a "shadow," and that it is the easiest thing in the world to follow up a man; but such is not the case. . . . It will not do to [merely] follow a person on the opposite side of the street, or close behind him. . . . Of course such a shadow would be detected in fifteen minutes. Such are not the actions of the real "shadow," or at least, of the "shadow" furnished by my establishment [the Pinkerton agency].[23]

Instead, Pinkerton goes on to explain, to shadow meant not merely to follow or mirror, but to enter fully into the criminal's world. A detective must do the work of establishing a new identity, circulating with the thief or embezzler's associates, and learning to "adopt generally the character of a fast man" (25). To shadow is an interesting verb: in material practice it meant to duplicate or copy criminal behavior; as a literary practice, it often meant injecting a darkness, perhaps even a shadow of guilt, into one's popular portrait of criminal licentiousness and excess. In print, shadowing thus meant not only to display crime but also to provide the reader with a safe or regulating distance.

As any fan of Dashiell Hammett's Continental Op knows, shape-shifting was the heart of the shadowing technique.[24] Labor unions and others, understandably, commonly equated such practices with provocation; genteel Americans sometimes regarded undercover work even by police officers as immoral. Yet although Pinkerton tended, in his writings, to celebrate a coordinated, quasi-military style for his operations, he readily understood how smaller, instrumental, less-intrusive techniques were useful in attaining private remedies. For instance, in tracking down an embezzler, he would employ the figure called a "roper" who first pulled the sucker into the (fraudulent) confidence game restaged by the agency (26). Recruiting men and women suitable for this work thus often meant dipping into a talent pool of operatives with already-shady résumés: work in vigilantism, fee-for-service recovery of property, or local political chicanery, for example. Track through the apprenticeship of the famous "cowboy detective" and Pinkerton Charlie Siringo, and one finds a story, like Abagnale's, blurring the lines between adventure, boy-sleuthing, and white-collar crime. Much as in the sensational cheap reading of this era, Pinkerton work often relied on class masquerade and the masking of secret identities. Siringo himself had gravitated to Pinkerton, while still in his teens, from the shady world of corporate cattle ranching, rustling, posse work, and vigilantism. Like the famous Molly Maguire provocateur, James

McParlan, Siringo developed his trademark skill in fraudulently adopting identities, working his way into gangs by posing as a criminal on the run, or informing on others from within prison.[25]

Usually, of course, these tactics were used to track down criminals (or sometimes simply political opponents) identified by Pinkerton clients. But in this deployment of boy delinquents—the character type also inverted by Flynt's reform—the shadowing strategy also recalls Michel Foucault's meditation on the integration of criminality, especially petty and mobile criminality, into policing and surveillance systems in the modern era. By the "delinquent" (*délinquant*), Foucault invokes not only the frequent offender, but the offender who leveraged his pending criminal penalty back into service of the state. The delinquent often uses informing (a term I suggest we should see as related to intelligence gathering) to get out of prison. In the layered rendering of *Discipline and Punish,* the static walls of a physical place (a prison) become permeable, and power itself becomes mobile, individuated. In Foucault's formulation, the delinquent becomes "a means of perpetual surveillance of the population . . . [of] the whole social field." Foucault's primary example, in fact, is Vidocq, the tramp-turned-detective who achieved "almost mythical importance" (283) among his contemporaries by putting former criminality in the service of the police apparatus:

> Vidocq marks the moment when delinquency, detached from other illegalities, was invested by power and turned inside out. . . . [T]he disturbing moment when criminality became one of the mechanisms of power. . . . The Shakespearean age when sovereignty confronted abomination in a single character had gone; the everyday melodrama of police power and of the complicities that crime formed with power was soon to begin. (283)

Delinquency becomes, in this way, a new form of power-knowledge, a "political observatory" (286) that moves across private and public boundaries, criminality and respectability alike. Like Vidocq before him, Flynt was mobilized into supervision (and even classification) of his own delinquent past and the criminal class he had once occupied. Like Pinkerton, Flynt even began to spy on other detectives who had been hired to watch tramps (*ML* 278). Private policing thus meant, apparently, ensuring the responsible actions of others. In other words, Flynt's services included assessment of areas vulnerable to crime and the persons responsible for guarding the potential security breach. In the loop at the heart of private security's own con game, he thus insured against the very risks he had exposed.

One caveat: the nineteenth-century term *delinquent* probably did not carry the connotation (or, eventually, the shorthand) of juvenility it would in the twentieth-century United States. And Flynt was, in many ways, on the path of petty criminality, or so it would seem. But precisely for these reasons, it is intriguing how—right at the moment late-Victorian culture began to argue over the emerging figure of the adolescent—Flynt marshaled his own juvenile biography into his new expertise, by making such small or "pedestrian" violations the subject of his alarm. As its punning title suggested, books like *Tramping with Tramps* worked both as a nostalgic rendering of his own youthful adventures and a compendium of newly scientific techniques like collecting underclass lingo, or describing a criminal type's *modus operandi*. (Eventually he would even append dictionaries of road slang to his studies.) The transposition in his own life, embodied through memoir into a reading experience, set the template. Having learned the "bluster and bluff" (*ML* 82) of confidence men in his character of Cig, he reapplied his verbal and physical disguises to his new craft as detective and, in another telling evolution, undercover muckraker.

In truth, as Lindner observes, it was probably the combination of happy-go-lucky bohemianism with reform goals that made Flynt so popular with middle-class readers (122). Along with an obvious facility for slang and street argot, Flynt's relish for the mystery of acting allowed him to mimic how criminals mastered the art of impression management, vital to a society of contract relations.[26] "Now you may or may not know it," he would write self-reflexively, "but the confidence man of the tip-top attainments cultivates the control of expression of his features with as much care as he does the professional beauty—this for the reason that his looks are among his most valuable assets" (*ML* 317). As Hodder described this art, "It was [Flynt's] habit to get under the guard of everyone he met, *to turn them inside out and inspect them* . . ." (quoted in *ML* 344–45). This practice also shaped his view of conning as the very heart of criminality generally. To Flynt, for instance, even the most impoverished of beggars were criminals, "voluntary" vagrants who conned the taxpayer into paying involuntary taxes (*TWT* 290).[27] Conversely, Flynt habitually equated the interest of his employers—for instance, the railroads—with those of the general public (*TWT* 308).[28] Turning the criminal into a man who victimized his targets made him into the anti-type of the more vigilant citizen that, reciprocally, Flynt's shadow man now came to model.

But here is where my earlier reflections on our own climate of contemporary fear and moral backlash come into play. To read only a grim vigilance in Flynt's storytelling is to truncate it at least by half. Flynt also appealed to readers by engineering a comic reduplication of the criminal act. Conning was now put in the service of tramping understood as recreation: re-creation of the vagrant's parasitism but also rediscovering, through undercover return, the leisure (or play) Flynt still loved. In other words, Flynt both modeled vigilance and allowed his citizen-readers to experience, through the virtual powers of reading, the pleasures that the road, and criminality itself, had once conferred upon him. Readers also partook of the new pleasure of knowing that his delinquent past was now a source of power. Flynt's own half-reformation was a matter of retelling (through writing) how he had learned to simulate what he had once done naturally. In a tactic terribly relevant to Abagnale, as we shall see, Flynt recounted how he had learned to become a fraud of a fraud.

Nostalgia also played a crucial role in Flynt's craft, as it affirmed the legitimacy of the homes that he said he was there to protect. At times, like Hawthorne's forlorn Wakefield, he would return to look in on his former life as a member of the educated middle class, relishing the concern over other lost boys' disappearances (*ML* 359–60). Perhaps the most revealing moment in Flynt's memoirs comes when he recounts a visit, while still a beggar on the road, back to a middle-class home:

> How odd it seemed! I almost felt at home, and had to be on my guard to keep up my role as a vagabond. For it was certainly a temptation to relieve myself then and there, and have an old-time chat on respectable lines. I had been so long on the road that I was really in need of some such comfort, but I dared not take advantage of it. So I answered their questions about my home, my parents, and my plans as professionally as I could, and spun my story, not entirely of fiction, however. . . . (*TWT* 162–63)

When Flynt learns that his hosts have lost a boy of their own, he is clearly moved: "I hope they have him now, for they certainly deserve surcease of sorrow on his account" (*TWT* 164). As a reformer, however, he must also chastise their sentimental impulse to charity: "There are people like this in every town, and it is the tramp's talent to find them." When he found them, Flynt said, he must make a "note" on them. "He thus becomes a peripatetic directory for the tramp world, which lives on the working world at a cost which it is worth while to consider" (*TWT* 164). But the text we're reading, of course, is the inside-out version of that former con. Now, as a tramp expert, Flynt has become the mobile observatory, creating a book that is much like a municipal ledger, emerging out of his own half-reformed delinquency. His new profession repays the host of his earliest rebellions—with pleasure.

II.

But what does this have to do with our own era—as it were, with our own moment of global economic dispersion, a persistent quest by corporations for public hegemony, and the ever-expanding privatization of security—and with the crime of identity theft, so often claimed to be a signature of our times? How would we describe, in terms relevant to Josiah Flynt, the services that Frank Abagnale provides?

In part, answering those questions begins with understanding Abagnale's context. Right as he came of age, corporate security consulting began its upward climb to its status, today, as a multibillion-dollar industry. Of late, security consulting businesses have grown from training and supplying menial and often poorly paid employees, such as bodyguards and private security personnel, to offering full-service operations that include protection against employee theft and embezzling, economic espionage, or cybercrime. The industry even encourages some industries to hire a Chief Security Officer (CSO). Meanwhile, since the 1970s, the panic over identity theft has contributed to this growth. Recently, both the FBI and the Federal Trade Commission have called identity theft one of the fastest growing white-collar crimes in the United States and a major source of consumer complaints to the government.[29] In truth, however, despite this public alarm, U.S. politicians have been reluctant to police identity theft through aggressive state or federal legislation. Fraud has traditionally been deemed a civil matter, and in the United States conservatives and liberals have resisted devices like national identification cards.[30] Recent legislation, therefore, has often focused as much on the illegal production of fraudulent documents as on personal identity theft, a distinction that points to terrorism as the main target.[31] Otherwise, the law has been content to rely on the traditional standard of *caveat emptor.*[32]

Such a state reluctance allows Abagnale to play the answer man. In this climate, he has thrived by nimbly shuttling between the preaching of consumer vigilance, the servicing of corporations, and the supplementing of state security and law enforcement. On the first front, as the author of several handbooks on personal security, Abagnale tutors individual consumers in the typical frauds performed by everyday confidence men: the lawn service that takes your personal check to the Internet and orders a new checkbook (*Art of the Steal* 29); thieves who steal payment checks from mailboxes left with their postal flags up (41); the smiling service provider who passes off phony gift certificates, for a small fee, in a mall (71–72). On the second front, Abagnale has invented various devices that secure contractual or financial obligations made by consumers with corporations; these devices protect companies that would otherwise bear the financial brunt of fraud. He has, for instance, designed SAFE checks for corporations; invented a water-resistant pen to thwart "check washing"; offered an identity-theft insurance program that reimburses the investigating and recuperating costs that victims might otherwise seek from banks and corporations; and consulted on the security of shredding machines. And again he has advised the FBI, as well as having consulted on the authentication of passports.[33] However, Abagnale's central faith is that real security depends not on these inventions but upon the responsible and vigilant consumer. Again, in Garland's term, he emphasizes personal "responsibilization." Abagnale frequently tells his reader that he or she is all too likely to be the weakest link in everyday transactions: as one subhead puts it, "Your first line of defense is you" (56). Or, even more fantastically, "If you're not doing anything about crime, you're encouraging crime."[34]

To a degree, this logic was a byproduct of defining identity theft primarily as an "opportunity crime," one created by breaches in victims' habits.[35] But more generally, Abagnale's self-help reflects the way that neoconservatism in the United States presses upon us the fatalistic sense that the state can no longer provide for our welfare. As if in miniature, Abagnale's platform seems to justify, or literally personify, the personal register in which so much of neoconservative crime talk constructs citizen vigilance. As some of our shrewdest analysts point out, identity theft is one crime category where we most often hear the recurrent lament that the state cannot or will not provide systemic solutions to our crime problems. As Gary T. Marx has put it, it is where we hear the "only you" refrain enjoining the citizen-subject to work on him- or herself, to manage risks at the personal level.[36] (If we become victims of identity theft, few of us would think to call the police, at least at first.) In such a climate, we are instead treated to advertisements about identity theft in which we are reduced to dreary lives and jobs. As if mocking a public service announcement from the government, a ventriloquized voice of an identity thief gleefully describes his or her spending spree with our credit card.

It is this context that allows Abagnale, as it were, to transpose the geographic mobility of the nineteenth-century shadow detective into something like an "indoorizing" of security, a scaling down into the personal life. He now enters into the interstices of the contract relation and, especially, personal consumption. Echoing Flynt's formulation, the former con man becomes the "peripatetic directory" of cons, a municipal service or manual made a private property for each of us. Abagnale is thus quite literally a private expert in that he secures the everyday, promises it peace of mind, and offers to guard individual identities in transactions commonly outside the state's protections. And he seems to do this, in part, by fanning fear through his catalogue of crimes. Although Abagnale's expertise more precisely reflects an ongoing category shift from identity *fraud* (counterfeiting an occupation or making up a person) to identity *theft,* he portrays such an act as more like a physical threat or violation. It is a burglary of selfhood. Indeed, as someone who narrates potential crimes to consumers, he melds the language of consumer protection to the vocabulary of victims' rights. In essence, he asks consumers to visualize their own potential victimization, but to see that victimization as redressed mainly by civil action on their own part.

In these respects, Abagnale's service philosophy threads its way through many of the larger themes of the neoconservative turn. A modern, marketplace-driven notion of risk management comes to seem as if it simply restores a bygone day of American self-help. And Abagnale's own individualism, his idiom of protecting the "little guy" from everyday small frauds, is an appeal that lends a "mom-and-pop" tenor to his consumer tutelage, an aura of resistance to modernity arriving, say, in the guise of electronic or Internet crimes. And cutting in almost the complete opposite direction, Abagnale's services (which often involve technological devices themselves, after all) also create different ways for corporations to track employees, or to secure against embezzlement or petty theft. He therefore contributes to vigilance *over* the public, not simply for or by them. In Abagnale's rendering, meanwhile, crimes against consumers are also byproducts of compulsion, metaphorically adolescent in character. And this is precisely why, as if crafting a first principle of American neoconservatism, identity theft crimes are defined as rooted in a permissive impulse culture.[37] As the counterpart of street thugs, who represent what neoconservatives cast as "predatory" criminality, the archetypal white-collar criminal becomes a computer hacker: the figure who seems to say that if a crime can be committed, it will be.[38] Crime on both fronts is thus cast as ever-present, something we have to learn to live with.

As with Flynt, however, underneath this fear-based approach, a more subtle appeal is being crafted. As Ian Loader has suggested, much of the contemporary discourse of private security also offers to empower the consumer as what Loader calls a sovereign citizen, often by creating social distinction and even pleasure around the acquisition of security. While citizens today still often look to the public police as a source of legitimate authority and crime management, the expanding security market encourages them to see the state as simply one player in that market. That is, as Loader describes it, the consumer is offered a choice of policing alternatives that he or she can use; he or she can express that preference without any necessary political justification; and, quite tellingly, he or she can exit from such protection if his or her consumer preferences remain unsatisfied. And thus, when security is a good not in the sense of a public value, but in the sense of a commodity, it offers a sense of power and control to the private buyer, a way to privately produce a separation between ourselves and an often-threatening world "out there."[39]

That service, on its face, might seem quite compatible with the larger cultural work performed by a text like *Catch Me If You Can*. Doing your duty as a risk-informed consumer certainly seems compatible with growing up, in the way we assume that Frank Abagnale, former identity fraud, has. But here again, the example of Josiah Flynt is a telling one. It turns out that shadowing the identity thief's own professional knowledge does not mean something as simple as disowning the past. Rather, in his as-told-to memoir, it means displaying that criminality, even enjoying the image of freedom that is supposedly being marked as criminal. To understand Abagnale's cultural work, in other words, we have to understand how the older voice of authority hacks into its alter ego, replicates, even counterfeits him, becoming a fraud of a fraud—and then puts the pleasure of duplication into our social imaginations. The "art" of the con thus may be a larger part of Abagnale's "deal" than we might otherwise suspect.

III.

First, however, I offer a meditation on Abagnale's particular framing of security within the larger crime context. Abagnale's equating of consumer vigilance with personal maturity, to be sure, might seem confined to the realms of middle-class consumption and corporate relations. Or, to put it another way, he might make it seem that those realms are distinct from, held apart from, the threat of "predatory" street crime. Yet, as I've already suggested, there are more continuities between private and public realms of crime control than we commonly suspect. The neoconservative turn has not been merely about sanctioning community groups or crime watches, encouraging vicarious participation in various crime wars, or fanning fear; rather, "responsibilization" has meant that citizens have been urged to internalize risk assessment, conceived quite broadly, into their adult identities. That is, it was now said, citizens must embody vigilance, take the assessment of crime's risk into their own minds and bodies, and thus carry the state's work within them, not unlike Flynt's mobile undercover agent (as I show, in chapter 1, Rudolph Giuliani actually proposing; or, in chapter 3, when communities are encouraged to join the cold case). As middle-class or consumerist as Abagnale's ethos might seem, therefore, his program was not at all incompatible with what was going on in the streets. Rather, it paralleled the other ways in which the call to "responsibilization" claimed to empower the consumer as a sovereign citizen.

Meanwhile, this charge mobilized public and private resources. As many commentators have realized, the not-at-all-ancillary effect of the neoconservative emphasis on "community involvement" has been the erosion of boundaries between private and public spheres around policing. As I have discussed in chapter 2, even tactical crime-busting programs like CompStat, aimed at street crime, took this blended philosophy into the streets. William Bratton was well-known in New York for presenting himself as "the CEO Cop," and for saying, simultaneously, that cops were "sales representatives" just as citizens were "consumers."[40] In many ways, the expansion of private security only reveals that neoconservative reforms, once having applied consumer management to public policing, now returned the favor, exporting lessons from public order-maintenance back to the personal spheres of spending, consumption, and leisure. What has increasingly emerged, as a result, is a kind of synergy between proactive crime prevention as such (old-fashioned actuarialism, with a long history in police management) and managing citizens as consumers of the security one provides. In a rhetorical parallel to the idiom of victims' rights, politicians have been willing, in turn, to proclaim private "rights" to such security.

The back-and-forth movement has many dimensions. One thinks, for instance, of the application of insurance or accounting principles to law enforcement and public policing; in the crossover (and back) of former police commissioners like Bratton into security consulting; the installation of public police stations in private buildings (e.g., malls); or in the construction of private-public partnerships like Business Improvement

Districts that structure park management around private security and user-friendly social services. Each of these designs offers the reduction of crime risk to citizens by conceiving them as consumers or stakeholders, in some cases literally paying for the service.[41]

This explicit reciprocity between public and private responsibilization is perhaps best exemplified by the effects of consumer "victimization surveys," much touted by thinkers like James Q. Wilson and Robert H. Rhodes. Initially, these were surveys that asked citizens to report upon their experience with crime and their fears of its occurrence; such surveys were used to provide an alternate means of recording crime's incidence beyond the state's own records. Police officials, criminologists, and crime commentators, in other words, no longer had to rely on records of crime displayed in Uniform Crime Reports. Neoconservatives commonly seized upon these surveys, which usually suggested that crime was more prevalent than previously thought, particularly during the affluent 1960s. Crucially, however, these surveys in themselves demonstrated that one way crime fear had manifested itself was in a broad-scale distrust of the state. These surveys thus became one quite concrete register of the surging importance of victims' rights, and the often-devious way that order-maintenance policing (in a veiled retort to feminist and community activism) claimed to "take back the streets" on behalf of the fearful.[42] Victim surveys could also be claimed as a democratic reform—and here, Simon's crime control as governance expressed itself—because they supposedly "spoke" directly for citizens. At their worst, conversely, victim surveys showed how easily crime busting could veer into public relations: when, for instance, neoconservatives argued that their reform sometimes meant that streets were not really safer (which data often demonstrated), but that it would make people *feel* so.[43]

Meanwhile, these claims to citizen sovereignty, as expressed through such surveys, had other devious effects. As various critics of risk management have argued, imagined fears now legitimated police action based upon them. Surveys also legitimated fears that might have been discriminatory in origin. Moreover, relying on victim surveys also installs a negative logic that can veer hysterically between magnifying the threat and then declaring its actual absence a sign of success.[44] And as Elizabeth Stanko has shown, it was also a simple step from asking citizens to name the public locations where they felt most threatened, to calibrating those fears to a demographic profile of citizens who were themselves reporting (in other words, viewing potential crime victims as a focus group). Early neoconservative advocates of a "victim-centered" justice, like Rhodes, were quite explicit on this point:

> Beyond its usefulness for assessing unreported crime, victimization surveying permits study of the victim himself. It has been argued that victims in some situations encourage crime and have a vital role in potential prevention. Examples are legion: vacationing residents who fail to cancel their newspapers or mail while they are away; intoxicated down-and-outers sleeping it off in a city park or street; the young girl who is unaccompanied late at night on a remote highway or dimly lit city street; and the defaulted banker, swindled in a desperate attempt to keep the institution's head above water. As we learn more of the victim's role in the criminal event, we may be in a position to prevent crime, not simply by deterrence or incarcerating offenders, but by encouraging potential victims to alter their behavior.[45]

And so, for example, a survey might well determine that the probability of being victimized—or, again, feeling threatened—was directly related to the amount of time one spent in public spaces.[46] From this, it was easy for crime managers to conclude that the populace should be policed differentially, inevitably making risk management a practice that produced benefits for some but not for all. Stanko, for instance, shows that victims said by such surveys to be at risk included those who spent time with "non-family members," a measurement wide open to differential application. Some citizens, that is, might be protected by public or private security because they were deemed to be "out with their friends"; others doing the same thing might be policed in what would be called a gang sweep. As in Abagnale's program, the survey meant that vigilant citizens were now designated as undercover agents. But now they had their fears tapped, not just their observations or actual experience.

A specific connection to Abagnale, meanwhile, also shows us that there is something more subtle at work in these devices of risk assessment than the simple reproduction of fear. Rather, for the consumer secured by these differential and often arbitrary practices, it was *leisure* that could be particularly made safe. That is, in practice, the philosophy of risk management often delineates a middle zone for the consumer, *between* often-disabling fear generated by crime talk or media, and a hypothetical condition of pure safety. This is a point about the current culture of "fear" that our criticism often overlooks. The idea embedded in the theory of "responsibilization" is that one internalizes the knowledge of a security presence so as, supposedly, to reduce fear, if one is willing to entertain the risk. To reward those of us who have, we might say, privatized a risk assessment in order to *take* that risk, not to refuse it. Here, "going out with one's friends," with one's credit cards securely insured by Frank Abagnale, captures much of what risk management has implicitly offered by way of securing pleasure.[47] The credit card, secured against an identity theft conceived much like personal assault, thus spoke volumes about how pre-political attitudes were embedded within the consumer ideal, conjoined with a redefinition of state authority.

It is not merely, then, that Abagnale's rakish imaginings contribute to the public's dismissal of the seriousness of white-collar crime; in fact, he complains about such public dismissals himself. Rather, in a telling modification on responsibilization, he adroitly reveals his past criminality in order to invoke nostalgia for the freedoms and personal (class) security of the very world his own marketing proposes to preserve. Recreating that no-longer-lost world is the cultural work of *Catch Me If You Can*.

IV.

Like Josiah Flynt's memoirs, *Catch Me If You Can* is a narrative of quickness, mobility, and movement: from city to city, con to con, recounting what Abagnale (again, through Redding) calls "Adventures in Crime" (63). The con man's favorite animals in this memoir are nimble tricksters, the jackrabbit or bumblebee (75). Meanwhile, particularly in this book form, *Catch Me If You Can* is not a narrative of simple revenge against the state.[48] Rather, as I have already suggested, Abagnale's turnabout becomes a story of responsibilization, of risk and rewards that ends up in the state's service. And in Abagnale's universe, to engage in risk management means to "entertain" crime in the sense of picturing or plotting what a criminal would be likely to do. It involves an imagining that invites a strain of pleasure as much as vigilance or fear.

Despite the future-oriented taunt of its title, *Catch Me If You Can* is a book shot through with nostalgia. As with Philip Gourevitch's *Cold Case*, it makes us feel as if the mobile, freer decade it recalls—the 1960s—is actually the 1940s. Importantly, in the memoir itself, we are never actually shown Abagnale's capture or incorporation into the FBI; instead, we luxuriate in his criminal past. Even the older security man's voice is saturated with wistfulness and with the use of retro diction such as "threads" or "goodies." A woman can easily be described as a "fox," or, in the collective, referred to as "broads" (5, 10, 15). For his own earlier line of work, Abagnale evokes the argot of "rackets," the slang term that, from the early twentieth century on, referred to both common professions and the elaborate swindles of criminals. As if we begin in the days of ward bosses and gambling dens, he even compares his father's world to that of Damon Runyon (9).

Catch Me, however, reaches even farther back in history. Both the book and the film adopt many conventions common to juvenile tramping narratives of the nineteenth century, including Flynt's. As I have said, we watch as young Frank first escapes from a reform school (17), flirts with jail, and then heads out on the road to seek his fortune. But again, as in many a Victorian good-bad-boy tale, that route is transformed into a journey of experience and personal self-development (20–21). As in a Horatio Alger tale, natural boyishness blurs into prankishness, and then prankishness seems like metropolitan savoir faire. We eventually discover that, like a dime novel hero, young Frank studies in libraries "as diligently as any investor studies the markets available to him" (128). He learns, the older man recalls, how to combine "personality, observation, and research" (130) into his criminal vocation. In one of his earliest cons, Frank poses as a cub reporter for a high school newspaper, only to trick a pilot into revealing airline security measures. Young Frank then sticks a logo from a plastic airplane model, appropriately enough, onto his first fake security ID. *Catch Me* also misses few opportunities to portray young Frank as a forlorn boy, driven by anxiety about a troubled home (in Abagnale's case, his parents' divorce). It even includes an element one sees in gangster narratives, where the young criminal is actually tutored in the urban world of boss politics and saloons (Abagnale's father being a New York Republican ward politician).[49] If anything, Spielberg's adaptation—set up, really, as a Henry Mancini–scored, 1960s "caper" film—would accentuate these elements even further, often by taking more liberties with Abagnale's upbringing than the memoir itself does.

Meanwhile, Abagnale's memoir begins to move nineteen-year-old criminality from the aura of adolescent high jinks into premature hypermasculinity.[50] Shifting gears from a fable-like and even a folklorish feel— that childish world of rabbits and bumblebees (28, 62, 75)—the young entrepreneur begins moving from woman to woman as well. Smoothing the transition, Abagnale begins to describe his own motivation as having always been hormonal. He begins his criminal career by using a tire-replacement and credit scam, for instance, to pay for gasoline so he can date girls (27). ("An inflated sex drive," the older man intones, "has no conscience" [16].) Thus, as in *Tom Sawyer,* conning is written off to normal male competitive instincts and good fun. At the same time, I think, it is difficult to overlook the developing tension that results between the narrator-adult and this maturing rascal. The inside, retrospective narrative voice that we recognize from *The Art of the Steal* coyly notes others' vanity, vulnerability, and gullibility; yet in the plot, young Frank can easily strike us, as he does his companions, as modest, generous, respectful, and polished. Likewise, we are sometimes reminded that the adult Abagnale is (and says he always was) deeply conservative in personal matters, having outgrown (we are told) his bumblebee days. The narrator avers, for instance, that he dislikes "women's lib" (11); yet as we move from "fox" to "fox," Abagnale is quick to defend his former bedmates against the charge of promiscuity (52).

Perhaps to neutralize this tension, *Catch Me* actually begins to depart from conventions we might associate with a con man narrative. Gradually it makes it seem as if young Frank had no marks (or leaves no marks) to speak of. With two very minor exceptions—a prostitute hoping to scam *him* (196–97) and one insufferable boss (211)—Abagnale never relishes in the classical "sizing up" or "busting out" that analysts like David Maurer famously posited as the signature elements of the confidence game. Abagnale even claims never to have stiffed an individual person (197).[51] But here is where the con man-boy seems to give way to the security expert shadowing these adventures. Removing the predatory tinge of his activities allows Abagnale to cast his former crimes as merely passing along the costs to companies or banks rather than their customers or employees. We thereby learn more of the loopholes (or breaches) in corporate or bank or airline security than we do of any mark's own propensities for larceny. Turned about in this fashion, Abagnale's memories become object lessons in what is commonly called the "low hanging fruit" theme of risk management. For instance, we are meant to conclude how easily the airlines "set *themselves* up" (59, my emphasis) by creating vulnerable accounting practices, loose arrangements to house flight crews, and so on.[52]

Along the way, as well, our young hero basks in the perquisites of the jobs he acquires rather than their labor as such. Time and again, naturally, he cites the "ego boosts" he gets from his adopted professions, as if rediscovering a normative-male competitive instinct anew. But he points more to the vicarious pleasures of these identities rather than their skills or authority per se. He doesn't love flying: he loves hotels, toadying waiters, and, as always, stewardesses. In point of fact, these faux identities are *not* stolen from another individual—a category shift again, disguised by our own hindsight. That absence of identity theft as we know it is why Abagnale can pass off his various counterfeiting or perquisite-thefts not as conning a person so much as taking funds from the corporations for which that person works. In this sense, the cross-cutting between sexual freedom and identity fraud in employment is instructive. In Abagnale's boyish retrospect, the labor of the job is actually hollowed out, as if its perquisites, or the leisure it might produce, feed back into the experience of the job itself. When posing as a doctor in an emergency ward, for example, Frank's boss tells him to just "do anything you want: just be here!" (86). In many instances, Abagnale actually passes in these occupations by playing the bad boy or the buffoon: not by mastering the craft, but by becoming Flynt's happy-go-lucky tramp artist. The workplace, in other words, is given a prelapsarian innocence, like the bedroom. There, the risks of sexual freedom (such as it is, in masculinist terms), reinfused with a little healthy masculine conning, can be restored by (a subtext never mentioned) the risk management of birth control pills.

In many respects, Abagnale's adoption of these identities, a shadowing of the everyday, returns us to the dream of professional status as itself a form of class exemption from hard labor, a motif we might now discern in those identity-theft ads mentioned earlier. It is as if the identity fraud's joy has restored the promise of pleasure in modern white-collar work. It is a joy that, say, worrying about malpractice insurance costs might actually threaten. Larceny becomes a way to refresh an everyman fantasy. Particularly in the recovery of the lost boy, criminality ostensibly allows readers (especially male readers) to re-experience the fruits of their labor and see work as the achievement of their desires. In tandem with his mobile-directory security self, the younger Abagnale can claim to simply be returning to consumers the pleasures that others threaten to take from them. He becomes, as it were, joyously delinquent on everyday responsibility. He allows readers to rediscover what the identity thief fraudulently adopts by hacking into their lives. Reciprocally, Abagnale tutors his future clients to catch themselves in fantasies of pleasure and implicitly reminds them what is at risk. Abagnale asks readers and consumers to make the larceny in their soul a more open secret and to take pleasure in it. But he does so *not* to summon its full repression but to entertain the pleasures sustained by taking measured risks. The consumer-reader is enjoined to make risk assessment in order to take that risk, not to refuse it. As Loader suggests, the idea is to produce security not through fear or moral suasion, but through a commodity that promises to produce pleasure and distinction—by, in effect, buying in.

Ultimately, in fact, what is remarkable about Abagnale's rewriting of risk is that it actually removes most, if not all, of the disastrous consequences that might result from young Frank's crimes. In one of his earliest airline flights, nineteen-year-old Frank is asked to take over the plane's controls—oh, no! But then we learn young Frank can simply turn on the automatic pilot (3–4). When he poses as that emergency room doctor—oh, no!—likewise, we soon learn that his assignment means that he won't actually be treating patients, just supervising interns (85). (In one of the book's more comic moments, the interns are simply grateful that he lets them be "real doctors" and actually treat the sick [92].) When he becomes a lawyer (106), he says he is happy *not* to have to try any cases (though in fact he may well have).[53] This is not, however, a simple minimizing of white-collar crime. Rather, Abagnale's fantasies of identity fraud *preempt* its risks while we are being entertained by his criminal craft. In an "adventure" with comic kinship to a film (and original Philip K. Dick story) like *The Minority Report,* the risk is already managed, in the shape of the fantasy itself. Spielberg is thus a very apt appropriator of Abagnale's memory, which seems like cryptomnesia in the first place. Reading Abagnale is very much akin to viewing those scenes in Spielberg films when the moment of danger is neutralized by the look of an amusement ride: the risk is entertained but neutralized, managed by the invisible hand of a nostalgic adult, still overlooking the kids. (As, for example, in the famous moment when threatening guns of the government, in the re-release of *E.T.,* were erased and replaced by walkie-talkies as the boys ride their bikes into the moon.) It is significant that Abagnale's signature milieu, in the end, was the hybrid, state-run yet mass private property space of the airport. (The venue, of course, has also intrigued Spielberg.) Even more significant is that this first public laboratory for modern risk management is here made akin to the second most influential location: Disneyland.

In the end, Abagnale's shadow narrative thus betrays a certain signature byplay between the uses of political nostalgia in our day, and the larger program of "freedom" that the neoconservative turn has claimed to restore. At first, *Catch Me* uses its juvenile conventions to forge an attachment to an entrepreneurial past. Much like Ronald Reagan or George W. Bush, Abagnale's boy-hero hearkens back to a world of open markets and professions. But is it not simply that Abagnale's fantasy takes us back to those days—whenever they were—when law, medicine, or (imagine) academia were such open markets that employers were simply hiring job candidates off the street. Rather, it is that his nostalgia works to invoke a longing for the freedoms and personal (class) security of the very world his own marketing proposes to re-secure. In this imagined past, the phrase "catch me if you can" refers to an existence supposedly beyond the reach of the liberal (and, with the figure of O'Riley, the paternal) state. Risk management offers to turn back the clock, to erase the new world disorder these days actually produce, as the Kroll executive admits. I might offer a few parting thoughts, therefore, about Abagnale's supposed recruitment by the FBI.

In Abagnale's version of events, the original site of his conversion to security consultant, it turns out, was the American prison. Having been first arrested in France, and then recaptured and placed in a U.S. facility, Abagnale claims to have manipulated the "civil rights scrutiny of prisons" (268–69) into a ruse to create special treatment for himself as a prisoner. His con was to create suspicion among his jailors that he was what he calls a "Bureau of Prisons prober" (271), an undercover inspector of the prison itself. In other words, he supposedly posed as the person he would become, a risk assessment specialist. But he tested the weakness of the system by posing as someone who could police it from the inside-out, to create distinction (and eventually freedom) for himself. Not surprisingly, then, in the book, he effects his final escape from our narrative inspection by posing as a friend of O'Riley. When surrounded in the final crisis moment, he poses as an FBI man to elude capture (272–76). All along, in fact, we can easily have the feeling that we have been reading, as it were, less an autobiography and more the résumé for an audition.

Spielberg's version, by contrast, would have us believe that Abagnale was reformed and recruited by the FBI. But as I have been suggesting, Abagnale's imaginary memoir—what else can one call it?—actually scripts a somewhat different courtship between private security and the state. Instead, he portrays a state so hot upon his paper trail that it hopes to learn to live with crimes that he has modeled. Instead of showing himself tracked down by that relentless, middle-of-the-road FBI Man—or revealing the fact that it was probably an FBI plea bargain that freed him from prison—in the book, Abagnale concludes his story by suggesting he eluded state incorporation. We are left to conclude, from his title, that he ultimately decided to catch *himself*. By turning away from the juvenile play of "kiting" checks to catching those who still do, young Frank will learn, we gather, to literally incorporate his fantasies and his talents, and fold himself into something more like a private-public contract. (It is Abagnale, after all, who lectures to the FBI, not the other way around.) In a sense, this is a fantasy in which the boy-hero and vagabond engineers his own (state) adoption, and now sells us freedom at the everyday low price of increased personal vigilance and security. Therefore, we might say, Frank Abagnale himself puts the con into neocon.

5

"Doing Time"
Keepers, Brothers, and the Prison Exposé

> "They're keeping him there till they think that he won't do the same thing again."
>
> —John Edgar Wideman, to his daughter Jamila

IN THE FIFTH CHAPTER of his *Newjack: Guarding Sing Sing* (2000), undercover journalist Ted Conover pauses, as many authors of prison exposé will, for a long historical interlude. Breaking stride from recounting his enlistment in the state of New York's training program for corrections officers, and then his ten months at the infamous maximum-security facility at Ossining, Conover instead takes his reader through the oft-retold phases of prison history. He begins with the Quaker-inspired innovation of the penitentiary in antebellum America, which drew European visitors like Charles Dickens and Alexis de Tocqueville, and then turns to describing the gradual, turn-of-the-century elimination of abuses like the cat-'o-nine tails, cold-water torture, and contract labor, counterpointed by the grim arrival of the electric chair in 1891. Then Conover recalls the work of twentieth-century reform wardens like Thomas Mott Osborne and Lewis Lawes, who installed job training, prison furloughs, and community programs, so many of which have been curtailed in our grimmer moment of bureaucratic stagnation and lockdown. In the end, what therefore is most startling about Conover's historical interlude is how nearly irrelevant it comes to seem. In the face of the collapse of prison's rehabilitative mission, that is, the effect of these historical antecedents seems purely bathetic or ironic. Conover presents the contemporary prison as a world hollowed out, drained of any function except as an empty space of pain and isolation, as if having been distilled to its essence: jail, warehouse, "keep." It is almost as if we have come not only to the end of history, but beyond it—in Conover's phrase—to the "scrap heap" of Time (208). To a prison that, though "storied and mysterious" (59), is a monument to liberalism's ruination.[1]

These days, the gesture seems apt. Prison in its many manifestations, old and new, public and private, from detention center to supermax, has come to stand as a material culmination of the neoconservative turn and its fatalistic premium on "learning to live with crime." Incarceration is intimately related to many of the tactics I have described in earlier chapters—informing that capitalizes on administrative plea bargaining, deceptive interrogation, pretext busts, warrant squads, and more—and a site of symbolic investment, a place where the premium on vigilance and control becomes manifest in the extreme. (Even Frank Abagnale argued for more punitive incarceration, though he himself was reformed through plea bargaining.)

But perhaps even more vexingly, the prison also seems to speak to public acquiescence about the costs these measures have exacted. Whatever stories prisons still hold for American readers, the dismantling of the rehabilitative rationale is actually an open secret. As Joseph Hallinan reminds us, a Harris poll from 1970 once showed that 73 percent of Americans believed the main goal of prison should be rehabilitation; by 1995, that number had dropped to 25 percent.[2] While hardly universal, this public fatalism seemed a sorrowful affirmation of two related planks in the neoconservative platform: the idea that prison should punish offenders and control crime in advance; and that its costs had to be accepted on behalf of at-risk neighborhoods. Indeed, prison exposé has been the one genre where the war on crime has gone beyond fear or political backlash. Rather, it is often argued, Americans have been systematically incorporated into the prison as an economic and political institution, into a "prison-industrial complex." And like the military-industrial complex before it, prison comes to signify a state of political stagnation—as it were, the permanence of the war on crime itself.[3]

This final chapter seeks to take the pulse of contemporary prison exposés by evaluating this recent argument, and then by looking more closely at two texts that bracketed the neoconservative turn: Conover's prize-winning account of 2000 and a memoir from a decade and a half earlier, John Edgar Wideman's *Brothers and Keepers* (1984). Though the prison is a hub of many social ideas and practices, I want to zero in, instead, on these two texts in light of the signature micropolitical tactic of *incapacitation:* the argument, so often made by neoconservatives, that prison could control crime by targeting repeat offenders and removing them from their neighborhoods. An idea that received renewed emphasis in the 1970s, incapacitation remains central to the public defense of the prison system, even in its most dismal, warehousing manifestations.[4] But beyond looking at this premium on "doing time," I also want to examine how our prison exposés "do" *our* time: that is, how they capture the political claims of the turn on which I have focused in this book. Ostensibly, the theory of incapacitation offered to turn back the clock to the prison's traditional function. On the other hand, the tactic actually brought together many of the forward-looking elements I have discussed: the imposition of actuarial thinking (targeting repeat offenders), the renewed premium on personal control and vigilance to manage risk, and the idea that a mixture of new federalism and privatized management might reconstruct the state's power.[5] And for all the talk about making incarceration legible to potential offenders, recent decades have witnessed new forces that have actually worked to limit what Americans could know about prisons.

To begin, I will focus on two related dimensions of recent prison exposés, the "concrete" (my pun intended) and the cultural. In the first sense, these exposés have shown us how prison operations have become a jobs program; in regions like upstate New York, the prison *literally* became something citizens had to learn to live with, just as, albeit in a vastly different way, the families and neighbors of those in prison did. But in the sense more central to this book, prison has also had its cultural dimensions rewritten, as part of the manufacture of consent. The prison solution reconstructed citizen affiliation with crime control even as it attached a specific tactic (incapacitation) to the criminal himself. In these senses, "doing time" behind prison walls meant rewriting both real communities and imagined ones, prisoners' hopes and family memories, present-day social relations and what we imagine they can be. Incapacitation's cultural effects were often redoubled behind prison walls. To inmates, that is, the tactic offered a bleak reminder of the choices in their own past and the lost legacies of communities whose memories they tried to carry with them.

Houses of correction, of course, present enormous challenges for journalistic exposés, and no single account can be comprehensive. Beyond their sheer scale and variation, prisons are typically secretive places, worlds of rumor and self-pleading, riddled with internal economies of privileges, punishments, violence, and information. Some exposés, as I will show, delineate the regional or national contexts of prison more fully than Wideman or Conover do; others delve more extensively into neighboring communities, or the post-prison experience; others capture prisoners' experience more thoroughly, including the brutality that is all too common. Yet in capturing the material and cultural meanings of incapacitation, the counterpoint between Conover and Wideman's memoirs can be especially instructive. As if re-deploying the tactics of Josiah Flynt, Conover uses undercover reporting to enter into the labor of corrections officers, thereby hoping to examine the physical and psychological state of vigilance at the point of contact with those deemed criminal. (And as we shall see, echoes of the streets outside get under even Conover's undercover skin.) Wideman's text, meanwhile—actually a meditation co-written with his own imprisoned brother Robert (Robby)—offers a startling repudiation of the restructuring of neighborhood memory and individual futurity within the neoconservative turn. From different positions in a critical American racial divide, both writers struggle to come to terms with what, in our culture of crime, has become something like a sanctioned underworld. The prison has become a place where, as an emerging complex of ideas about the state would have it, criminals could be placed in a condition that immobilized them—as the Widemans' memoir puts it, frozen in their "dull, inferior portion" (195) of time.

I.

A more contemporaneous but equally dispiriting interlude for Conover's book might have begun with Susan Sheehan's *A Prison and a Prisoner* (1978), a portrait of the Green Haven, New York, maximum-security facility in the years following the Attica uprising of 1971.[6] As on so many crime fronts, the 1970s proved to be a turning point in prison management and in the political conditions shaping crime genres, including exposés of the "prison-industrial" complex.

Writing for *The New Yorker* before this template was at her disposal, Sheehan had made use, instead, of her magazine's trademark chiseled restraint. Her goal was to deflate reader expectations generated by, among other influences, Hollywood prison melodrama. Instead of depicting "men with furrowed brows, bent heads, or plaintive eyes" (38), for example, Sheehan chose to deadpan prison life: the absurdities of its bureaucracy, wholly inadequate psychiatric resources, and even guard brutality (92). Yet reading Sheehan back from our time, we also realize she had arrived at a darkening moment. At first, in the immediate aftermath of the Attica uprising, the New York state legislature had actually experimented with the liberalization of prison management: with a relaxing of prisoner-movement and lockup rules, freeing up phone and mail privileges, and allowing typewriters and tape recorders in cells. Green Haven had even added a gym and a law library, and then inaugurated a formal grievance procedure for inmates. Conover and Wideman would be especially interested to discover that the liberalization of prisoners' visitors' rooms (under the banner of prisoner "resocialization") was also experimented with. But soon, the tide shifted. In the summer of 1977, under the leadership of State Corrections Commissioner Benjamin Ward, New York officially repudiated the objective of rehabilitation. The state then instituted draconian cost cuts, abolished honor blocks, reestablished lockdown procedures, and curtailed the freedom of movement prisoners had briefly enjoyed. Sheehan would only remark obliquely upon the mood of "uncertainty and disarray" (162) resulting from these changes. But of one thing she was sure: the retrenchment had "sent the morale of the guards soaring" (162), even though increased inmate supervision often meant more work. (In fact, in the next twenty years, U.S. prison employment would double.)

All this, of course, was but a prelude to the massive prison boom of our time—a national boom extensively documented by a flurry of general-interest exposés: most prominently, aside from Conover's memoir, Joseph Hallinan's *Going Up the River* (2001); Christian Parenti's *Lockdown America* (1999); Cristina Rathbone's *A World Apart* (2005); Andi Rierden's *The Farm* (1997); and Eric Schlosser's influential *Atlantic Monthly* essay, "The Prison-Industrial Complex" (1998). A deadly counterpoint lay behind all of these accounts. As prison support programs of all kinds would be eviscerated, they would be replaced by devices that would effectively dragnet the poor (and often the nonviolent) into the world of the penitentiary: mandatory minimum-sentencing laws, "relevant conduct" and conspiracy clauses, three strikes provisions, and more. In New York State alone, the prison boom resulted in the quintupling of its incarcerated population. Inside the prison, meanwhile, one would see the institution of administrative segregation and twenty-three-hour keeplock, practices that, in many ways, would define Conover's tenure as a guard. New York's map would itself be split between older facilities like Sing Sing and newer, upstate prisons, many built under Democratic governor Mario Cuomo, ostensibly under the aegis of "community development." Urban and minority prisoners would effectively be exiled from their neighborhoods and families, to be watched over by largely white guards from the regions surrounding the newer facilities. Schlosser's essay, though it focuses mainly on prison privatization, describes how Cuomo's new prisons displaced the traditional economies of the areas into which they were placed. In upstate New York, it is the downturn in farming, mining, and manufacturing that provides the opening for development. (One West Virginia county with two new facilities, Joseph Hallinan similarly tells us, has more prisoners than coal miners [203].) Meanwhile, the incarceration of women—documented in Rathbone's *World Apart*—often became the locus of an underground economy of cosmetics, prohibited food, and most disturbingly, sexual exchanges with guards. Contradicting some of the principal tactics I describe in my first three chapters, Rathbone shows that it is low-end members of the drug economy (often women) who cannot bargain their way into informing (99–100), and that nonviolent inmates serving mandatory-sentence drug time aren't eligible for work release—whereas murderers, pedophiles, and arsonists are (138–39).

Thanks to these writers, as well as a persisting clamor of alarm by academics and activists, the story above may seem a distressingly familiar one.[7] Nevertheless, documenting the prison boom has been achieved against considerable odds. It is easy to overlook the ratcheting down of journalists' rights of access to prisons since the mid-1970s. Following a trio of Supreme Court decisions—*Pell v. Procunier* (1974), *Saxbe v. Washington Post Co.* (1974), and *Houchins v. KQED Inc.* (1978)—state governments and prison officials have been given broad discretion to limit or, in some cases, prohibit journalists' entry or face-to-face contact with inmates. Particularly in the 1990s, as government officials tightened controls over prisoner mobility, reading material, and access to lawsuits, state and local wardens erected a variety of restrictions for journalistic access. One could be denied entry based on whether one was a print or broadcast reporter, whether one conducted interviews in person or on the phone, and more. Some locales even created restrictions based on the content of articles (for instance, whether the story proposed would benefit the corrections department itself). Wardens, legislators, and tough-on-crime governors such as California's Pete Wilson legitimized these prohibitions by complaining about the media's tendency to create celebrity prisoners at the expense of suffering victims.[8] The change in climate is made no more evident than by contrasting Sheehan's account with its successors. Sheehan was given unobstructed access to the prison of her choice. Taken to "every part" of the prison she "asked to see at a moment's notice," she was allowed to spend "countless sixteen-hour days" interviewing prisoners, sometimes in their cells and out of earshot of guards, who could be an entire floor or two away (vii–viii). In 2002–4, by contrast, Rathbone was forced to wage an eighteen-month legal battle merely for *access* to female prisoners in Massachusetts. Because of byzantine state regulations, even though Rathbone won her court battle, no journalist had yet conducted an unsupervised inmate interview when she went to print.[9] New York's Department of Corrections refused Ted Conover access to its training academy, thus compelling him undercover, where he concealed his ruse from all but a few close friends. Later, his book had entire portions excised before it was allowed to circulate in prisons themselves.[10] Given these restraints, again, the revival of prison exposé has been remarkable.[11]

What interests me here, however, is the form in which this story has often been told. Naturally, the given of these accounts is the war on crime itself, generated by fearmongering politicians indifferent or even oblivious to the social costs of the prison boom. But even more commonly, prison building on the outside and its underground expressions on the inside are cast as reflections of the supply-side greed of economic irrationality, of a capitalist West finally freed from its cold war constraints and Great Society idealism. This foundation produces a story of economic and political alignment, or what in cultural analysis is sometimes called an "economistic" interpretive style.[12] Statistical recitations or ironic facts are typically used to puncture recent trends: for example, the fact that between 1988 and 1998 New York State prison spending soared some $761.3 million, offsetting the entire range of cuts for state and city colleges; that over 60 percent of women incarcerated nationwide are more than one hundred miles from their children or families; that Colgate now markets a translucent toothpaste tube to thwart the smuggling of contraband or weapons.[13] The emergence of private prisons, in particular, has served to give much of contemporary prison portraiture an ironic, future-perfect aura. Schlosser's essay, for instance, begins by contrasting the "granite" and "Gothic stonework" of prisons much like Conover's with the sleeker California State Prison at Sacramento. More recently built, this prison—already overcrowded before it was finished, Schlosser tells us—presents a "stark and futuristic" portent. Ironically, Schlosser observes, *private* corrections corporations are making prisons into the greatest "public works" program of our time (77).[14]

As this kind of irony suggests, examinations like Schlosser's also signaled the retooling of an older style of exposé, a revival of early-twentieth-century muckraking.[15] That is, in illustrating the capitalist economy's indifference to the public good, the prison system became at once a political boss system and an underworld unto itself. In these analyses, prisons epitomize a confluence between political opportunism by state and local officials (notably in impoverished rural areas), private corrections corporations, and federal policymakers—what would have been called, one hundred years ago, a political "nervous system." Although politicians wax poetically about "small government and the virtues of the free market," Schlosser observes, they seize upon the public fear of crime to "encourage increased spending on imprisonment regardless of the actual need" (58). Much as in muckraking portraits of the boss system, prison contracts became symptomatic of a decentralized octopus, even public-private "fiefdoms" extending into the New York countryside (53). As it were, prisons are symptomatic of a new public shame *outside* of the cities and driven by fear *of* them. Meanwhile, incarcerated criminals, sometimes manning telephone banks or laboring in fast-food production, become what Walter Lippmann once called the "secret servants" of the mainstream.[16]

As in classical muckraking as well, greed works here to create both literal effects and metaphorical irony, as the profit motive produces a system of fixed demand with arcane results. On the one hand, Hallinan shows, draconian cost cutting produces the dreary functionalism of the new prison architecture, along with terrors within. But *Going Up the River* also shows that supply often exceeds the demand. Again, for Hallinan, as for Schlosser, prison building is a jobs-creation program, an engine of local development, and (irony at work again) environmentally safer than older industries; however, like a tourist business, it must always fill beds. Prisons even provide employment, Schlosser argues, that is labor-intensive, year-round, recession-proof, and again non-polluting (and in several southern states, non-union). Prison employment also keeps the young men in town close to home by offering high salaries and benefits; little wonder, then, that local politicians seek it out. No problem when the supply of criminals drops off: supermax prisons, once built to house the worst of the worst, can be made to lower eligibility requirements to sustain their capacity (Hallinan 204–5). The hyphenated prison-industrial modifier therefore puns off Dwight Eisenhower's original formulation. Much like the now-collapsed Soviet Union, the fear of crime provides a more reliable threat than actual crime rates, which actually fell during the prison boom. And as with the national security apparatus, political influence-peddling takes hold: revolving doors between state corrections officials and private consultants, indifferent wardens provided rhetorical cover by politicians, and kickbacks coming from corporations in search of prisoner-consumers or laborers.[17]

Like any narrative form, this "macro" approach has its strengths and its drawbacks. It would be silly to deny the power and scope of these narratives: one comes away convinced of a national redrafting of social and political resources around the prison. Although prisons can be isolated (geographically and from public consciousness), they are nevertheless integral to the political and economic status quo. And guard unions have been, in some cases, beneficiaries of this new social compact. In addition, these exposés, particularly Schlosser's, effectively show how prisoners' rights can be eroded (even more than they already have been) when they are farmed out to private corporations exempt from meaningful state oversight. We also see how local communities are re-inscribed by the prison into a *racial* divide, keeping watch over prisoners from nonwhite communities, though this subject needs still fuller treatment.

Nevertheless, the "prison-industrial complex" paradigm may overreach in certain ways. It may make us forget that commercial operations have been integral to prisons at least since the 1920s, that private prisons are still vastly outnumbered in our prison system (including New York State), and that corrections officials (as in New York) have, in some instances, resisted privatization precisely because it *is* anti-union. Because prisons under "private management" are often relatively small, it is not clear how economies of scale might affect their profitability. Nor does it need to be said that the United States seems to be having little trouble finding external replacements for the threat of Communism.[18]

Meanwhile, as incisive as these exposés often are, one wonders if they actually countermand the public resignation that has too often marked the neoconservative turn. The exorbitant costs of the prison boom may indeed, as Jason DeParle has suggested, eventually erode even conservative support; bribery, cronyism, or incompetence may also produce a reaction. And as Christian Parenti points out, the pressure prison growth puts on social services is also not always welcome in the locales asked to bear the burden. But to put it baldly, exposing that prisons are horrible or expensive places may not, on its face, undermine public attitudes, much less trump the claim that incapacitation serves as a form of crime control.[19] That is, we may avoid confronting the tradeoff that voters outside prison walls may still be willing to countenance. As effective as it has been, therefore, the "prison-industrial" critique may continue to struggle for public traction.

All that being said, these limits may also shed light on Conover's or Wideman's more personal, smaller-scale contributions. It is striking, for instance, how dependent even the best of these macro accounts are on a rather statistical rendering of Conover's subject: prison labor. That is, the prison-industrial critique often casts corrections work as a job with measurable salaries or benefits but less often as the *labor* it actually might entail. We could still know more about what it is to work as a keeper, to buy in to security not only with one's consumption (as with Frank Abagnale), but with the work of one's days. In addition, what (in my Introduction) I have called the tactical point of power between guard and prisoner—the heart of that labor—remains, despite legitimate concerns about brutality, an elusive quarry, difficult to connect to its historical moment. Schlosser is surely right that there is a massive contradiction between the current celebration of the free market and the accompanying "eagerness to deny others their freedom" (77). In my view, however, it has always been easier to describe this contradiction than to explain precisely how it has been implemented. We may, in fact, partly mistake the nature of the intellectual justification that neoconservatives have attached to the prison boom: the logic of incapacitation as crime control, the rationale revived by the RAND Corporation and articulated by thinkers like James Q. Wilson.

Admittedly, Wilson's "Incapacitation" chapter, the fifth in *Thinking about Crime* (1977), is not famous as its second "Broken Windows" chapter. But we need to connect the two. The Broken Window thesis provided the template for the turn to community policing under the banner of restoring the traditional functions of the beat cop. Wilson and his coauthor, Kelling, postulated that a broken window left unattended in an at-risk neighborhood signaled the community's larger indifference to order and hierarchy. That is, the window became a symbol, read in common by citizens and criminals alike, of a decline in neighborhood authority, manifested in the loss of informal social controls formerly exerted by elders, long-term residents, local businessmen, and cops. Such a decline necessitated, Wilson and Kelling argued, a return to "back to basics," order-maintenance policing and community watches, even when such an ethos brought tactics that went beyond the strict boundaries of the law.[20] In turn, so too was prison incapacitation proposed as a mode of control exerted upon repeat offenders who demonstrated, or so it was claimed, the loss of that internalized communal control. Incapacitation was the tool designed to recuperate this lost social authority of the neighborhood at the level of the subject, the inmate.

The crucial point, I think, is that incapacitation was only compatible with the tenets of neoconservatism with one important twist. Liberty could be revered only if, at the same moment, the incapacity of some citizens to grasp its promise was also fatalistically acknowledged. Economic "cost" was thus linked emotionally to the "cost" of preserving that liberty—which meant, in a deep contradiction, removing it from those who had demonstrated their unsuitability. Incapacitation became the dominant crime control justification, for example, not because, as in common misunderstanding of "three strikes," punishment was a moral or symmetrical response by the state. It was not a "conservative" solution, akin to punishing a recalcitrant child, although some police or community members might interpret it that way.[21] Rather, incapacitation's logic was actuarial: three strikes were a predictor of a fourth or a fifth crime, a risk that incapacitation could supposedly countermand. Philosophers of punishment like Ernest van den Haag were quite frank in saying that incapacitation was no longer a matter of proportionality but of protecting the polity. Nor was it assumed to be cheap for the state to work this way; rather it was a cost that had to be borne to protect the liberties of the non-incarcerated.[22] One should underscore how literal the term *to incapacitate* was: to remove the power to act. Prison thus becomes the taking of prisoners out of the time when they otherwise might commit another crime. The measurement for success became, in Wilson's hands, predicting what these criminals would do (as he puts it) if they were "otherwise free" (146). In terms of governance, incapacitation was quintessentially the deprivation of liberty.

Meanwhile, despite the claims about prison's legibility to a future criminal pondering his choices, an important transformation had taken place. It is apparent that, whatever the invocation of the prison's traditional aura, the contemporary, post-Attica moment actually charts a movement away from the conservative standard of punishment fitting a crime. In theory, now, the punishment should supposedly fit the criminal (as his history or profile was charted, for instance, in the grids of sentencing guidelines). Wilson and the RAND Corporation did not, for instance, argue for the wholesale lengthening of sentences; rather, they recommended targeting them at those who committed the most crimes. What this future-perfect, circular logic disguised, obviously, was that incapacitation was tantamount to punishing offenders for crimes that, by definition, they would never commit. This was why it was incredible when Wilson asserted, so confidently, that his argument for incapacitation did not require "any assumptions about human nature" (145). In this sense, control was its own good. Economic costs or prisoner's rights took a back seat to this fundamentally cold risk assessment.[23]

Were all this not horrifying enough, this rationale was also claimed to benefit the very neighborhoods from which inmates themselves had originally come. Depriving repeat offenders of liberty was claimed to preserve the future order of the communities they left behind; their criminal past was used to legitimate control of the future. For prisoners themselves, therefore—as if offering a different turn on Conover's collapse of history—incapacitation actually meant making their criminal past a permanent state. This is a point about "doing time" that a prisoner in Conover's *Newjack* himself makes, and—as my chapter epigraph suggests—a tragedy that John Edgar Wideman's memories of his brother will also bring out into the open.

II.

Ted Conover's assignment to the classic venue of Sing Sing might seem to have taken him off the beaten path of other recent exposés. As he acknowledges, his downstate, nineteenth-century institution, staffed predominantly by urban and nonwhite guards, was quite different from those prisons built by upstate New York's "growth industry" (41, 60).[24] And in response to New York's restrictions on journalistic access, Conover also seems to have retooled his trademark undercover technique. Formerly preferring a looser, discursive idiom, he now decides to evoke a more intense, sensational literary style appropriate to Sing Sing's labyrinthine world of spiders and feral cats. That is, while many contemporary writers disdain any resemblance to what Peter Brooks calls melodrama's aesthetics of astonishment and apostrophe, Conover seems to have invested even more deeply in them. He turns back to the style of reportage emphasizing verification through physical registers of experience, secret witnessing, and intense bodily sensations.[25] His depiction of Sing Sing's "storied and mysterious" (59) past even recalls the sensational idiom of Victorian underworld narratives. *Newjack* echoes the work of not only Josiah Flynt or Jacob Riis but also of Nelly Bly, whose undercover narrative, *Ten Days in a Mad-House* (1887), might be said to have gone inside the nineteenth-century's reform faith in asylums.[26]

At first reading, Conover seems fully at home in these inheritances. Classic undercover excursions are fond of threshold moments, as well as patterns of surprise followed quickly by fears of emotional drowning or the loss of identity. Collaterally, underground realms are presented (as in Rathbone's title) as a "world apart" existing in parallel to the mainstream but out of sight. The undercover spy commonly has his or her privileged education unwritten, must learn a new underworld argot, and become so immersed that he or she often feels marooned even when returning home. The opening chapter of *Newjack* is likewise called "Inside Passage," as we cross over the threshold entrance to the cellblock, pushing away its cobwebs (40). The concrete and steel and brick create a hard and resonant sound chamber (9); some outbuildings remind Conover of colonial ruins (66). In all, Sing Sing is laid out for us in a "stupefying vastness" (8) that stands for the spirit of "neglect" itself (4).

As this casting suggests, meanwhile, the narrative is carried by a passionate, heart-on-its sleeve voice. Sheehan had used her *New Yorker* style to muffle attribution, talk indirectly about prison beatings, or obliquely call up the retrograde elements in guard culture (including racism) she found permeating Green Haven. Her pointillism produced a pacific effect, emphasizing the tedium and lethargy of prison life.[27] By contrast, Conover's tactics of immersion make his body visible, his voice always first person, his identity always under threat. He thus tends to favor the idiom of astonishment rather than deflation. Mad inmates are described as "bugs" by guards; the cellblock is likened to a Pandora's box of "swarming" inmates (11). The final lines of his text, calling up his own phantoms, liken guards to plantation house slaves who secretly relish the idea of their Big House being burnt down (309).[28] Freewheeling and free associative, his heart often pounding, Conover aims for a visceral response, an identification on our parts. His prison knowledge, he means to show us, is not constructed out of the customary circuit of interviews or even journalistic observation; rather it is gathered by actually having become one of Sing Sing's own identities.

In an interview with Robert Boynton for *The New New Journalism* (2005), Conover makes clear why he feels he can make this claim. He does so while explaining why he didn't seek out an advance book contract before starting out: "The . . . reason I didn't want a book contract was so that it wouldn't look like I was serving two masters. After the book appeared, I didn't want New York State officials to be able to accuse me of *pretending* to be a guard, while actually working on a book for my publisher. When I was a guard, I wanted to be 100 percent a guard" (13). A rationale like this—which, let it be said, will not convince every reader—points to Conover's fundamentally humanist assumption: as he says in his first book, that the "other" is, inside, "one of us."[29] Conover seems to claim that moving through New York's training course for corrections officers, literally qualifying for the job and then shouldering the responsibilities of a regular shift, made all traces of "undercover" pretense disappear.[30] The story we follow, therefore, is of a newjack (rookie guard) gradually initiated into "group feeling" (48), much in the familiar narrative movement of what James Clifford calls ethnographic realism. In fact, Conover himself wants to call his technique "participant observation" (18) in this sense.[31]

Such assumptions often give *Newjack* its vivid emotional impact, and yet also undermine some of its interpretive claims. Even the most self-aware of writers can easily fall victim to the disabling rhetorical inheritances of this technique. As many readers know, the undercover tradition rather infamously displays patterns that exoticize the "other" world, or that foster identification with the mobile traveler rather than the inhabitants under scrutiny. Undercover voyagers often express dismay when saying "farewell to civilization" and then betray a sense of release when returning "home" to it.[32] *Newjack*'s rhetoric, as I've suggested, often strays into these reflexes.[33] That being said, we should also recognize that the undercover journey does not always generate such uncritical identification by the *reader*. Rather than "buying in" to an illusion of full immersion, readers of Conover's narrative are just as likely to recognize what Kate Baldwin has called a "continual 'error' of identity" in his role playing. That is, often simply due to his narrative position, we are repeatedly made aware of the gaps (educational, cultural, physical) between Conover and other guards.[34] Conover does enter into the "manufacturing" (training) of prison "keepers." But paradoxically he can do so only while smuggling in a different identity, one more connected to his own readership than the guards themselves. Reformist undercover writing, in fact, has often been more about modeling mediation of the underworld, as much as has been recreating the experience of any of its inhabitants. That is, Conover is more accurately modeling keeping while also looking at it.[35]

Conover's desire to overcome the play of "surfaces" of a simple prison tour (21), therefore, results in something like a double vision. At one level, his desire to use the undercover strategy to get inside guarding is quite reminiscent of David Milch's tutelage under Bill Clark, or Gourevitch's under Andy Rosenzweig. We are encased in another micropolitical venue, in this case the prison cellblock. And yet, that double vision also allows us to see that we are initiated into the blue fatalism of everyday citizens who, themselves, simultaneously serve as law officers and stand-ins for the public. Conover's own mixed status ends up, in other words, capturing important dimensions of corrections officers who are, he says, like forgotten soldiers "on the front lines of our prison policies" (18). He calls them society's "proxies" (18) as well as society's "last representative[s]" to inmates themselves (207).

In many ways, in turn, guarding is defined, from the get-go, by its inability to cross this divide, by its lack of access to prisoners' experience. While Conover expresses sympathy for the "soul ache" (41) of inmates, he is fully aware that their lives remain, quite literally, locked away from him. In addition, he shows us that the alienation of keeping partly derives from the impersonality demanded by his job. On the cellblock floor, everyday routines block the forming of personal relationships (223), and personal histories of inmates are supposed to be left undiscussed by guards (88). In this sense, his casting of Sing Sing as a perpetual present tense for both parties is quite apt. "The past seemed like so much noise," Conover writes, "when you were trying to deal with the difficult present" (223). The guards' ID badges omit first names, supposedly to limit manipulation or verbal abuse by inmates (85). Even the most sympathetic depictions of prisoners in *Newjack,* therefore, seem but pale reflections of the guarding regime. Conover admits as much when he closes his book: he tells us of a prisoner who has tattoos on his entire body, Spanish translations of passages from Anne Frank's diary that speak of "turning my heart inside out, the bad part on the outside and the good part on the inside" (293). As we've seen, that is precisely what a guard is asked to do, as well. In a particularly telling moment—an important contrast to Wideman's memories, as we shall see—he describes his mixed emotions upon seeing prisoners' families interact with their husbands or sons in the Visitor's Room. Particularly when he observes the females who remain loyal to their imprisoned men, Conover can only voice the confusion of the keepers who have, in the prison boom, seized upon their jobs as the means to a more secure future. "The CO's couldn't figure [that loyalty] out," he writes, "because those [inmates] would never *support* the women, and the goal of solvency animated officers' entire lives" (155).[36] As Conover says in a reflection on both his journalistic and prison labor, "work in so many ways *becomes* our lives" (318). Guards also don't share their occupation's secrets when they're off the job; to outsiders, they are often likely to lie about what they do for a living (21).

In my view, Conover's dual burden of keeping undercover and mastering the labor of keeping may magnify this absorption in work. The undercover reporter's fears of his own vulnerability can easily double back on his interpretation of the subject's (in this case, the guards') consciousness; carrying the additional fear of exposure can also add to the stress Conover means to represent.[37] Moreover, going undercover sometimes means constructing what might be called a "model" figure of the subject being impersonated. One must internalize rules so fully that breaking them seems that much less imaginable.[38] As a result, work brings its own blinders. For all of *Newjack*'s veering into the melodrama of astonishment, we don't actually see impromptu beatings or much day-to-day corruption in the society of the guards. In fact, we hear more about all of that in Sheehan's comparatively downbeat account.[39] Conover himself admits that his fears of intruding on other guards' privacy kept him from cultivating friendships with them outside of work (316ff.)—a limit, again, on how truly "participatory" his ethnography can be. His ever-vigilant guard is, by definition, someone who has little time off, who is never "himself" either on the job or off it. This may all contribute to the way *Newjack* often casts Sing Sing as what is sometimes called a "total institution," a place where the guard's duty is simply equivalent to his or her self-preservation (96). Because he is both reporter and guard, Conover's attention isn't free to wander; if he fails, he fails at both jobs. In this sense he really *is* a guard—on guard.

As I will argue shortly, this conflation may create other interpretive problems as well. But it also clarifies why, to Conover, Sing Sing comes to seem like a scrapheap of its own designers' intentions, a place reduced to the essence of guarding. It is made virtually equivalent to its work of administering what he calls "that strange practice of 'doing time'" (247). It should therefore not surprise us that he feels the guard-inmate relationship hasn't changed much over the course of history (207). In his historical interlude, he quotes the dark prophecy of Tocqueville and Gustave de Beaumont, who themselves seem to have written about Sing Sing's eclipsing of time:

> One cannot see the prison of Sing-Sing and the system of labour which is there established without being struck by astonishment and fear. Although the discipline is perfect, one feels that it rests on fragile foundations: it is due to a *tour de force* which is reborn unceasingly and which has to be reproduced each day, under penalty of compromising the whole system of discipline. The safety of the keepers is constantly menaced. In the presence of such dangers, avoided with such skill but with difficulty, it seems to us impossible not to fear some sort of catastrophe in the future. (176)

This passage is perhaps *Newjack*'s keynote: the prison is reduced by its own routine to its cycle of keeping. Perpetual vigilance always seems ready to collapse into its antithesis, chaos; each day, therefore, control is summoned up again. And thus we see how the regime of incapacitation, a supposedly traditional function of prison, produces a future-perfect eclipsing of time behind walls. Quite effectively, I think, *Newjack* shows us that the prison becomes actuarial cynicism made into a concrete manifestation of the outer society's fatalism about prisoners' past criminality and how it is re-imposed upon them in the now. Countermanding the antique feel of Sing Sing's cobweb world, one prisoner suggests that the outer world is "'planning prison for somebody who's a child right now'" (233). And he's right.

Meanwhile, as a representative of that outer world gone inside, Conover attempts to show us how that plan is executed. As I've said, his internal voice frequently registers an "error" or gap by pointing to his aversion to military discipline (17), to his curiosity and other guards' lack of it (221), or to his knowledge that they'll be transferring upstate and he won't (169). But on the other hand, he also participates in these guards' work culture. He is actually initiated not into official New York State mandates about guarding, as much as the shop-floor accommodation with those ideas. Much like chroniclers of municipal police training, Conover casts New York State's correctional training program as a bookish academy that is actually out of touch with the demands of the "street" or, here, the cellblocks. The program is called, early on, a place of "institutional denial" about the "moral weirdness" (42) of prison, oblivious to the needs of those it claims to train as "peace officers" (33).[40] Whereas other writers of the prison exposé emphasize connections between the prison and the outside economic system, Conover stresses the distance between public proclamations and the everyday micropolitical practices of corrections work. Much like a double agent, he asks us to witness not just how such incapacitation is enforced but how enforcing it feels.

We also engage darker elements of this thin blue line. He limits his storytelling mostly to what his body can be present to. Yet in turn, Conover's portrait, like Milch's or Gourevitch's, also takes us into the effects of vigilance on the psyche of the enforcer. Conover thus echoes the gallows humor among guards (inmate conjugal visits are called the "Felon Reproduction Program" [159]). Or he follows the lead of comrades who tell him *not* to log a "use of force" incident with an inmate they deem insane (146). In this way, Conover illuminates a blue-collar resistance to the "white shirts" of wardens and politicians (95), showing us a guard culture both better and worse than what the state's training dictates. In *Newjack*'s line of sight, indeed, we are taught that guards and inmates reciprocally restructure the rules handed down to them. At the academy, for example, he was taught not to talk to prisoners; on the prison floor, he learns that the job is all about talking (69). Previously given tedious rules to memorize, he discovers the value of maintaining the appearance of inmates' compliance in a way he hopes is not degrading to them (255). The point, perhaps, is thus not only how the stress doubles up on Conover as investigator *and* actual guard. What also produces stress in corrections work, it seems, is the unstable balancing of managerial imperatives with the actual demands of labor; the constant threat of violence beneath the routine, from guards and from inmates; and the corruption among guards that can result from the necessary ceding of some of their power on the cellblock floor.[41] Whatever *Newjack*'s limits, this results, I think, in a much richer and also more frightening portrait than that of a no-frills functionalism the "prison-industrial" critique might convey. And, in turn, much more than any theory that claims it needs no account of human nature.

To add to the turmoil, the outer half of Conover's identity, the part that is a proxy for many of his readers, creeps back under his undercover skin. His anxious heart, we might say, becomes tattooed on his own adopted identity, as he experiences what often seems like a perpetual state of dread on the job. "Keeplock" becomes a verbal conflation that expresses fatalism and fear, even gratitude about the collective security of guarding in a group. Albeit often with disarming candor, Conover speaks frankly about the thrill he gets in seeing his guard team subdue a prisoner (134–35, 275–76), or how he found himself wondering of any given inmate, constantly, "Could I beat him in a fight?" (247). Perhaps the most telling symbol becomes not the baton but the emergency pin on each guard's radio, a pin that always seems about to be pulled (62). Before long, Sing Sing becomes, Conover admits, simply equivalent to living with fear (95). Over time, guards who initially seem unduly cautious or insensitive come to seem like veterans, primarily through a series of anecdotes that unveil, for instance, their experience as POWs (116) or, more tellingly, of having been taken hostage by prisoners in the past. Attica, the epitome of these fears, becomes quite like Bill Clark's imaginative rewriting of Vietnam. "At some level," Conover says of one superior officer who had been taken hostage by inmates in the past, "[the older guard] Wickersham hated our innocence and wanted to cure it through abuse"; soon, however, he seems only to be "insuring himself against repeating the experience" (117). As if this man individuates Tocqueville and Beaumont's daily *tour de force,* one's superiors become veterans much as in a war narrative. Wickersham's experience seems only to validate the rookie's own fears of the dangers ahead of him. Fear of inmates, or fear of failing on the job, ends up amounting to the same thing—or, we might say, learning to live with the prison's incapacitation of inmates' identities.

However, here is precisely where we arrive at the downside of Conover's citation of Tocqueville and Beaumont's prophecy. As persuasively as that vision captures the prison's regime of control, it also runs the interpretive risk of making that regime seem fearful primarily because it menaces the safety of the keepers. To his credit, Conover fully recognizes that this flip side to impersonating "society's last representative" means carrying with him its social fears, including white or majoritarian racial fears. He understands, for instance, that "minority officers' allegiance to the system was constantly being tested in ways that white officers' was not" (285). While we often mistake undercover writing for an invisibility strategy, *Newjack* again shows us otherwise: Conover actually feels his whiteness made more visible behind prison walls, not less. (The most frequently used prisoner nickname for him, "Barney Fife" [226], speaks volumes.) And when Conover flashes back, in the aftermath of a cellblock melee, to the Rodney King beating, the image he calls up is that of Reginald Denny (273).

These fears suffuse even the best of liberal intentions. Along with pointing to the injustices of Rockefeller drug laws (204), as well as the need to restore prison education programs, *Newjack* rightly draws our attention to a sclerotic bureaucracy that fails to offer guards training in counseling. This is especially shocking given the number of prisoners now in need of serious psychiatric care (43, 208). But in the absence of political will for such resources, it is startling that the most Conover can do is propose that we humanize the keeper. Specifically, his working experience leads him to hypothesize that the best correction officers are those who make themselves akin to beat cops (89, 219). One is certainly struck by the fragility of this analogy: a cellblock is not a neighborhood of consenting, free citizens; guard labor is predicated on control and confinement, not civilized exchange; and so on. But beyond even those limits, it is telling how Conover's liberal intentions end up in an ideological neighborhood so like the mythological constructions of neoconservatism.[42] It is as if he intuits, that is, the other end in the chain of control (the street) that architects like Wilson had described. The result may be a sentimentalizing of his fellow guards and their own desire to be friendly counselors, against the grain of so much of what he has shown us. Stepping out of the rules of the undercover game, where facts are only supposed to be directly felt or seen, Conover wants to believe that, like him, his fellow guards want training in counseling even more than economic security. Though denied that schooling, Conover writes that "in their hearts, I think the officers wish it wasn't so" (208).

To be fair, we don't know if they do or they don't.[43] At its best, *Newjack* dramatizes the burdens that keeping might exact on their lives, and the paranoia that could be produced by the regime they helped to create.

Albeit economistic in its own way—in its focus on the guards' premium on solvency—the book also reminds that the costs of maintaining such vigilance are not experienced equally by all. But one of the reasons we don't fully know the inside of their hearts, a dialogue with *Brothers and Keepers* might suggest, is that Conover hasn't calibrated his story of "doing time" by looking outward. That is, he hasn't fully looked at the communities incorporated into the prison-industrial complex—communities of guards *or* prisoners—and engaging their memories of what life had been like *before* learning to live with the prison. In accepting Conover's humane pleas, we are still liable to feel that these lost histories, not only the collapse of liberalism, haunt his portrait of Sing Sing—a past still present to *Newjack*'s perpetual present tense.

III.

Written nearly two decades earlier, and from the other end of the Visitor's Room, John Edgar Wideman's *Brothers and Keepers* could hardly seem more different from Conover's *Newjack*. A scathing portrait of the incipient forces gathered around his black brothers as the neoconservative turn grew in force, Wideman's memoir presents prison guards as conscious agents of humiliation, proxies of a "crusade, a war on crime" (80), who degrade those they have already punished. As John puts it, "[w]hat politicians demanded in the free world was being acted out inside the prison" (80). Yet Pittsburgh's Western Penitentiary, where his brother would be sent—and remains today, despite a tortured appeals process—is not just the end point of Robby's sorrow. It is the actual starting place, the setting of John's remembering. There, John must face, again, Robby's straying into adolescent rebellion: into petty theft, drug use and drug-dealing, and finally, robbery homicide.[44] The memoir thus both represents John's visits to Western and recreates their past together through the lens of prison life. In turn, the book connects the project of incapacitation to these brothers' lost neighborhood of Homewood.

Although *Brothers and Keepers* has a long historical, retrospective interlude, much like *Newjack*'s, a more local, microcosmic history is embedded in Robby himself—one might say, as he endures his own private Attica. Paralleling the broader historical trends of his era, Robby was incarcerated right after Western's own prison strike (following upon the death by asphyxiation of an inmate in 1980). He was then subjected to a new "get tough policy" instituted by a younger generation of guards. The new regime includes more strip searches, more cell shakedowns, and more humiliation. Robby also flirted with Islam, and then backed away when it only seemed to double the surveillance he was subjected to. As John begins his visits, Robby has been assigned to "administrative custody" in the "Behavioral Adjustment Unit" (81–84)—in other words, to administrative lockdown. Thus the entire donnée of *Brothers and Keepers* is the ethos of control and incapacitation. But by definition, the book can therefore achieve neither catharsis nor release.

Instead, *Brothers and Keepers* is a more lyrical and provisional book, a fluid text John creates in collaboration with Robby. Whereas *Newjack* evokes prison's perpetual present and its hard surfaces of steel and concrete, the Widemans' is a more historical, improvisational, and bluesy narrative, bending material and temporal realities. The memoir is built around the call-and-response of African American spirituals, the back and forth of blues ("Got two minds to leave here. Just one of them telling me to stay" [40]), and even the folktale byplay of the plantation "briarpatch" (39) between a rational "John" (the bear) and Robby (rabbit, the trickster). Blood and racialized "brothers" converse with "keepers," a term referring to guards and family members and the wider social powers around them.[45] The book's dialogic structure also evokes a series of metaphorical transfers, puns with violence, or riffs upon words' secret stories that so often evoke the underworlds of crime: "mugging" (21) for the camera, a "slammer" that "sure as shit . . . slams us together" (47), or a play on "the length of your sentence" (25). Prison solitary, or the "hole," becomes a place where the boys' mother witnesses the unfairness of a "whole" assault upon her neighborhood and family; as the memoir says, "[s]he's peeped their hole card" (72). The blending of John's and Robby's voice also means that the "you" (and the "you-alls") used by this memoir evokes—at times simultaneously—the conversation between these siblings, a direct appeal to readers, a social generalization, or interior monologue by either brother. John, for his part, reexamines the open secret he always suspected, what he calls the "rape" of Homewood in the years of their youth (40). Robby tends more to revisit how the ethos of the war on crime imposed itself upon the choices he made.

Complicated riffs on time and "doing time" quickly become the organizing motifs of the memoir. If *Newjack* tried to evoke Sing Sing's impossible routine of days, the Widemans' book time-bends the central contradiction of the retributive calculus itself. At one point, the book verbalizes the social rationale of "doing time," offering a bitter rendering of its era's dominant ideology: "A narrow sense of time as a material entity, as a commodity like money that can be spent, earned, lost owed, or stolen is at the bottom of the twisted logic of incarceration. When a person is convicted of a crime, the state dispossesses that *criminal* of a given number of days, months, years. Time pays for crime. By surrendering a certain portion of his allotment of time on earth the malefactor pays his debt to society" (52). But then, as if we are listening to the dialogue of a minstrel show, another Wideman voice speaks up:

> But how does anyone *do* time outside of time? Since a person can't be removed from time unless you kill him, what prison does to its inmates is make time as miserable, as unpleasant, as possible. Prison time must be hard time, a metaphorical death, a sustained, twilight condition of death-in-life. The prisoner's life is violently interrupted, enclosed within a parenthesis. . . .
>
> Yet the little death of a prison sentence doesn't quite kill the prisoner, because prisons, in spite of their ability to make the inmate's life unbearable, can't kill time. . . .
>
> In spite of all the measures Western society employs to secularize time, time transcends the conventional social order. Prisoners can be snatched from that order but not from time. Time imprisons us all. (35–36)

Thus again material and cultural constructions of the prison come into play. Here, time itself serves to negate the simple cultural calculation that "time pays for crime" (35). In prison, to be sure, "Time's all you got" (91). But it's never your own.

To enlarge upon this contradiction, the Widemans give voice to the conflicts the process of mutual remembrance creates. As John wades into Robby's past, and also into his own—sadly, we learn, not the same thing—John feels overwhelmed by the unfolding of time. "My imagination creates something like a great seashell," he writes, "enfolding, enclosing us." The image of the shell evokes a structure both comforting, like a brothers' shared secret, and yet daunting as well, with repeated inward turns and revisions: "Its inner surface is velvet-soft and black. A curving mirror doubling the darkness . . . time stolen from time in the hole" (87). Like the figure of the parenthesis in the long passage quoted above, the shell shape alludes to the plot of the memoir as well. By moving from the "Western" provinces of Laramie (where Robby first escapes to seek John's help), back to the "Western" penitentiary so near their home, the linear story is made to circle back and inward. The book begins with Robby's capture, moves into the first section called "Visits," and then shifts haltingly back into Robby's crime, in the section called "Our Time."

"Our Time," of course, invokes the vexed memories this collaboration calls up. The phrase refers not only to the time into which any of us are born, but to the factors that shape our identities: birth order, how close to holidays we are born, or how close to historical events. As but one example, Robby swerved into drug use (117) in 1968, the year that Martin Luther King was shot. That year was also the historical moment when, as John tells it, the "net" of economic deprivation settled down upon Homewood (40). The phrase "Our Time" also calls up the hubris, competitiveness, and desperation of late adolescence. That is, the phrase refers to the relish young men often take in their young manhood, their supposed "time" of achievement and establishing an identity. As it happens, though, this is the precise moment that John's and Robby's paths diverged. In Robby's case, "our time" meant trying to be the "star" of a perpetual party, then a local Superfly, then a petty con man and self-appointed "stone gangster"; in John's, it meant going to college. John was consequently no longer there to look out for his brother, having escaped into what he describes as the "cage" of his own upper-middle-class freedom (203). In other words, the brothers did not really share "their" time at all. We discover that John actually has to be retold the key events by which Robby became a criminal; the "you" of the narrative functions, now, more as a gentle brotherly correction. Robby's earlier charge of "Big Brother" (9) similarly implicates John both in judgmental observation and in Orwellian betrayal: for escaping Homewood. "I wasn't around for all that," John admits (67).[46]

John and Robby do, however, share a sense of what the net of deprivation has done to their family. John's departure into the world of the keepers illustrates the phenomenon that sociologists like William Julius Wilson call the loss of "old heads" in disadvantaged neighborhoods.[47] It is a story paralleled by the death of an older, more level-headed brother-surrogate for Robby named Garth (62). As the Widemans' mother remembers, Garth's death triggers Robby's turn to more reckless criminality, as does the waning of his own father's strength. And so, in a story articulated by the "Broken Windows" mythology, we see the decay of many of the forces that might have kept Robby in check. In fact, John's memory of neighborhood decline is keyed to the disintegration of the local A & P, and even to a "plate-glass window that gets broken and stays broken" (75), the very symbol around which the crime-control case was being built.[48]

Yet if the Wideman brothers seem to be diving into neoconservatism's own shallow pool of social memory, they actually rewrite the meaning of this symbol. For one thing, in the twilight of Pittsburgh's steel industry (40–41), the Widemans understand that a broken window is liable to be a sign of a closed factory, not merely of impulsive vandalism or neglect. Even more to the point, the spaces left by disappearing landmarks remain haunted by memories and thus are sites that *continue* in the neighborhood's own consciousness. As John Wideman says in one interview, they are a "world that's carried around in people's heads"—places of personal connection, of belonging.[49] *Brothers and Keepers* also uses the "net" or "rape" of Homewood not to denote a simple hollowing out of the ghetto—economic or social decline—but to suggest an attack, and thus to recall the imposition of new controls, the new "law and order" (72) ethos itself. Like Robby's school, guarded by metal detectors after the summer of 1968, the "keeping" of the ghetto therefore anticipates the prison itself— lorded over by violence and betrayal, and by corrupt figures of authority like drug-dealing cops.[50]

Most importantly, the Widemans cast this transformation with an entirely different generational backdrop than the apologists for order-maintenance did. In the past, Robby and John's father would, indeed, have taken it upon himself to personally avenge a family insult (73–74). But their mother, by contrast, carried on a stronger family tradition of forgiveness, of extending what the boys remember as "the benefit of the doubt." It was a matter, John said in one interview, of always taking a "longer, slower look at people and situations," calling on "your better side and try[ing] to get your ego out of it."[51] Or, what the Wideman boys remember as an ethos of seeing with others' eyes: "You tried on the other person's point of view" (69). (John's daughter is said, in a telling mutual recognition between the brothers, to have their mother's eyes [18].) As Robby is brought down partly by his own recklessness, family bitterness ensues, and the capacity for extending doubt is momentarily forgotten. After a time, however, their mother "realized her personal unhappiness and grief were inseparable from what was happening *out there*" (75), and the anger subsides.

Recouping this fragile legacy from their mother is crucial, we begin to recognize, to the entire subject of imaginatively engaging the prison. "Visiting," a residual ethos brought to the North during the Great Migration, actually comes to stand for that legacy. Like "revisiting" in memory, visiting the prison becomes a process of remembering, or rejoining the social relation through writing with Robby, and hopefully seeing with his eyes.

This reconnection, in turn, challenges the literal, more vexed visiting of the keepers' turf in the penitentiary. Of his earliest encounters with Western's inmates, for example, John writes that "I want to learn from their eyes, identify with their plight, but I don't want anyone to forget I'm an outsider, that these cages and walls are not my home" (46). What begins as an evocation of tension at *not* being in Robby's "home," or his memories, or even his actual historical past, gradually turns to John's re-initiation as an institutional visitor, one who must learn the keepers' rules anew. Just as Conover extrapolated from his own immersion, John must also imagine, since one's own eyes are not enough. The "visit," in other words—doing some time with Robby—becomes a trope about imaginative engagement. Yet the trope also reminds us of the determining limits on our imagining: limits imposed by one's fears, one's ego, one's personal history, and more.

John learns, as I have said, about incapacitation. He discovers quickly that the guards have tremendous power, of course. Yet he also speculates that they are bored, "numbed by routine" (49), looking to avoid hassles and to just stick to their job; here, he intuitively anticipates Conover's findings. And like most visitors, John must import analogies more familiar to him: the prison seems, for instance, like a funeral parlor (185), the Visitor's Room itself like a "coffin" (218). Or, passing through a prison metal detector, John remembers that he had been stopped in an airport in the early 1970s, since his racial profile supposedly fit that of an "air pirate" (185).[52] John also uses a story that Robby has told him about a temporary extension of control given inmates over the Visitor's Room itself:

> You said the prisoners complained about the state of the visitors' facilities and were granted, after much bullshit and red tape, the privilege of sprucing them up. But when it came down to supplies or time to work on the project, the administration backed off. Yes, you can fix up the place. No, we won't provide decent materials or time to do it. Typical rat-ass harassment. Giving with one hand, taking away with the other. If the waiting room's less squalid than it was three years ago, it's still far short of decent and it's turning nasty again. The room thus becomes one more proof of the convict's inability to do anything right. We said you fellows could fix it up and look what a crummy job you did. . . . Like you fucked up when you were in the street. And that's why you're here. That's why keepers are set over you. (51)

In other words, control granted to inmates becomes another lesson in control over them. Indeed, many times John imagines that the purpose of the

Visitor's Room was to humiliate him in the same way Robby has been, to force the visitor "to become an inmate. Subjected to the same sort of humiliation. Made to feel powerless, intimidated by the might of the state" (52).

Reading passages like these might easily lead to the conclusion that John identifies with Robby. John indeed cannot help but feel tied to Robby; in that involuted shell design again, the prison recapitulates the net of Homewood, but this time they are together in it. As it were, slammed together by the virtual space of the Visitor's Room. Nevertheless, this desire for solidarity—or what John calls his "Soledad George Jackson fantasy" (191)—is made ridiculous by the end of visits, and more. John knows he's *not* really in Robby's skin. Imagining he is, even for a moment, might only be a way to hide from himself and his own past (77). In John's view, the fantasy only exposes the brothers' shared habit of compartmentalizing, an egocentrism that still keeps them apart, "each one alert," both "trembling behind the vulnerable wall of our dark skins" (222). A pose of sentimental empathy can also disguise the competition between the brothers (87–88, 202), or the guilt John feels about Garth having taken his big brother role. Instead of these rhetorical identifications, therefore, the stronger moments in *Brothers and Keepers* work toward re-listening to Robby's story. In what Gertrude Stein would have called the "time of the composition," in other words, it is the differences between the brothers that unlock the meaning of their time together, in the prison and outside of it.

Certainly, John's university-trained, more self-consciously political voice has its contributions to make. In a telling debunking of the emergent logic of neoconservatism, for example, John recasts prison through the lens of governance, revealing it as a gross distortion of majoritarian rule. He recalls the history of slavery to invoke this enduring wound, adapting the infamous reasoning behind *Dred Scott* (1857): "*Prisoners have no rights,*" Wideman reasons, "*that the keepers are bound to respect*" (187). Like slavery, then—as a regime of law extending beyond the South as such—the prison must express the total, encompassing vigilance reflected in such legal reasoning:

> As the keepers decide what time prisoners must awaken, when they may clean themselves, when they may eat, to whom they may speak, how they may wear their hair, which patches of ground they may march across and how long they may take crossing them, as the keepers constrict space and limit freedom, as the inmates are forced to conform to these mandates, an

identity is fashioned for the prisoners. Guarding the inmates' bodies turns out to be a license for defining what a prisoner is. The tasks are complementary, in fact inseparable. (188)

Along with invoking the "keepers" of slavery, such a reading obviously also calls up the imagery of a zoo or prison camp, territorial and regimented to an extreme. Western is every bit the "total" institution that Sing Sing is in *Newjack*.

On the other hand, what John may learn from Robby is that this control is not the strict "rule-based" regime that it pretends to be. To Robby, the prison is more a "fun-house mirror" that makes rules themselves arbitrary, "more perverse" than a predictable imposition of authority (183). If the prison were simply about rules, even upside-down ones, one could learn to live with it. Instead, it becomes a place where everything is distorted, and the inmate—by his submission and his fear—must encounter a grotesque reflection of himself. And if he doesn't internalize this image, the Widemans suggest, he's often put in even more danger (183). "Nothing is what it seems. You must always take second readings, decode appearances, pick out the obstructions erected to keep you in your place. Then work around them" (221). In other words, what Conover experiences as a regimen produced by the daily round of incapacitation is now provisionally "seen" (with Robby's eyes) as something even more arcane. *Brothers and Keepers*' image of the mirror is thus further revised. As is the "you":

> You, the custodians, formulate whatever rules, whatever system you require to keep the prisoners in custody. You must stand between them and us. You are not a connection between the free world and the prison world but a chasm, a wall, a two-sided, unbreakable mirror. When we look at you we see our selves. We see order and justice.... When prisoners gaze into the reverse side of the mirror they should see the deformed aberrations they've become. (189)

After reading Conover, we are perhaps likely to feel that, like other "peace officers," prison guards are the handy symbols of the broader public cry for order. But in this passage, Wideman ends up depicting the literal, on-site keepers not as Conover does—not just as "proxies." Rather, they become a one-way mirror that blocks the Homewood tradition of trying on the other's point of view. Therefore the prison does not, as in the future-perfect fantasies of its neoconservative keepers, become an institution that saves the old neighborhood; rather, it attempts to eclipse that home, driving the tradition of "you-alls" and shared "eyes" into the lockdown of each brother's memories. But perhaps like time itself, this tradition cannot really be "owned"—by any one person, that is. It can be revisited only by its collective inheritors. In *Brothers and Keepers,* it can be viewed only collaboratively, and even then, only through a bending light.

IV.

We can never really know whether John Edgar Wideman successfully captures the world on the other side of the mirror, the prison as experienced by the incarcerated. Like *Newjack*'s strategy of undercover immersion, the time-bending, collaborative technique of *Brothers and Keepers* is merely an attempt to cope with prison's intractable barriers to an outsider's observation and understanding. Indeed, the proliferation of analogies in both texts—whether a prison is called a zoo, compared to the condition of slavery, made into a funhouse—demonstrates how elusive the prison experience can be. In contrast to exposés that investigate the broader or "macro" span of the prison-industrial complex, both books are also more personal and more intent upon the relationship between the guard and prisoner. Yet both are inevitably the work of visitors. Lest we conclude that these authors have somehow gotten us further "inside" than other exposés, we should remember that both of them encounter, in different senses, the limitations of their own skin, as well as their kinship with keepers of all kinds. In narratives like these, therefore, James Clifford's reminder about the doubly partial nature of cultural description—"partial" in the sense of invested, and also meaning incomplete—is all the more germane.[53] Nor can these books' micropolitical focus do more than complement and complicate accounts of the "net" descending upon neighborhoods like Homewood.

At their core, these books come up against one of the fundamental tensions in depicting the prison-industrial complex: the challenge of capturing how a site so "out of the world" nevertheless reflects the larger social system that created it. Prison's portraitists must explain how the release of controls upon capitalist enterprise, in our day, has been accompanied by the imposition of new controls upon others. Indeed, this is a contradiction akin to those I have discussed earlier in this book: how to justify using criminal informants in the name of "zero tolerance" about law and order; how to validate the work of public police officers in terms of extralegal order-maintenance; or how to create a new architecture of security, paradoxically, in the name of personal sovereignty and consumer freedom. Conover and the Widemans remind us, as well, that "learning to live with crime" has meant vastly different things for different citizens and communities. The phrase refers not only to the choices we make as voters, or as adolescents in "our time," but to whose jobs are integrated into the prison system, or to who is forced to sustain a relationship with a loved one behind bars. The cold calculus of incapacitation has meant, as well, that prison is not simply about retribution or "payback" for individual crimes, despite what politicians or even the system's critics often insist. Rather, prison's culture of keeplock and Alice-in-Wonderland arbitrariness suggests a doubling up on prisoners' pain through the control device of incapacitation. As the Widemans' allegory of the Visitor's Room "reform" suggests, prison becomes a perpetual reminder, in one final turn of the phrase, of the prisoner's incapacity to better himself.

In such a light, therefore, we also might carefully measure our understanding of Robby Wideman's continuing survival in prison—his choice, in particular, to complete a prison degree program (239). His endurance is not meant, I think, to serve as exemplary of the "model" prisoner, one who has survived by internalizing control, or reflecting it back, as his keepers supposedly want. That might be the story we would prefer to tell ourselves.[54] Much more tellingly, bending incapacitation's own collapse of time to a different argument, *Brothers and Keepers* contends that Robby survives by being who he always was. As John says, "[t]he character traits that landed Robby in prison are the same ones that have allowed him to survive with dignity, and pain and a sense of himself as infinitely better than the soulless drone prison demands he become. Robby knows his core is intact: his optimism, his intelligence, his capacity for love, his pride, his dream of making it big, being somebody special" (195). In fact, this core includes doing the very thing Conover's keepers can't imagine: Robby falls in love again, doing so without telling the girl he loves that he's in for life, ignoring time as he always has. Ever the rebel and trickster, Robby survives, paradoxically, through his *in*ability to accept his fate. In prison, he only redoubles his refusal to accept that "dull, inferior portion" handed out to black boys in the Homewood streets (195), which to him had meant passively taking his welfare check and waiting to die (132).

In the end, *Brothers and Keepers* calls up a series of social memories that countermand the emergent mythologies of what I have called the neoconservative turn. The memoir serves as a powerful repudiation of the central myth of the prison's timeless function, its supposed turning back of the clock to protect what neighborhoods like Homewood were said to have lost. It is not only that the Wideman brothers still recall the "benefit of the doubt" they found in their *original* keepers, their parents—in the "old heads" that, in another generational involution, the brothers are now themselves becoming. More to the point, *Brothers and Keepers* shows that Robby retains a repository of neighborhood values that, at least in his case, do survive the incapacitation of doing time. And Robby, in turn, repudiates the actuarial predictions that others have made about his own future. Because his crime skills, his impulsiveness, and his sense of specialness remain, they help him survive, or endure, prison's special degradations. Turning us through the curving shell one last time, *Brothers and Keepers* tells us that Robby's past was never a dismal predictor of what his real future could be. In this sense, he is a keeper for all of us.

Epilogue
Public Secrets

I.

During the writing of this book, I often found myself thinking about a scene from Danish author Peter Høeg's international crime thriller, the mystery entitled *Smilla's Sense of Snow* (1993). In fact, it is a moment cited by Philip Gourevitch in the book (*A Cold Case*) I discuss in chapter 3. The scene takes place in Copenhagen, as Høeg's protagonist, the part-Inuit, transplanted Greenlander whose name gives the book its title, investigates the death of a young neighborhood boy she had once befriended. Smilla is not a professional detective; she is, or so the official investigation can designate her, merely a private party, and thus (for once) a citizen. But she follows the trail of this murder nonetheless, and, returning to her apartment, she runs into the special investigator who *is* officially in charge. We soon learn that this investigator, now reaching the end of his career, is a mordant man who feels that he is little more than "a pebble" in his government's shoe. Upset by Smilla's interference, he begins to lecture her about the pressures of a career in the Ministry of Justice, about the skills one must cultivate, and about the loyalty that working in a bureaucracy requires. And then he drops a line that is intended to bring her up short. Most people, he says, comply with what the Ministry wants. "I can tell you," he adds, "that most people secretly find it a relief to have the state divest them of the trouble of being an independent person."[1]

My thinking about this remark has changed over time. At first, we might attribute the investigator's aphorism to a trademark convention in the police procedural. That is, the maxim reflects how this mystery genre centers on the detective's arts—and so would much of our criticism argue. But rather than accepting this comment as a reflection of a genre formula, I was more interested, at first, in the ways that it illustrated the authority we commonly invest in the state's management of crime. Drawing upon a logic erected within his criminal justice system, Høeg's investigator is reminding Smilla of the rules of a certain political game: how the state customarily takes it upon itself to prosecute a wrong on the private citizen's behalf. In this way, the investigator invokes what in cultural analysis is commonly called "ordination," a sorting out of who is in charge of what. Indeed this is how Gourevitch's police detective, Andy Rosenzweig, apparently reads this comment.[2]

Over time, however, as my own work progressed, I realized that the investigator's maxim didn't really capture how *Smilla's Sense of Snow* proceeds. Instead, he complains that times are changing: when a crime breaks out these days, the detective seemed to say, citizens need to be reminded about where the traditional boundaries have always been. And, more to the point, Smilla herself must be told not to disrespect those rules. (To apply an American colloquialism to my own title, the subtext of his motto now seemed: "live with it.") Smilla, meanwhile, didn't seem particularly ready to accept that her interests were compatible with the investigator's own. Rather, she appoints herself part of what, these days, we call the victim circle, even though she is not a blood relation of the boy. And were this not complicated enough, Høeg also begins to introduce elements of criminality on *both* sides of the divide the investigator's maxim would construct. Having little love for the authority of the Danish state, Smilla hugs the detective upon his departure, only to pick the wallet from his pocket. Even before that, the investigator has gotten into the apartment by filching its original key, an act implying that the state has more at stake in covering up this boy's death than solving it. We've already seen that the investigator is not, in fact, from the homicide division at all.

Of course, all that is how the plot thickens, and how Høeg's procedural blurs over into noir. I don't mean to suggest that his ideas about criminality and political authority were somehow magically revealed to be akin to my own. Rather, it was simply that, shaped by my growing understanding of the neoconservative turn in the United States, I could no longer chalk up such an episode to literary convention, plot complication, or even the static political allegory I had begun with. Rather, Høeg's microcosmic drama illuminated a process in which crime and its management became sites for re-negotiations in political contracts between citizens, victims, cops, and criminals alike. The scene crystallized how formal governments in nations or states or municipalities rewrite the terms of their governance through crime, and how citizens often construct new rights or responsibilities in reply. And, at a deeper layer, Høeg's scene suggested how executing the seemingly rational or impersonal imperatives of duty, law, and moral certitude might actually end up mimicking criminal deception.

And yet, what was ultimately most striking was how Høeg's detective seems not just to challenge citizen authority; he claims to have already taken it into himself and expects that most members of the public will be grateful for his having done so. Or, more accurately, he seems to have imaginatively projected his own claim to professional authority into the public he serves, and then tried to draw a sense of legitimacy from his own projection. More than anything else, it was this inner dimension of "learning to live with crime" that was now most important to me. It seemed to echo a claim commonly voiced in American neoconservative ranks over the past four and half decades: to have discovered the public's own secret fears and desires, to have made those desires into policy, and thus effectively to have spoken *for* that public.[3] In this sense, something rather startling had happened in American life. What had started out as transformations in crime control, or even under-the-radar responses to assumed fears, soon became something like "open secrets": practices intimately connected to a restructuring of political consent.

II.

At its heart, this book has been driven by a desire to understand the cultural and political transactions described above. During the neoconservative turn, I have argued, transactions in and through crime control have taken place around themes like community vigilance, personal "responsiblization," consumer sovereignty, or victims' rights; such themes have often been accompanied by a fatalistic sense that crime is inaccessible to large-scale solutions (that is, other than building more prisons). Risk management, especially, has become a mechanism crucial to the politics of allotting both the amount of crime that we supposedly must countenance and the measures we must supposedly tolerate to control it. In the meantime, the time-honored idea of "paying for crime" has been literalized into an effort to actually quantify crime's costs (usually in terms of jail time; more literally, to measure the costs to businesses in citizen fears, through victimization surveys; most literally, in asset forfeiture following convictions, or even cash payments to victims). Collaterally, there has been an across-the-board attempt to punish a criminal for the ostensibly foreseeable consequences of his actions, whether it means his original decision to join an organized crime family, sell drugs, or violate a neighborhood's sense of order. I have also tried to use crime narratives to show some of the ill effects of neoconservatism's learning to live with crime: for instance, how using the Mafia as a template for the wider crime campaign made it into a war supposedly waged on behalf of everyday life; how the spiraling logic of victim surveys only augments the cycle of fear and markets security consciousness too often based on policing phantoms; and how incorporating criminal intelligence into crime control, whether through informants or cold case patterns or experts like Frank Abagnale, often ends up making everyday experience seem like a condition of vulnerability, a ripe field for "opportunity crimes." And at a deeper layer, I have tried to show how so many of these tactics only perpetuate inequalities in our criminal justice system by making a criminal's actuarial past part of what is assumed to be an inevitable future for all of us.

As part of this inquiry, I have also tried explore crime narratives that open up these transactions by retelling the stories generated in crime control itself. That is, I have stressed how crime narratives often involve "second-order" storytelling, collaborative acts whether consciously recognized as such, or not: retellings of an informant's tale, marshaled into the policing and prosecution of organized crime; of a confession prompted or shaped by police interrogators; of a victim's story that, as Høeg's investigator suggests, has already been sponsored and reshaped by state authorities. Working from the contact zones in which these stories are often first encountered, I have tried to attend to the vocabularies, pre-political attitudes, and legal frameworks that writers must negotiate. We see such negotiation in the interplay of the corporate reading of organized crime with Nicholas Pileggi's mechanic's tale of Henry Hill; in the cold case claim to have re-infused meaning into so-called "meaningless" murders; in the way, as Ted Conover realizes, sites like Sing Sing are often already "storied"; and so on. I have also tried to explore the impact of the neoconservative turn on cultural memory. And, let it be said, to explore a cultural forgetting that has also accompanied this turn: about racial divisions in the 1960s, about the real legacies of Vietnam, or about the long-standing inequality outside prison walls that is hardly redressed by what goes on inside them.[4]

Thinking about the connections between crime vocabularies, crime management practices, and cultural memory suggests that we might approach political legitimization—or what I would prefer to call the construction of "terms of consent"—as more than simply a matter of forging ideological agreement about criminal justice as such. Crime stories also reconstruct cultural attitudes about ethnicity, mobilize longings for lost neighborhoods or lost childhoods, and even entertain ideas about pleasure or self-assertion; all too commonly, these stories invoke a respect for law that coexists uneasily with more covert admiration for criminal transgression.[5] Even the characters of seemingly formulaic stories about crime reveal this more complicated mosaic. A cop like Bill Clark, like *NYPD Blue*'s Andy Sipowicz, surely carries brutality into his daily work, and a longing to assert his professional, quite conservative certainty in the interrogation room. But his partner, David Milch, is attuned, as well, to less predictable registers of Clark's personality: his taciturnity, his self-identified Irish-cop fatalism, his memories of having left unfinished business in Vietnam. And Milch is careful, therefore, to re-partner Sipowicz's labor to that of the Puerto Rican Bobby Simone, so as to solicit the more cosmopolitan and pluralist values of *NYPD Blue*'s viewing audience. In the world of lead detective Lily Rush of Meredith Stiehm's *Cold Case,* likewise, we are certainly reminded of crime's enduring costs with an almost ghostly certainty and sorrow. Nevertheless, it is always necessary that the pain of the crime victim be opened up, so that it may be appropriated into an ever-vigilant, populist, and sleepless state where, as Elizabeth Stanko has written, all "Victims R Us." (Or a world where, as Alice Sebold tells us, members of a suburban family feel they are at the epicenter of a war.)[6] Henry Hill is important not only because of his inside knowledge of the Mafia. Rather, it is because he is a street sparrow of a consumer society, playing its angles, galling his bosses, and always looking for his golden parachute. Much like Frank Abagnale, Hill also expresses a longing for the decade that remains, in the polemics of neoconservatives, a seedbed of the permissiveness that supposedly generated so much crime in the first place.[7]

Learning secrets from criminals, or learning how the law has come to live with them, thus proves to be a tricky process for my writers. Many older templates for depicting crime—the gangland drama, the shadow narrative, the street sparrow adventure, the underworld voyage—persist into the twenty-first century, and their sensational idioms often persist with them. Even when a residual muckraking impulse ironically exposes crime's mirroring of the mainstream, a much older, quasi-anthropological approach tends to hold sway: one that depicts the world of cops or crooks (or, in Conover's case, the world of prison guards) as a culture unto itself into which the writer is initiated.[8] To be sure, this approach, whether it leads to a writer's immersion into cop or gangster culture, or to his cultivation of an informant, often elicits valuable insights. Thanks to these writers, we know much more about everyday crime workers, about the structure of mob families and the codes of police work; we know more about con men who paste icons of status and sexuality into their counterfeit identities, or about the ways that prison guards or cops feel about their labors. Yet there are pitfalls to this particular approach as well. An individual informant can be conflated with the larger criminal culture or organization from which he has been extracted, or exiled. What might be called a tendency to "read for culture" can itself make crime look habitual, a product of internalized, shared norms by which the informant has supposedly lived (even though, by informing, he may be violating them).[9]

Like other struggles between confessor and interrogator, meanwhile, the initiation of writers has many back channels and countercurrents that are inherited from the crime-control setting itself.[10] Criminals can push back against their handlers, rationalize their violence, re-describe a witness protection program as extortion, or hold on to their adolescent gangster dreams. In some instances, the satiric deflation of criminal enterprise is a reflection of law enforcement processes that are themselves reducing criminals in scale. The debunking of mob or gang rituals, similarly, might seem necessary journalistic work, especially in detaching the stigma of organized crime from particular ethnicities. In some cases, however, this miniaturizing tactic expresses a brittle nostalgia for the "little guy" or small operator, or the "good old days" of a supposedly more stylish, or more "meaningful," crime era. (What is a "meaningless" crime, one might ask?) Similarly, the various styles of investigative shadowing—and here I mean not only journalistic immersion, but the imaginative projection into criminality—produce many insights and vicarious pleasures. Yet the shadow of the citizen himself can often infuse the process, pulling the writer back toward the needs of social order or personal security. The informant or proxy can also turn the tables, recapturing the writer's own imagination. My hope is that my final chapter on *Brothers and Keepers*, therefore, is read not just as a coda regarding neoconservatism's hegemony. Rather, I intend that chapter to be an *interpretive* riposte to the literary collaborations discussed in each of my earlier chapters. We should be guided especially by he intricate musings in *Brothers and Keepers,* on the multiple meanings of freedom and time, of the walls between writers and criminal transgressors, and the only-temporary visiting of narrative. I hope these musings remind us of the inevitable struggle between sympathy (brotherhood) and restraint (keeping) that emerges whenever writers try to convey what any of us can know about crime.

It also needs to be acknowledged that contemporary crime writing is too various to be encompassed by any single study. My small sample is almost exclusively the work of male writers, most of them white-identified; I have said little about how representative my genre samples are, or how different audiences might read them. I have emphasized journalistic codes at the expense of mystery formulae, true crime over fiction, micro-encounters over macro trends. And my chapter list fails to exhaust the range of crime-control practices that are equally vital to recent decades. Undercover police work, for instance, seems to have experienced a revival of late; electronic surveillance, a subject well documented in British and U.S. cultural studies, has also affected many areas of crime control. Private prison management and prison transfers raise many more issues than I address in chapter 5. I say nothing in my chapters about immigration detention and border policing; about the increasing integration of criminal justice, welfare, and immigration; or about the new dimensions of ethnic and religious profiling engendered by the war on terrorism.[11] And I hope that my own conscious decision to subordinate the management of street crime is not taken as an attempt to discount its continuing importance or complexity—particularly when street gangs seem to be ever-more part of organized-crime drug cartels, and therefore entangled in the politics of our borderlands.[12]

The study of crime narrative is also hardly the only entryway into the relationship between crime, its management, and political legitimization. Nevertheless, I remain convinced that it remains a vital way to explore the complex claims regarding state power and democratic consent at the heart of the neoconservative turn. Some readers might argue, for instance, that some of the tactics I have been calling "under-the-radar" were, after all, fully discussed in public. The Broken Windows theory, they might say, was famously broached in the *Atlantic* magazine; scholars and civil rights advocates have been vocal in their objection to the ills of coercion in interrogation; the prison-industrial complex is supposedly there for all to see. In this regard, I am reminded of a rejoinder Lincoln Steffens once offered, in regard to his own work. The kind of exposé he was writing, Steffens observed, was not the sensational kind that revealed a system operating in the darkness; rather, he said, *Shame of the Cities* was an exposition on what citizens already "know and stand" for.[13] The real paradox of the neoconservative turn, I think, is that its tactics offered the *appearance* of having received public vetting, and yet were premised on near-invisibility in terms of their everyday implementation.

Indeed, from the get-go, these tactics were attractive precisely for their reduced visibility. The Broken Windows analogy, for example, made it seem as if consent was to be constructed through the register of public symbolism, or "thinking about crime" that took place in those much-publicized community meetings. In practice, the philosophy actually legitimated aggressive and often extra-legal practices by police *in place* of rigorous legal or civilian oversight. Similarly, the furor over coercion and brutality in interrogation might seem to have brought the practice into the open. I'm glad that it has. Yet the more difficult matter is that this furor may have unwittingly provided cover for the tacit acceptance of (the false alternative of) police deception.[14] And for all the benefits of raising public awareness about crime victims, we might reexamine the ends to which the comforts of an often-therapeutic vocabulary are mobilized. As Smilla recognizes, just because a prosecutor embraces a victim's suffering, or makes it a public emblem of crime's costs, does not mean their interests are compatible. For instance, a supposed support of victims has been used for what Frank Rich has called "closure mongering": advocacy of the death penalty.[15]

The ongoing social rewriting of our prisons, the culmination of this sorry master narrative, remains the most startling illustration of how supposedly "open secrets" have accompanied a narrowing of meaning, oversight, and debate. As Eric Schlosser shows, the incorporation of citizens into the economic operations of prisons is one of the most telling manifestations of public dependence on the war on crime. (For Conover, it threatens to create a veritable gridlock of "keeplock.") Yet despite neoconservative claims to the fatalistic "openness" of this development, multiple silences have been imposed upon the ways citizens are commonly asked to imagine prisons. For example, when I discuss the notion of "doing time" with my college students, they are certainly ready to argue over quantifiable sentences, and to debate how long a criminal should or shouldn't serve out his or her sentence. These students often challenge the terms of neoconservative discourse with their own sense of justice. But when asked what a prisoner would be *doing* in prison, no matter what span of time had been chosen, a silence not uncommonly opens up. It is as if, implicitly, the rationale of crime control (incapacitation), of doing time outside the polity, had taken this issue off the table.[16]

III.

This silence, which takes us back to Høeg's investigator and his assumptions about public dependence on the state, therefore poses another dilemma for a book like this one. In the fickle attention span of American politics, crime can itself seem a subject that has now receded from public view. Talking about "the crime problem" may only invoke, in other words, a condition that Americans have learned to live with. As I suggest in my Introduction, this is one of the persisting contradictions of the past forty-odd years: crime persists in our reading and on our television sets and movie screens, even when it was barely mentioned in the 2008 presidential campaign. In fact, it is fair to say that many of my own readers would associate the term *neoconservative* more with shadowy players in American foreign policy—and after all, it is said, terrorism is now the main concern of our day.[17] In this regard, therefore, I feel compelled to tell one last crime story.

My tale begins with the appearance of General Michael Hayden, just appointed as George W. Bush's Director of the Central Intelligence Agency, on the *Charlie Rose* show in October 2007. Hayden had arrived, of course, to talk about the war on terror, specifically to explain the approach he was taking in the wake of the intelligence fiascos of 9/11 and the run-up to the war in Iraq. He spoke about the low morale of his own workforce at Langley and the importance of getting his people back to work—and out of the newspapers. Gliding over what it might mean to have an upbeat CIA, Hayden preferred to stay in the mode of caution, much like Høeg's investigator. "I said this in my confirmation hearings," he reminded Rose. "There is no worse place for an intelligence service like the CIA to be, than on page one above the fold in your daily newspaper. That's a distraction to the kind of work the agency has to do." He then went on to enumerate the tools of his trade, in his opinion, best kept out of public view (or, again, review). His guiding premise emerged in a discussion of Great Britain's partnership with the United States:

> HAYDEN: Because of my experience at that time as the director of the National Security Agency, [my idea] was that [terrorism] was not, in its essence, primarily a law or enforcement issue. This was an armed conflict. . . .
>
> ROSE: Well it is said that the British have been successful because they

> believed it is a police effort, and that's why they've been able roll up some of those people they have. . . .
>
> HAYDEN: Right. And the British are wonderful partners. And we share information with them intimately. And their success is our success and vice versa. [But r]olling up people on the verge of an attack on Great Britain is not a comforting measure of success in this war. You know, if we try to defeat this enemy at the moment of attack, and it may be just that. It may be the moment of attack. . . .
>
> . . . [S]omeone else had commented, well you could put [a terrorist suspect] into a judicial process. That's the question that I see an awful lot of friction on.
>
> . . . I don't think we have anything to fear by putting them into a judicial process, if that is possible, but that cannot be our only approach to this problem. . . . Back to the premise . . . this is not a law enforcement activity.

For a military man, of course, this might seem like an understandable distinction. It allowed Hayden to invoke the *Army Field Manual* in dealing with terrorist defendants, and to draw the homeland boundary even as he distanced himself from U.S. laws or treaties about rendition, torture, and the rest.[18] But from my vantage point, of course, Hayden was hanging his entire argument on a distinction without a real difference. For if anything, the extensive recalibration of the criminal justice system I have described in this book had *itself* been predicated precisely what Hayden held out for himself: the legitimating necessities of a "war."

Moreover, despite Hayden's insistence, one could find many traces of the domestic war on crime in his own campaign. For example, I found myself remembering how the imaginary terrain of an *NYPD Blue* interrogation room, pre-9/11, would flip inside-out, and an episode like "Prostrate Before the Law" would turn into a story about a terror cell. Or how Gourevitch's Andy Rosenzweig would model the ever-vigilant citizen on a war model. Or that security experts like Frank Abagnale would see business rise when identity theft panic would be fueled by terrorist tactics. And certainly there was a ringing in my ears when, after writing on the Whitey Bulger scandal of the late 1990s, I began to hear national security officials (Hayden among them) tout the supposedly forgotten merits of "human intelligence." (In Hayden's world, as in Giuliani's, a spy and an informer are often one in the same.)[19]

In turn, the currents between counterterrorism and criminal justice Hayden preferred to deny might actually run in both directions. The domestic war on crime I have described in this book might, in fact, help us interpret recent tactics on the terror front. These crime narratives can suggest, for instance, that the mass orchestration of battlefield detentions in Afghanistan and Iraq may have been designed to gather intelligence through generating informants; that the terrors of Abu Ghraib may have led directly from the assumption that prisons and plea bargaining would be used for interrogation; that interrogation was probably used, in a deadly circle, to engender such informing, so as to (as in cold case investigations) infiltrate otherwise-hostile civilian populations. These connections suggest that the rhetorical linkage so often made between achieving security and political stability in these foriegn venues plays off the "peace" we have made, so uneasily, with own domestic phantoms. And certainly there are other crosscurrents.[20]

In the end, however, perhaps the most suggestive element of all was Hayden's presumption that a declaration of war legitimated the separation of his tactics from judicial interference. In this absurdly long view, failures in prosecuting terrorists might actually be, to someone like Hayden, beside the point. To him, the preemption of attacks would be the more important pre-juridical objective. Indeed, Hayden's musings suggest that pre-juridical capture, detention, and even the war on terror's notorious erection of legal indeterminacy—once again, a "doing time" frighteningly outside of time—are all designed, in *both* wars, precisely to forestall the operations of law as such. And thus, in the shadows of Hayden's rhetorical juggling of secrets and open confessions, it was no longer so easy to see which war was the epilogue of the other.

Again, perhaps my own musings only begin to suggest how many subjects are beyond the scope of this book. On a more hopeful note, we might also consider why, like Høeg's investigator, Hayden would make such an appearance at all: why, that is, he would seek the public's (or at least Charlie Rose's) understanding of practices he otherwise defines as off limits. Hayden's testimony, to be sure, suggests that the calm but belligerent insistence on the homeland only serves to isolate the United States from its allies, that the tactic of rendition is not separable from torture, and so on. But his appearance also reminds us that headlines have indeed preceded him, however much as he would hope to remove his workforce from public storytelling. In other words, as much as he would discount democratic consent, he is there, after all, partly seeking it. These more fluid fronts to this complex turn in our political life—"fronts" not only in the sense of battlefronts but also in the sense of facades and front men who describe these battles to us—offer any number of continuing challenges to our writers and to those of us who write about them. And, as Steffens might have it, challenges to the continuing cause of exposing secrets while recognizing that some are already open to us.

Notes

Introduction

1. I am indebted to Stuart Scheingold for highlighting the phrase I have chosen for my book title; see his "Constructing the New Political Criminology: Power, Authority, and the Post-Liberal State," *Law and Social Inquiry* 23 (1999): 857–95; see esp. 886. For an instance of the common use of "learning to live" in political discourse, see Thomas E. Cronin, Tanzia Z. Cronin, and Michael E. Milakovich, *U.S. vs. Crime in the Streets* (Bloomington: Indiana University Press, 1981), 164. Epigraphs are from Robert P. Rhodes, *The Insoluble Problems of Crime* (New York: John Wiley & Sons, 1977), 257; and Alice Sebold, *The Lovely Bones* (Little, Brown, 2002), 184, apparently a Greek aphorism adapted by Colette's *Les Heures Longues* (1917).

2. Simon's central argument was offered in "Governing Through Crime," in *The Crime Conundrum: Essays on Criminal Justice,* ed. Lawrence M. Friedman and George Fisher (New York: Westview Press, 1997), 171–89 (subsequent quotations in text), and later expanded into *Governing Through Crime: How the War on Crime Transformed American Democracy and Created a Culture of Fear* (New York: Oxford University Press, 2007).

3. For the phrase "specific gravity," see Phillip Rieff's discussion of George Orwell in the *Columbia Journalism Review* 46 (November–December 2007): 28–30.

4. Cf. Raymond Williams, "Culture Is Ordinary" (1958), reprinted in *Resources of Hope: Culture, Democracy, Socialism,* ed. Robin Gable (London: Verso, 1989), 3–18.

5. For one helpful overview that posits this disenchantment theme, see Malcolm W. Feeley, "Crime, Social Order, and the Rise of Neo-conservative Politics," a review of David Garland's *The Culture of Control: Crime and Social Order in Contemporary Society* (Oxford: Oxford University Press, 2001), in *Theoretical Criminology* 7 (2003): 111–30; subsequent quotations in text.

6. For these summaries, I am indebted to Michael W. Flamm, *Law and Order: Street Crime, Civil Unrest, and the Crisis of Liberalism in the 1960s* (New York: Columbia University Press, 2005); Frank J. Weed, *Certainty of Justice: Reform in the Crime Victim Movement* (New York: Aldine De Gruyter, 1995); Stuart Scheingold, *The Politics of Street*

Crime: Criminal Process and Cultural Obsession (Philadelphia: Temple University Press, 1991); and Malcolm W. Feeley and Jonathan Simon, "Actuarial Justice: The Emerging New Criminal Law," in *The Futures of Criminology*, ed. David Nelkin (London: Sage Publications, 1994), 173–201. On profiling, see Morgan Cloud, "Search and Seizure by the Numbers: The Drug Courier Profile and Judicial Review of Investigative Formulas," *Boston University Law Review* 66 (November 1985): 843–921; and Simon, "Governing Through Crime," 177–82.

7. Samuel Walker, summarizing a consensus view he challenges, in "Wars on Crime—Struggles for Justice: Conflicting Trends in American Criminal Justice, 1970–1995," in Friedman and Fisher, 193–94.

8. On neoconservative philosophy and its implementation in order-maintenance policing, see esp. Bernard Harcourt, "Reflecting on the Subject: A Critique of the Social Influence Conception of Deterrence, the Broken Windows Theory, and Order-Maintenance Policing New York Style," *Michigan Law Review* 97 (November 1998): 291–389.

9. Robert Reiner, "Media Made Criminality: The Representation of Crime in the Mass Media," in *The Oxford Handbook of Criminology*, ed. Mike Maguire, Rod Morgan, and Robert Reiner (New York: Oxford University Press, 1997), 189–231. See also Mary Beth Oliver, "Race and Culture in the Media: Research from a Media Effects Perspective," in *A Companion to Media Studies*, ed. Angharad N. Valdiva (Malden, MA: Blackwell, 2003), 421–36; Clinton R. Sanders and Eleanor Lyon, "Repetitive Retribution: Media Images and the Cultural Construction of Criminal Justice," in *Cultural Criminology*, ed. Jeff Ferrell and Clinton R. Sanders (Boston: Northeastern University Press, 1995), 25–44; James M. Carlson, *Prime-Time Law Enforcement* (New York: Praeger, 1985); and Paul G. Kooistra, John S. Mahoney, and Saundra D. Westervelt, "The World of Crime According to 'Cops,'" in *Entertaining Crime: Television Reality Programs,* ed. Mark Fishman and Gray Cavender (New York: Aldine D. Grayter, 1998), 141–58.

10. For a typical acknowledgment of crime's persisting presence in American primetime TV, see, for instance, Allison Romano, "Crime Pays, Again and Again," *Broadcasting and Cable* 135 (8 August 2005): 18.

11. See Elayne Rapping, *Law and Justice as Seen on TV* (New York: New York University Press, 2003); and Jeffrey Toobin, "Annals of Law: The 'CSI' Effect," *The New Yorker* 83 (7 May 2007): 30–35

12. For important studies in this regard, see Claire Bond Potter, *War on Crime: Bandits, G-Men, and The Politics of Mass Culture* (New Brunswick, NJ: Rutgers University Press, 1998); and Lee Bernstein, *The Greatest Menace: Organized Crime in Cold War America* (Amherst: University of Massachusetts Press, 2002). A number of other studies have also theorized the relationship of crime narrative to the welfare state, and thus might well be seen as leading into the period I am describing; see, for example, Sean McCann, *Gumshoe America: Hard-Boiled Crime Fiction and the Rise and Fall of New Deal Liberalism* (Durham, NC: Duke University Press, 2000); Paula Rabinowitz, "What Film Noir Can Teach Us about 'Welfare as We Know It,'" *Social Text* 18 (Spring 2000): 135–41; and Leonard Cassuto, *Hard-Boiled Sentimentality: The Secret History of American Crime Stories* (New York: Columbia University Press, 2009). For many insights on the recent era (including the role of victimology), see Mark Seltzer, *True Crime: Observations on Violence and Modernity* (New York: Routledge, 2007).

13. Stephen Brauer, "Moving Beyond Genre: The Critical Reception of Detective Fiction of the 1930s," in *Working Papers on the Web* 6 (Spring 2004), http://extra.shu.ac.uk/wpw/thirties/thirties%20brauer.html (accessed 15 July 2009).

14. For a class-based, left perspective on this crisis of governance as "counterinsurgency by other means" (167) moving from political crackdowns to control of "floating

populations" created by economic restructuring, see Christian Parenti, *Lockdown America: Police and Prisons in an Age of Crisis* (New York: Verso, 1999). See also the superb analysis in Ruth Wilson Gilmore, *Golden Gulag: Prisons, Surplus, Crisis, and Opposition in Globalizing California* (Berkeley: University of California Press, 2007).

15. On risk and actuarialism, cf. Feeley and Simon, "Actuarial Justice," and Barbara Hudson, *Justice in the Risk Society* (London: Sage Books, 2003), 45ff. I discuss the place of commonsense, actuarial logic in the history of public policing in my *Cop Knowledge: Police Power and Cultural Narrative in Twentieth-Century America* (Chicago: University of Chicago Press, 2000), 69–70 and passim.

16. Describing this "turn," I mean to speak of a constellation of approaches, described by the scholars above, coming of age in the post-industrial moment in the United States. I mean to reflect, as well, the influence of classic work such as Stuart Hall, et al., *Policing the Crisis: Mugging, the State and Law and Order* (New York: Holmes & Meier, 1978). "Governing through crime," Jonathan Simon wrote in the late 1990s, ". . . might be looked at as a response to this crisis, both a reaching back to real or imagined strategies for maintaining what appears to be a precarious social order, and reaching forward towards new platforms" to manage it ("Governing Through Crime," 177). The awkward but necessary term "responsibilization," which refers to cultivating citizen vigilance, comes from David Garland; see his "The Limits of the Sovereign State: Strategies of Crime Control in Contemporary Society," *British Journal of Criminology* 35 (Autumn 1996): 445–71, esp. 452–55; and his *Culture of Control*. See also Stanley Cohen, "The Punitive City: Notes on the Dispersal of Social Control," *Contemporary Crises* 3 (1979), esp. 354–57.

17. Although my distinction of "*neoconservatism*" is relatively rare in cultural and literary criticism, it is a commonplace in criminological discourse. James Q. Wilson's revised edition of *Thinking about Crime* (New York: Vintage, 1983) contains all of these themes and was the keynote neoconservative text of this era. But see also Rhodes, who cites Reinhold Niebuhr's maxim about democracy in his book title and epigraph (3); and Ernest van den Haag, *Punishing Criminals: Concerning a Very Old and Painful Question* (New York: Basic Books, 1975). I have discussed Wilson's importance in *Cop Knowledge*: see 177ff. Compare Cronin, Cronin, and Milakovich, *U.S. vs. Crime in the Streets*, 74; Scheingold, *The Politics of Street Crime*, 12ff.; and William Ker Muir, Jr., *Police: Streetcorner Politicians* (Chicago: University of Chicago Press, 1977), esp. 54–55, 122–23. Though she prefers the term *conservative*, I have also followed the argument in Rapping's *Law and Justice as Seen on TV* that there has recently been a "blurring" of "left, right, and center" (78ff.) in cultural and political debates about prison penology. Rapping's discussion of victims' rights, like Seltzer's, has also shaped my discussion in chapter 3.

18. Michel Foucault, *"Society Must Be Defended": Lectures at the College de France, 1975–76*, trans. David Macey (New York: Picador: 2003), 30, 28.

19. Simon, "Governing Through Crime," 177, 178. Simon and others sometimes call these "micropractices"; see, for example, "Actuarial Justice," 174. An effective recounting of Disney's influence in urban planning is Sharon Zukin, *The Cultures of Cities* (Cambridge, MA: Blackwell, 1996). Simon draws in part on the work of Clifford D. Shearing and Philip C. Stenning, "Modern Private Security: Its Growth and Implications," *Crime and Justice* 3 (1981): 193–245.

20. Garland, *Culture of Control*, 2. The key point is that these tactics often challenge Foucault's theoretical premises and approach. See Richard V. Ericson and Kevin D. Haggerty, *Policing the Risk Society* (Toronto: University of Toronto Press, 1997), 55.

21. On this point about differential orders, see Ericson and Haggerty, *Policing the Risk Society*, 43.

22. I have expressed my concerns about some of the best work in this area; see my review in *American Literature* 76 (2004): 196–99.

23. On these surveys, see esp. Richard F. Sparks, "Surveys of Victimization: An Optimistic Assessment," *Crime and Justice* 3 (1981): 1–60.

24. Scheingold, "Constructing the New Political Criminology," 864.

25. On the "pre-political," see Feeley and Simon, "Actuarial Justice," 190ff; Ian Loader, "Consumer Culture and the Commodification of Policing and Security," *Sociology* 33 (May 1999) 373–92; and the work, generally, of Pierre Bourdieu, especially *The Field of Cultural Production*, ed. Randall Johnson (New York: Columbia University Press, 1993).

26. Or, as Simon observes: "There is doubtless some link between the conservative ascendancy and the trend toward governing through crime, but there are also reasons to doubt that the former explains the latter. For one thing contemporary liberals also find themselves drawn toward punishment as a locus for governments. Laws and institutional rules punishing racist speech, domestic violence, sexual harassment, and pornography, for example, have become major agenda items for some liberals. Likewise, 20th-century conservatives often embraced noncriminal approaches to governance as an alternative to social instability. It is interesting that in a period of conservative ascendancy during which the right has articulated aspirations to govern through patriotism, work, and family, as well as crime, it is largely with respect to crime and punishment that there has been significant legislative success" ("Governing Through Crime," 175).

27. Sheldon Wolin, *The Presence of the Past* (Baltimore: Johns Hopkins University Press, 1989), 185.

28. Gary T. Marx, "Soft Surveillance: The Growth of Mandatory Volunteerism in Collecting Personal Information—'Hey Buddy Can You Spare a DNA?'" in *Surveillance and Security: Technological Politics and Power in Everyday Life,* ed. Torin Monahan (New York: Routledge: 2006), 49.

29. The animosity between Hoover and RFK is well described by Richard Gid Powers, *Secrecy and Power: The Life of J. Edgar Hoover* (New York: Free Press, 1987), 399ff.; see also his discussion of Nixon's attack on Clark, 445. But only by separating out the war on organized crime can Powers argue that RFK and Hoover had diametrically opposed approaches (400) to crime more generally.

30. Feeley and Simon, "Actuarial Justice," 175–76.

31. See Franklin E. Zimring and Gordon Hawkins, *Incapacitation: Penal Confinement and the Restraint of Crime* (New York: Oxford University Press, 1995), 72.

32. For Didion's argument, see Joan Didion, "Insider Baseball," *Political Fictions* (New York: Vintage Books, 2001), 41–43. The essay originally appeared in *The New York Review of Books* in 1988. Dionne's label first appeared in "Saving Cities: Is 'Kojak Liberalism' the Answer?" *The Washington Post,* 15 June 1993. Dionne, not unimportantly, actually cites neoconservative Nathan Glazer. On neoliberal adjustments to crime, see Eric Schlosser, "The Prison Industrial Complex," *Atlantic Monthly* (December 1998): 58–77; see esp. 56–57 on Mario Cuomo.

33. See Shearing and Stenning, "Modern Private Security," esp. 226–29.

34. Wilson, *Thinking about Crime,* 127–28.

35. See *Cop Knowledge,* 177ff.

36. See, in particular, Foucault's formulation concerning Vidocq, discussed in my chapter 4.

37. Wendy Lesser, *Pictures at an Execution: An Inquiry into the Subject of Murder* (Cambridge, MA: Harvard University Press, 1993), 4.

38. My approach here has been influenced by the critique of realist ethnography; see,

for example, James Clifford, *The Predicament of Culture* (Cambridge, MA: Harvard University Press, 1988), and George Marcus and Michael M. J. Fischer, *Anthropology as Cultural Critique: An Experimental Moment in the Human Sciences* (Chicago: University of Chicago Press, 1996).

39. I refer to "explanation forms" as the term is used in Gene Wise, *American Historical Explanations* (Minneapolis: University of Minnesota Press, 1980). In his discussion of the Kefauver Committee, similarly, Lee Bernstein has pointed out how the committee enlisted existing conventions of gangster narrative to make its work legible to the voting public. See Bernstein, *The Greatest Menace,* 137.

40. Cultural criminologists often call for work that is ethnographically grounded in the experience of communities, and I would agree. See, for example, the call in *Making Trouble: Cultural Constructions of Crime, Deviance, and Control,* ed. Jeff Ferrell and Neil Websdale (New York: Aldine De Gruyter, 1999), 358–59.

41. As Hall et al. suggested, dependence of reporters on "official" sources, for instance, permits institutional definers to "command" the field of possible meanings (*Policing the Crisis,* 58); compare Reiner, "Media Made Criminality," 222. See also Ian Loader, "Consumer Culture and the Commodification of Policing and Security," *Sociology* 33 (May 1999): 373–92. I have also been influenced by James Clifford's remarks on Hayden White in *On the Edges of Anthropology: Interviews* (Chicago: Prickly Paradigm Press, 2003), 13. This framing of crime has proved essential to the "facts" supposedly in evidence in public discourse: see esp. Elizabeth A. Stanko, "Victims R Us: The Life History of 'Fear of Crime' and the Politicization of Violence," in *Crime, Risk and Insecurity,* ed. Tim Hope and Richard Sparks (London: Routledge, 2000), 17, 19; and Sparks, "Surveys of Victimization."

Chapter 1

1. Dick Lehr and Gerard O'Neill, *Black Mass: The Irish Mob, the FBI, and a Devil's Deal* (New York: PublicAffairs, 2000). Epigraph from Burton B. Turkus and Sid Feder, *Murder, Inc.: The Story of "The Syndicate"* (New York: Farrar, Straus and Young, 1951), ix.

2. For reviews and discussions of *Black Mass*'s influence, see Ralph Ranalli, "New Rules on US Informants Call for Scrutiny, Safeguards Changes Reflect the Fallout from Bulger-FBI Case," *Boston Globe,* 12 January 2001; Shelley Murphy and Thanassis Cambanis, "Connolly Convicted, But Jury Acquits Ex-agent of Most Serious Charges," *Boston Globe,* 29 May 2002; William Bratton's review of *Black Mass* in the *Boston Globe,* 13 August 2000; Selwyn Raab and Ralph Ranalli, "US Tightens Rules on Informants," *Boston Globe,* 9 January 2001.

3. For a typical example of such a history, see Thomas Repetto, *Bringing Down the Mob: The War Against the American Mafia* (New York: Henry Holt, 2006). For a treatment with a superb eye to the cultural context, see Bernstein, *The Greatest Menace.*

4. Ronald Goldfarb, *Perfect Villains, Imperfect Heroes* (Sterling, VA: Capital Books, 1995); Pete Early and Gerald Shur, *WITSEC: Inside the Federal Witness Protection Program* (New York: Bantam, 2002).

5. I have discussed this case in "'Where's Whitey?': Ethnic Criminality and the Problem of the Informant," *Crime, Law and Social Change* 43 (March 2005): 175–98.

6. On the FBI program, see esp. Ralph Ranalli, *Deadly Alliance: The FBI's Secret Partnership with the Mob* (New York: HarperTorch, 2001).

7. For Hoover's repeated use of informants, see Potter, *War on Crime,* esp. 188ff.

8. Atlanta statistics and informant costs from Mark Curriden, "Making Crime Pay: What's the Cost of Using Paid Informers?" *American Bar Association Journal* 77 (June 1991): 42–46. DEA described in Dick Lehr, "The Information Underworld Police Reliance on Criminal Informants is a Dangerous Game for Both," *Boston Globe*, 16 October 1988. Fee limit in Curriden, "Making Crime Pay"; FBI testimony from DEA agent quoted in Brian McGrory, "Drug War's Odd Couple: Informants and Police," *Boston Globe*, 15 April 1994.

9. For overviews of these trends, see Peter S. Canellos, "Many Warrants, Little Scrutiny: Police Statements about Informants Go Unchecked," *Boston Globe*, 6 March 1989; Curriden, "Making Crime Pay." Reports link federal agencies to other informant controversies as well. See, for example, Ralph Ranalli, "FBI Reportedly Hid Key Evidence Documents Show It Knew of Deegan Slaying Plot in '65," *Boston Globe*, 21 December 2000; Joseph P. Fried, "Prosecutor Says FBI Agent Misled Superiors about Informer," *New York Times*, 4 March 1997; and Selwyn Raab, "The Mobster Was a Mole for the FBI," *New York Times*, 20 November 1994.

10. In a way that also suggests currents across partisan lines, Richard Nixon's first appointee as the Law Enforcement Assistance Association's (LEAA) chief administrator would be Charles Rogovin, formerly of President Lyndon B. Johnson's Organized Crime Task Force. Under Rogovin, Nixon's District of Columbia Crime Control bill (1971) would model many of the tactics of the coming war on drugs—for instance, so-called "no knock" warrants, the expansion of preventive detention measures, mandatory sentences, and even expanded wiretapping. See Cronin, Cronin, and Milakovich, *U.S. vs. Crime in the Streets*, 83. Rogovin himself endorses these aggressive tactics in Charles H. Rogovin and Frederick T. Martens, "The Role of Crime Commissions in Organized Crime Control," in *Handbook of Organized Crime in the United States*, ed. Robert J. Kelly, Ko-lin Chin, and Rufus Schatzberg (Westport, CT: Greenwood Press, 1994), 389–400. On the general context of pretext busts to achieve warrants, see my discussion in chapter 2 and Stephen D. Mastrofski, "The Prospects of Change in Police Patrol: A Decade of Review," *American Journal of Police* 9 (1990): 1–79.

11. A *Frontline* documentary in 1999, for example, reported that over the prior five years, nearly one-third of the people sentenced in drug-trafficking cases in the federal system had reduced their sentence through informing. See the *Frontline* report entitled "Snitch," aired on January 12, 1999, transcript available at http://www.pbs.org/wgbh/pages/frontline/shows/snitch/etc/script.html (accessed 5 December 2009). On this general climate, see my *Cop Knowledge*, 145–48. On the police practice of "losing" informants intentionally, see Thomas A. Mauet, "Informant Disclosure and Production," *Arizona Law Review* 37 (Summer 1995): 563–76; Evan Haglund, "Impeaching the Underworld Informant," *Southern California Law Review* 63 (July 1990): 1405–47. On witness protection, see Curriden, "Making Crime Pay."

12. Giuliani in his 1994 introduction to Robert Daley's reissue of *Prince of the City* (New York: Warner Books, 1994), ix. I discuss these scandals, and the corporate emphasis of the Knapp Commission Report on police corruption, in "Undercover: White Ethnicity and Police Exposé in the 1970s," *American Literature* 77 (June 2005): 349–77.

13. See Sean Murphy, "Boston Police Curbing Use of Drug Informants," *Boston Globe*, 6 May 1990; McGrory, "Drug War's Odd Couple"; Peter S. Canellos, "Payments by Police in Question," *Boston Globe*, 26 May 1989.

14. The Supreme Judicial Court as qtd. in Murphy, "Boston Police Curbing Use of Drug Informants"; cf. Doris Sue Wong and B. J. Roche, "Lewin Is Found Not Guilty: Verdict Ends Tainted Case of Slaying of Detective," *Boston Globe*, 26 October 1990. See also Sean Murphy, "Sorting Out Informants to Be Key in Decision on Lewin Indict-

ment," *Boston Globe,* 5 March 1989. As an unidentified Boston officer told the *Globe:* "It's physically impossible to do the work required to get a warrant every day. So sometimes you have a nonexistent informant saying something that's obvious." As qtd. in Canellos.

15. I refer here to the Albert Lewin and Accelynne Williams cases. In addition to the above, see Toni Locy, "Bungled Raid Raises Questions on Reliability of Police Informants," *Boston Globe,* 27 March 1994; Sean Murphy and Toni Locy, "Three Supervisors Transferred for Fatally Bungled Raid," *Boston Globe,* 12 May 1994; the report of District Attorney for Suffolk County, Ralph C. Martin, *The Death of Reverend Accelyne Williams* (Boston: Commonwealth of Massachusetts, 1994); Boston Police Department, Office of Internal Investigations, *Report to the Community Regarding 118 Whitfield Street, Dorchester* (Boston: May 1994); and the Boston Police Department's *Response to Questions Posed by the Police Practices Coalition* (1993).

16. I am drawing here on historian Alan Block's argument that changes in organized crime commonly mirror changes in civil society and the political economy. As Prohibition would famously demonstrate, what the state declares illicit often only clears territory for the underground entrepreneur; put a tax on cigarettes in one locality, and a Mafia entrepreneur like Henry Hill is only too happy to bootleg them from another. Alan A. Block, *East Side-West Side: Organizing Crime in New York City* (New Brunswick, NJ: Transaction, 1994); Alan A. Block, "History and the Study of Organized Crime," *Urban Life* 6 (January 1978): 455–74.

17. The RICO provision would be drafted primarily by Kennedy protégé G. Robert Blakeley (Repetto, *Bringing Down the Mob,* 96).

18. Peter Maas, *The Valachi Papers* (New York: Putnam, 1968); Nicholas Pileggi, *Wiseguy: Life in a Mafia Family* (New York: Pocket Books, 1985). All further citations from both books in text.

19. Robert Warshow, "The Gangster as Tragic Hero," in *The Immediate Experience* (Garden City, NY: Doubleday, 1962), 97–103.

20. The FBI's top echelon program signaled Hoover's own understanding of the significance of this front to the larger public sentiment about crime. (He had already begun, as well, to embrace electronic surveillance for nefarious purposes.) On this animosity, see note 29 in my Introduction.

21. The renaming of Hoover's division is mentioned in Repetto, *Bringing Down the Mob,* 71.

22. A succinct summary of the corporate model used by law enforcement after the Kefauver Commission (as well as the 1967 Task Force on Organized Crime of the President's Commission on Law Enforcement and Administration of Justice) is provided by Francis A. J. Ianni, "The Mafia and the Web of Kinship," *The Public Interest* 22 (Winter 1971): 78–100, esp. 93–94. The model was most famously articulated by Donald Cressey in works such as *Theft of the Nation: The Structure and Operations of Organized Crime in America* (New York: Harper and Row, 1969). For examples of a strict application of this corporate model, see Timothy Carter, "Ascent of the Corporate Model in Environmental-Organized Crime," *Crime, Law and Social Change* 31 (1999): 1–30; and James B. Jacobs, *Gotham Unbound: How New York City Was Liberated from the Grip of Organized Crime* (New York: New York University Press, 1999).

23. For a succinct historical overview, Peter A. Lupsha, "Organized Crime in the United States," in *Organized Crime: A Global Perspective,* ed. R. J. Kelly (Totowa, NJ: Rowan and Littlefield, 1986), 42ff.

24. Thomas Byrnes, *Professional Criminals of America* (1886; rpt. New York, Chelsea House Publishers, 1969), 13–14.

25. Lupsha, "Organized Crime in the United States," 33; Turkus and Feder, *Murder, Inc.*, 74ff.
26. Lupsha, "Organized Crime in the United States," 33, 49.
27. Potter, *War on Crime*, 78.
28. See Warshow, "The Gangster as Tragic Hero," and David E. Ruth, *Inventing the Public Enemy: The Gangster in American Culture, 1918–1934* (Chicago: University of Chicago Press, 1996). The fullest discussion of the fraternal theme in the gangster narrative is Jonathan Munby, *Public Enemies, Public Heroes: Screening the Gangster from Little Caesar to Touch of Evil* (Chicago: University of Chicago Press, 1999), 47, 52–54.
29. See Ianni, "The Mafia and the Web of Kinship," esp. 91–92; Jacobs, *Gotham Unbound*, 136; Letizia Paoli, "The Paradoxes of Organized Crime," *Crime, Law, and Social Change*, 37 (2002): 51–97.
30. Although the formulation preceded him, this model is most famously used in Daniel Bell, "Crime as an American Way of Life," in *The End of Ideology* (Glencoe, IL: Free Press, 1960); contrast Block, "History and the Study of Organized Crime," 474, note 5.
31. Vincenzo Ruggiero, "Drug Economics: A Fordist Model of Criminal Capital?" *Capital and Class* 55 (Spring 1995): 131–50. On the emergence of the business motif in gangster representations, see Ruth, *Inventing the Public Enemy*, 37–62; an even more corporate and "syndicate" stamp in American film is comprehensively discussed by Ronald W. Wilson, "Gang Busters: The Kefauver Crime Committee and the Syndicate Films of the 1950s," in *Mob Culture: Hidden Histories of the American Gangster Film*, ed. Lee Grieveson, Esther Sonnet, and Peter Stanfield (New Brunswick, NJ: Rutgers University Press, 2005), 67–89.
32. Maas, *The Valachi Papers*, 77, 84, 98. Criminologists disputed the characerization of a formal "war." See Block, "History and the Study of Organized Crime."
33. Gay Talese, *Honor Thy Father* (New York: World Publishers, 1971).
34. Turkus and Feder, *Murder, Inc.*, 68. The authors reserved the term *Mafia* for non-Americanized, more local mobs and also analogized the newer structure to a federation or "states' rights" organization.
35. On Dewey's precedent, see Michael Woodiwiss, *Crime, Crusades, and Corruption* (New York: Barnes and Noble, 1988), 54ff. On the reorientation toward gambling, see Goldfarb, *Perfect Villains, Imperfect Heroes*, 38.
36. On these matters, see Paoli, "The Paradoxes of Organized Crime"; Ianni, "The Mafia and the Web of Kinship"; and Ruggiero, "Drug Economics."
37. See Goldfarb, *Perfect Villains, Imperfect Heroes*, esp. 57–58, 72.
38. For this point, and my understanding of RICO generally, I am indebted to William R. Geary, "The Social Construction of RICO" (PhD diss., University of Delaware, 1997).
39. These problems are documented in Early and Shur, *WITSEC*, esp. 75–76, 88–89, 113, 164.
40. As qtd. in Goldfarb, *Perfect Villains, Imperfect Heroes*, 149.
41. See Early and Shur, *WITSEC*, esp. 32–33, 66–68. The RICO mandate is quoted on 91–92.
42. Stephen Crane, "The Blue Hotel," in *Stephen Crane: Prose and Poetry*, ed. J. C. Levenson (New York: Library of America, 1984), 183.
43. See, for example, the narrative stemming from Joseph Pistone's undercover work: *Donnie Brasco: My Undercover Life in the Mafia* (New York: New American Library, 1987).
44. Here, as in chapters 2 and 5, I rely on Albert Stone's idea of the "telling occasion": see Albert E. Stone, "Collaboration in Contemporary American Autobiography," *Revue Française D'Études Américaines* 14 (May 1982): 151–65.

45. On this point and the general climate, see Bernstein, *The Greatest Menace*, esp. 174.
46. Block, "History and the Study of Organized Crime," 470.
47. Valachi in Permanent Subcommittee on Investigation of the Committee on Government Operations, *Organized Crime and Illicit Traffic in Narcotics: Hearings Before the Permanent Subcommittee on Investigation of the Committee on Government Operations*, U.S. Senate, 88th Congress First Session, Part I (Washington: U.S. Government Printing Office, 1963), 166. Cf. Repetto, *Bringing Down*, 82–83.
48. Permanent Subcommittee, 181ff.
49. Joseph Valachi, "The Real Thing: The Exposé and Inside Doings of Cosa Nostra by Joseph Valachi, Member Since 1930," Typescript in Peter Maas Collection, John F. Kennedy Library and Museum, [1963?]. Subsequent citations in text.
50. Initially, Maas achieved an agreement to publish Valachi's story, overriding the Bureau of Prisons' own restrictions. But under public pressure from Italian pride organizations, the government reneged and went to court to stop its publication. Maas then compromised: he agreed to use only materials gathered from in-person interviews with Valachi and *not* to include the gangster's charges of double-dealing by the Bureau of Narcotics. In an undated letter to Maas after the publication of the book, Valachi writes, "I must tell you I was shocked to read and find out that you have left out all I said about the framing and corrupting narcotics agents. . . ." Peter Maas Collection, John F. Kennedy Library and Museum.
51. On this limit to Valachi's knowledge, see James Morton, *Supergrasses and Informers: An Informal History of Undercover Police Work* (London: Little, Brown, 1995), 134.
52. See Walter Lippmann, "The Underworld, Our Secret Servant," *Forum* 75 (January 1931): 1–4.
53. Cf. Maas, *The Valachi Papers*, 255, and Permanent Subcommittee, 94–95.
54. In an interview in *Publishers Weekly*, Pileggi compares using Hill to creating "an anthropological study—watching wiseguys in Samoa, in a sense." Joseph Barbato, "Nicholas Pileggi," *Publishers Weekly*, 7 February 1986, 56–57. See also the comments of Scorcese on the "everyday" and the "documentary," as qtd. in Constantine Verevis, "Way of Life: *Goodfellas* and *Casino*," in *Gangster Film: A Reader*, ed. Alain Silver and James Ursini (Pompton Plains, NJ: Limelight, 2007), 209.
55. See also Barbato's interview with Pileggi; and Carol E. Rinzler, "Pileggi on the Record," *Cosmopolitan* 200 (January 1986): 30–31.
56. Nicholas Pileggi, "Gangbusters: The Brooklyn Strike Force Makes War on Crime," *New York*, 25 July 1983, 24–31. See also his "Open City: The Bad Guys Are Winning the War on Crime," *New York*, 19 January 1981, 20–26, and "The Mob and the Machine," *New York*, 5 May 1986, 36–41.
57. McDonald, as qtd. in "Gangbusters," calls it "casualness" (23).
58. The Vario family was a branch of the Lucchese mob. See also Barbato, "Nicholas Pileggi."
59. See Pileggi, "The Mob and the Machine."
60. I found the term *street sparrow* in Lorenzo Carcaterra's memoir *Sleepers* (New York: Ballantine, 1995). I have discussed this memoir in "Lost Boys and Recovered Classics: Literary and Social Memory in Lorenzo Carcaterra's *Sleepers* (1995)," *Journal of American Studies* 42 (2008): 107–31.
61. Horatio Alger, *Ragged Dick and Struggling Upward*, ed. Carl Bode (New York: Penguin, 1985), 10, 20.
62. Barbato, "Nicholas Pileggi," 57.

63. This central insight was best associated with Herbert Gutman, notably in *Work, Culture, and Society* (New York: Vintage, 1977).

64. I am thinking here of *Ragged Dick*'s thief and thug character Jim Travis, who is often mocked for blaming the social order rather than seizing his opportunities. "Maybe you was an innocent victim of oppression" (66), Dick sneers.

65. Henry Hill and Douglas S. Looney, "How I Put the Fix In," *Sports Illustrated*, 16 February 1981, http://vault.sportsillustrated.cnn.com/vault/article/magazine/MAG1124224/index.htm (accessed 13 December 2009).

66. Hill eventually lost his protected status in WITSEC: see Leonard Buder, "Protected U.S. Witness Commits New Crimes," *New York Times*, 23 September 1986.

67. On these cases and the restrictions states and cities attempt to impose around criminal speech, see Sam Roberts, "Criminals, Authors, and Criminal Authors," *New York Times*, 22 March 1987; Alan Feuer, "Questions on How to Allot 'Underboss' Profits Persist," *New York Times*, 13 October 2001.

68. On differentiating witnesses, see U.S. Department of Justice, "Department of Justice Guidelines Regarding the Use of Confidential Informants," January 8, 2001, http://www.usdoj.gov/ag/readingroom/ciguidelines.htm (accessed 13 December 2009).

69. For example, these new guidelines prohibit the exchange of gifts, or engaging in any business transactions with an informant. And they say that "A Federal Law Enforcement agent shall not socialize with a CI"—"*except to the extent necessary and appropriate for operational reasons*" (emphasis mine). Contingency fees dependent upon the "conviction or punishment of any individual" are prohibited—though apparently, if one reads the news properly, contingency fees following asset forfeiture are not (in other words, creative bookkeeping). Of course it is said that an agent shall not "authorize a CI to engage in any activity that would constitute a misdemeanor or felony"—a guideline that certainly would seem to hinge on the definition of "authorize," since the first way to blow an informant's cover would be to prevent him, suddenly, from being a criminal.

70. These contradictions are not restricted to these guidelines. As defense lawyers such as Alan Dershowitz have complained for some time, the use of paid informants raises severe questions for criminal trials as such: imagine, he said, if the defense put paid witnesses on the stand. Dershowitz has also claimed that RICO statutes force informant cooperation: see his testimony in Curriden, "No Honor Among Thieves," *American Bar Association Journal* 75 (June 1989): 52ff. See also The Honorable Stephen S. Trott, "Words of Warning to Prosecutors Using Criminals as Witnesses," *Hastings Law Journal* 47 (July/August 1996): 1381–432. Earlier handbooks about the use of asset forfeiture similarly reprint boilerplate agreement contracts that are what the agency calls, somehow, "no deal deals." *Asset Forfeiture: Informants and Undercover Investigations* (rpt. 1992; Washington, DC: Bureau of Justice Assistance, 1990).

71. One sees this emphasis, for instance, in Jeffrey Scott McIllwain, "Organized Crime: A Social Network Approach," *Crime, Law, and Social Change* 32 (1999): 301–23; Block, "History and the Study of Organized Crime," 466–71; Ianni, "The Mafia and the Web of Kinship," 94–95. On social networks and one gang experiment, see John Seabrook, "Don't Shoot: A Radical Approach to the Problem of Gang Violence," *New Yorker*, 22 June 2009, 32–41.

Chapter 2

1. On the centrality of *Police Story* to network planning, see Todd Gitlin, *Inside Prime Time* (New York: Pantheon Books, 1985). I have discussed Wambaugh's vision in

Cop Knowledge, 94–129. Epigraph from "The True Test," *Homicide* (NBC), Season 5, Episode 63, 22 November, 1993, with Pembleton referring to the interrogation room.

2. For one of the best discussions of the modern procedural, see Larry Landrum, "Instrumental Texts and Stereotyping in *Hill Street Blues:* The Police Procedural on Television," *MELUS* 11 (Fall 1994): 93–100.

3. Toobin, "The 'CSI' Effect."

4. David Simon, *Homicide: A Year on the Killing Streets* (New York: Houghton Mifflin, 1991), 197.

5. Seltzer, *True Crime*, 14–15 and passim.

6. Obviously, I am drawing on Elaine Scarry's argument about torture in *The Body in Pain* (New York: Oxford University Press, 1985); "spectacle of power" is discussed on 27; see also 56.

7. For police officers' support of the show, see Frank Absher, "Arresting TV," *St. Louis Journalism Review* 32 (April 2000): 7, Clifford Krauss, "NYPD Blues Praise TV Version," *New York Times*, 25 March 1994; and Lucas Miller, "Watching the Detectives," *New York Times*, 1 March 2009.

8. The public controversy is reflected by the reactions of Richard Clark Sterne, "NYPD Blue," in *Prime Time Law*, ed. R. M. Jarvis and P. R. Joseph (Durham: Carolina Academic Press, 1998), 87–104. While praising aspects of the show, Sterne also criticizes "its failure to face up to police brutality as an issue," among other matters (95). For similar critical views, Lee Siegel, "Why Cop Shows are Eternal," *The New Republic*, 31 March 2003, 25. As I shall discuss, NYPD Commissioner William Bratton also weighed in: "Legal rules such as the Miranda guidelines are intended to curb police excesses. But those guidelines seem to disappear in the heat of an adrenaline rush and fear. Only constant supervision and training can prevent abuses and mistakes. . . . The glorification of the type of policing practiced by Detective Sipowicz on *NYPD Blue*, where the end always justifies the means, cannot be tolerated." William Bratton, "The Legacy of Detective Sipowicz," *Time*, 6 March 2000.

9. A fuller slice: "For me, democracy is a patent delusion. It's an ideal, but this society is far from democratic, nor can it be . . . the reason I revile lawyers is they exploit the obvious and easily exploited difference between myth and fact . . . the Constitution victimizes people who are law-abiding by making available to lawyers these fictions. That everyone needs their Miranda rights, that everyone needs fair representation. That's bullshit. Monsters don't deserve any of that stuff. And cops are hired by society to gloss over that." Milch, in his interview with Laura Schiff, "Maestro in Blue," *Creative Screenwriting* 4 (Winter 1977): 6. Milch's first script for *Hill Street Blues*, which earned a prior HUMANITAS prize, also concerned a coerced confession: see Gerald E. Foshey, "Trial by Fury: David Milch's Breakthough Spec-Script," *Creative Screenwriting* (Winter 1977): 11–20. Simon's *Homicide* also contains an excellent discussion of police deception in which he, too, calls *Miranda* "a symbol and little more, a salve for a collective conscience that cannot reconcile libertarian ideals with what must necessarily occur in a police interrogation room" (70).

10. As qtd. in Kathyrn Eigen, "'NYPD Blue' Producer Talks Crime," *Yale Daily News*, 24 October 1996.

11. Milch, in the Schiff interview, "Maestro in Blue."

12. See Peter Brooks, *Troubling Confessions* (Chicago: University of Chicago Press, 2000), and John Conroy, *Unspeakable Acts, Ordinary People* (New York: Knopf, 2000).

13. For the debate over *Miranda*'s legal implications, see, for instance, *The Miranda Debate: Law, Justice, and Policing*, ed. Richard A. Leo and George G. Thomas III (Boston: Northeastern University Press, 1998).

14. For excellent analyses in this vein, see B. Keith Crew, "Acting like Cops: The Social Reality of Crime and Law on TV Police Dramas," in *Marginal Conventions*, ed. Clinton R. Sanders (Bowling Green, OH: Bowling Green University Popular Press, 1990): 131–43; Rapping, *Law and Justice as Seen on TV*, 236–51; Robin Anderson, "'Reality' TV and Criminal Justice," *The Humanist* (September/October 1994): 8–13. See also Rapping's discussion of the ideological confusion behind the prison series *OZ*, 88ff.

15. Robert Handt, "Articulation Theory and Public Controversy: Taking Sides over *NYPD Blue*," *Critical Studies in Mass Communication* 14 (1997): 1–30.

16. Some twenty-five years in existence, the HUMANITAS prizes were launched by Catholic priest and producer of Paulist Productions, Father Ellwood Kieser. See Jack Wintz, O.F.M., "The Humanitas Prize: Encouraging Hollywood's Best," *St. Anthony Messenger*, 10 May 2001, http://www.americancatholic.org/Messenger/Nov1999/feature1.asp (accessed 15 December 2009). For Dick Wolf's views on the Brady bill, see his "Ratings for Content or Control," *Los Angeles Times*, 4 August 1997.

17. In one content analysis, *NYPD Blue* showed an average of 2.7 civil rights violations per episode. These violations were relatively evenly distributed: the failure to give a Miranda warning, physical abuse, and promises of leniency. See Sarah Eschholz, Matthew Mallard, and Stacey Flynn, "Images of Prime Time Justice: A Content Analysis of 'NYPD Blue' and 'Law & Order,'" *Journal of Criminal Justice and Popular Culture* 10 (2003–4): 172. Compare Susan Bandes and Jack Beermann, who also focus on Miranda violations on this series. These law professors argue that the principal objective of an *NYPD Blue* interrogation is to have the suspect avoid "lawyering up"—as it were, getting "to" the "I did it." "Lawyering Up," Tarlton Law Library, Law in Popular Culture Collection, http://tarlton.law.utexas.edu/lpop/etext/bandes.htm (accessed 16 December 2009).

18. David Milch and Det. Bill Clark, *True Blue: The Real Stories Behind NYPD Blue* (New York: Morrow, 1995); hereafter cited in text. As in my first chapter, I rely here on Stone, "Collaboration in Contemporary American Autobiography."

19. See my discussion of the film version of *The Naked City* that established the basis of these TV series, in *Cop Knowledge*, 57–93.

20. See Peter Maas, *Serpico: The Cop Who Defied the System* (1973; rpt. New York: HarperCollins, 1997), 22.

21. For an overview of the "rapid response" model in policing, see Robert Fogelson, *Big-City Police* (Cambridge, MA: Harvard University Press, 1977), 219–42. On the popular-cultural connections to this ethos, see esp. Richard Gid Powers, *G-Men: Hoover's FBI and American Popular Culture* (Carbondale: Southern Illinois University Press, 1983), and Potter, *War on Crime*.

22. On police pay, see Fogelson, *Big-City Police*, 205ff., 278–79.

23. In the early 1930s, the "third degree" had been the subject of the famous Wickersham Report. Subsequently, in Richard Leo's estimation, it appears to have declined through the 1940s and 1950s. See The National Commission on Law Observance and Enforcement, *Report on Police*, no. 14 (Washington, DC: U.S. Government Printing Office, 1931). For a fuller discussion of this historical context, see Richard A. Leo, *Police Interrogation and American Justice* (Cambridge, MA: Harvard University Press, 2008), esp. 41–77. Contrast, however, the depiction in a noir film like "Murder, My Sweet" (1944). In many episodes of *The Naked City*—see, for example, "The Sweetly Smiling Face of Truth," airing 25 April 1962—suspects merely had "statements" taken with a stenographer present.

24. On this contradiction, see Frances Fox Piven, "The Urban Crisis: Who Got What, and Why," in *The Politics of Turmoil: Essays on Poverty, Race, and the Urban Crisis*, ed. Richard A. Cloward and Frances Fox Piven (New York: Pantheon, 1974), 314–51. More-

over, Robert Moses's leadership had resulted in "redevelopment" tilted largely in favor of middle- and working-class whites at the expense of the poor and the nonwhite. Norman I. Fainstein and Susan S. Fainstein, "Governing Regimes and the Political Economy of Development in New York City, 1946–1984," in *Power, Culture, and Place: Essays on New York City*, ed. John Hull Mollenkopf (New York: Russell Sage Foundation, 1988), 161–99.

25. Police precincts on TV are commonly more diverse than in real life: contrast Landrum, "Instrumental Texts and Stereotyping in *Hill Street Blues*," with James Barron, "Survey Places New York Police Last in Hiring of Black Officers," *New York Times*, 8 October 1992. The earliest description of this ethos of police "minorityism" can be found in Joseph Gerald Woods, "The Progressives and the Police: Urban Reform and the Professionalization of the Los Angeles Police Department" (PhD diss., UCLA, 1973), 481.

On the isolation of the PBA in the context of diminished machine power, see esp. Fogelson, *Big-City Police*, 199–200. See also the comments on the precinct as a boss system, in the interview with Commissioner Murphy by Frederick O'R. Hayes in *New York Affairs* 2 (1974): 88–111. Compare the description of sergeants' power in Jonathan Rubenstein, *City Police* (New York: Farrar, Straus and Giroux, 1973), 395–96.

26. Contrast the Supreme Court ruling in *Dickerson v. United States* (2000), which suggested to many that the recitation of Miranda principles on TV had embedded the procedure in our national consciousness.

27. *The Knapp Commission Report on Police Corruption* (1972; rpt. New York: George Braziller, 1976); subsequent quotations in text. See also Murphy's comments to Hayes, 92.

28. I discuss this climate in *Cop Knowledge*, 142ff. On the "nothing works" lament, see Jerome Skolnick, *The New Blue Line: Police Innovation in Six American Cities* (New York: Free Press, 1986), 4–5; and Jack Greene, "Foot Patrol and Community Policing: Past Practices and Future Prospects," *American Journal of Police* 6 (1987): 1–16.

29. Part of the rationale against committing detective division resources to vice policing was that so few gambling or numbers "round ups" led to convictions, much less jail time. In 1970, for example, there were more than 9,000 arrests in New York for common gambling; only seventy people went to jail. See Jonathan Rubenstein, *City Police* (New York: Farrar, Straus and Giroux, 1973), 378. And in addition to the reaction against undercover work—which I discuss in chapter 3—eyewitnesses and confessions were, for a time, thought to be much more effective in leading to successful prosecutions than extensive detective work. See Peter W. Greenwood, *The RAND Criminal Investigation Study: Its Findings and Impacts to Date* (RAND Corporation, July 1979). On the long-term impact of the RAND findings and other social science investigations of these years, see *Cop Knowledge*, 141–48.

30. This corporate emphasis itself reinforced the idea of using internal informants, much as I have suggested (in chapter 1) that they were used for fighting organized crime. That is, the Knapp Report hoped to create a climate where police managers could more easily enlist a former offender's help to break through the precinct-based code of silence. The report thus recommended against unduly punishing cooperating former offenders. The report argued, in fact, that they should be allowed to resign from the force in good standing (23–24).

31. On these cuts, see James Lardner and Thomas Repetto, *NYPD: A City and Its Police* (New York: Henry Holt and Company, 2000), 278–80.

32. Arthur Niederhoffer, *Behind the Shield: The Police in Urban Society* (Garden City, NY: Anchor Books, 1967), 85.

33. See, again, Murphy's comments to Hayes, *The Knapp Commission Report*, 103.

On the LEAA's focus, see Malcolm W. Feeley and Jonathan Simon, "Actuarial Justice: The Emerging New Criminal Law," in David Nelkin, ed., *The Futures of Criminology* (London: Sage Publications, 1994), 173–201.

34. Bratton's renovations, as well as the controversies over his success, are well summarized in Peter K. Manning, "Theorizing Policing: The Drama and Myth of Crime Control and the NYPD," *Theoretical Criminology* 5 (2001), esp. 319–24. As to working under Bratton, see the account in Edward Conlon, *Blue Blood* (New York: Riverhead Books, 2004), 275.

35. See Bratton, "The Legacy of Detective Sipowicz."

36. See James Lardner's portrait of Bratton, "The C.E.O. Cop," *New Yorker,* 6 February 1995, 45–57. On the aggressive policies at work here, see Lardner and Repetto, *NYPD,* 319; Mastrofski, "The Prospects of Change in Police Patrol"; and Greene, "Foot Patrol and Community Policing." On speeding up warrants, see Conlon, *Blue Blood,* 417; Conlon is the cop quoted on running for warrants, 13, 79.

37. On the centrality of "intelligence gathering" to Bratton's approach, see George L. Kelling and Catherine M. Coles, *Fixing Broken Windows* (New York: Touchstone, 1997). See Scarry's dismissal of the idea that torture is motivated by seeking information, *The Body in Pain,* 28ff.

38. Richard A. Leo, "From Coercion to Deception: The Changing Nature of Police Interrogation in America," *Crime, Law and Social Change* 18 (1992): 35–59; Richard A. Leo and Welsh A. White, "Adapting to *Miranda:* Modern Interrogators' Strategies for Dealing with the Obstacles Posed by *Miranda,*" *Minnesota Law Review* 84 (December 1999): 398–472; and Jerome H. Skolnick, "Deception by Police," *Criminal Justice Ethics* 1 (Summer/Fall 1982): 40–54.

39. Debra Young, "Unnecessary Evil: Police Lying in Interrogations," *Connecticut Law Review* 28 (Winter 1996): 425–77. Leo and White ("Adapting to *Miranda*") also offer a full rendering of this battery of tactics.

40. That visit is described in *True Blue,* 136.

41. "Box in a box" as described in Bourdieu, *The Field of Cultural Production,* 37–38.

42. As one can see from Jimmy Breslin, *I Want to Thank My Brain for Remembering Me* (Boston: Little, Brown, 1996), 123–25, the columnist promoted Clark as the investigator who broke the Son of Sam case; the overlooked cop Dom Carillo in Breslin and Schaap's fictional account of the case, *.44,* may well be based on Clark.

43. On these strategies in Lansky's career, see Albert Fried, *The Rise and Fall of the Jewish Gangster in America* (New York: Holt, Rinehart and Winston, 1980), 238ff.

44. Warren on the high function of technique in Robert Penn Warren, "The Unity of Experience." Originally in *Commentary* (1965); reprinted in *Ralph Ellison: A Collection of Critical Essays,* ed. John Hersey (Englewood Cliffs, NJ: Prentice-Hall, 1965), 21. On these traditions in Romantic aesthetics, see Raymond Williams, *Culture and Society, 1780–1950* (1958; rpt. Edinburgh: R. R. Clark, 1961); and David Lloyd and Paul Thomas, *Culture and the State* (London: Routledge, 1998); subsequent citation in text.

45. On the rhetoric of the poet-critic, see James S. Leonard and Christine E. Wharton, "Breaking the Silence: Collaboration and the Isolationist Paradigm," *Author-ity and Textuality: Current Views of Collaborative Writing,* ed. James S. Leonard et al. (West Cornwall, CT: Locust Hill Press, 1994), 28.

46. The repudiation of Vietnam-style militarization is a common theme of neoconservative advocacy of police reforms; see Wilson, *Thinking about Crime,* 84–85; Kelling and Coles.

47. By "un-alienating" I mean a narrative assertion of humanity and effectiveness that

restores the police's place among a public or a political system that often disowns them. See *Cop Knowledge,* 57–93.

48. The impact of Clark's own experience is evident here. As the *New York Times* told it, "He joined the police force in 1969; his first assignment—even before he attended the Police Academy—was to infiltrate the Young Patriots, an organization of white radicals who, he soon discovered, were planning to bomb several New York landmarks." Andy Meisler, "Out of N.Y.P.D., Into 'NYPD Blue,'" *New York Times,* 7 November 1995.

49. See my discussion of the con game and "belief" in chapter 4.

50. This impulse is famously described by Jerome H. Skolnick, *Justice Without Trial* (New York: Wiley, 1966).

51. On this ethos in film, see Susan Jeffords and Lauren Rabinovitz, eds., *Seeing Through the Media: The Persian Gulf War* (New Brunswick, NJ: Rutgers University Press, 1994). On the Vietnam ethos in police culture in the 1960s, see *Cop Knowledge,* 94ff.

52. Landrum, "Instrumental Texts and Stereotyping in *Hill Street Blues,*" 99.

53. See note 25 above.

54. On this broader controversy, see Verne Gay, "NYPD Blue Embroiled in Another Controversy: This Time It's Racism," *New York Newsday,* 14 November 1994; Greg Braxon, "'NYPD' Figure tries to Clarify Race Remarks," *Los Angeles Times,* 10 November 1994; and Ellen Edwards, "Black and 'NYPD Blue,'" *Washington Post,* 4 November 1994.

55. The latter analogy is not mine; rather it comes from Nathanael West, "Some Notes on Violence," *Contact* 1 (October 1932): 132.

56. When Milch took to illustrating in interviews what he meant by a cop's "exclusionary rhetoric," he pointed to those moments when detectives, describing perpetrators they had arrested, resorted to hand signals to identify the racial category of such suspects. Milch describes this technique in his interview with Schiff: "A lot of times they don't speak at all. A cop will be telling a story and say, 'I collared the perpetrator. [Milch passes the palm of his hand in front of his face as he speaks.]' What that means is he was black. That's a gesture that means black, so the cop doesn't have to be accused of being a racist. Or he'll say—[Milch touches two fingers to his left shoulder.]—'I collared the perpetrator.' Two—putting two fingers on your body—is another way of saying black, because when you make out an arrest form, one is Caucasian, two is black, and three is Puerto Rican. So those are all protective gestures." Schiff, "Maestro in Blue," 6; brackets in original.

57. As qtd. in Schiff, "Maestro in Blue," 10.

58. On this Romantic tradition regarding "Fancy," see Williams, *Culture and Society 1780–1950,* 104–7.

59. See William Ian Miller, "Clint Eastwood and Equity: Popular Culture's Theory of Revenge," in *Law in the Domains of Culture,* ed. Austin Sarat and Thomas R. Kearns (Ann Arbor: University of Michigan Press, 1998), 161–202.

60. Cf. Scarry, *The Body in Pain,* 57.

Chapter 3

1. Isaac Bashevis Singer, "A Crown of Feathers," in *The Collected Stories of Isaac Bashevis Singer* (New York: Farrar, Straus and Giroux, 1982), 352–71. This story is translated by the author and Laurie Colwin.

2. Philip Gourevitch, *A Cold Case* (New York: Farrar, Straus and Giroux, 2001). Singer quoted on 129, 133; "speaks for the dead" from 21. All further citations in text.

3. Bill McCay, *Tom Clancy's Net Force: Cold Case* (New York: Berkeley Jam Books, 2001). The other titles were Stephen White, *Cold Case* (2001 rpt.; New York: E. P. Dutton, 1999), and Linda Barnes, *Cold Case* (New York: Delacorte, 1997). Sue Grafton's *Q is for Quarry* (2002) is also a cold case mystery, as is Robert Parker's *Back Story* (2003).

4. On Stiehm's background, see note 24 below.

5. Hosted by Richard Crenna, this show was coordinated between a Glendale, California, police officer and an Irvine-based Internet service. See "Web Site Plays Key Role in Quantity and Quality of Show's Leads, Says CBS Cold-Case Co-Producer," *Business Wire*, 12 May 1997. See also "Epoch Networks and CBS Producers Create Web Site for First Interactive Reality-Based Television Program," *Business Wire*, 12 March 1997. A live-action crime-stoppers show, *America's Most Wanted*, had likewise become entwined in James Ellroy's own storyline.

6. As one example of this union, see John Ellement, "Boston's Cold Case Squad Hails Mother's Love in Breaking Case [of] Fugitive Who Fled Country," *Boston Globe*, 31 October 1995. The victim Web sites are well known: see, for instance, the Web site for Martha Moxley at http://marthamoxley.com (accessed 29 December 2009). By "victim circle" I follow the conventional meaning, referring to those closely associated with and including the victim of crimes.

7. A classic formulation of this ethos is Hillary Waugh, "The Human Rather than the Superhuman Sleuth," in *The Murder Mystique: Crime Writes on Their Art*, ed. Lucy Freeman (New York: Frederick Ungar, 1982).

8. On the symbolic effects of material police work, see. Ian Loader, "Policing and the Social: Questions of Symbolic Power," *British Journal of Sociology* 48 (March 1977): 1–18.

9. See my Introduction, 9–10.

10. See my Introduction, 15–16.

11. The relevance of this idea to the extension of *prison* time is not at all coincidental: as I will argue in chapter 5, advocates of prison incapacitation made a similar argument about the supposed forseeable effects of confinement in the prison itself.

12. *CSI* and other shows, for instance, often feature a rapid fingerprint, DNA, or photographic database that "scans" available records and then almost instantaneously signals a "match." In fact, many conservatives resist the integration (or federalization) of such records, particularly around firearms; the speed of return is greatly exaggerated; the word *match* is rarely used by such experts. See Toobin, "The 'CSI' Effect."

13. Soliah was convicted in a Symbionese Liberation Army bomb conspiracy. See James Sterngold, "Waffling Again, 70's Radical Asks to Change Guilty Plea," *New York Times*, 15 November 2001. On other cases, see Major Mike Richmond, "OSI Cold Cases Become 'Hot' Topic," and Lisa Prevost, "Greenwich's Other Murder: 1984 Case Reopened Amid Spotlight on Moxley Slaying," both from the Moxley Web site. That site attributes Prevost's article to the *Boston Globe*, 1 April 2001.

14. James Ellroy, *My Dark Places* (New York: Knopf, 1996).

15. John Ellement, "Unsolved Crimes Get a Fresh Look," *Boston Globe*, 28 February 1992. As Savoye notes, special squads still raise the prospect of elitism and internal second-guessing, reviving long-standing associations of detectives with Internal Affairs. Craig Savoye, "Across US, a Police Push to Solve Old Crimes," *Christian Science Monitor*, 5 February 2001.

16. Charles L. Regini, "The Cold Case Concept," *FBI Law Enforcement Bulletin* 66 (August 1997), http://www.fbi.gov/publications/leb/1997/aug971.htm (accessed 1 January 2010). Subsequent citations in text.

17. See Ellroy, *My Dark Places*, 193. See also Stefani G. Kopenec, "High-Tech Heats Up Cold Case Trails," *Los Angeles Times*, 19 November 1995.

18. See Regini, "The Cold Case Concept," and Brian MacQuarrie, "4 Years After Murder, Squad Makes a Cold Case Hot," *Boston Globe*, 8 October 1997.

19. The NYPD story is told in Stacy Horn, *The Restless Sleep: Inside New York City's Cold Case Squad* (New York: Viking Penguin, 2005), 14–23.

20. Matt Bai, "Cold Case Confidential," *Newsweek*, 12 January 1998, 70; Stewart Ain, "Nassau's Cold Case Squad Picks Up Chase," *New York Times*, 21 November 1999. See also Savoye, "Across US, a Police Push to Solve Old Crimes."

21. And thus even in those early days, the Boston department was clearly cooperating with federal agencies such as the IRS or the FBI's Violent Fugitive Task Force. A startup date of 1991 is used by Ellement in "Unsolved Crimes Get a Fresh Look." See also the reference in "Fugitive Convicted after 13 Years," *Boston Globe*, 10 November 1995, and John Ellement, "'Cold Case' Squad Finds Man Sought in '82 Killing," *Boston Globe*, 12 April 1994; Brian McGrory, "Fugitive in '67 Murder Is Tracked to Md. by Cold Case Squad, Arrested," *Boston Globe*, 29 April 1994.

22. See "No Bail for Man 26 Years on Run," *Boston Globe*, 19 May 1994. For another case, see Brian MacQuarrie, "4 Years after Murder, Squad Makes a Cold Case Hot," *Boston Globe*, 8 October 1997.

23. These characterizations are taken from Ronald Smothers, "The Heirs of Holmes, Hot on the Trail," *New York Times*, December 2, 1997; and Kopenec, "High-Tech Heats Up Cold Case Trails." One also thinks of recent science fiction films like *Time Cop* (1994), in which a cop eventually averts his own wife's murder in the past, or the television series *Seven Days* (1998); *Journeyman* (2007); *Waking the Dead* (2001–9); and the British and U.S. versions of *Life on Mars* (U.K., 2006–7, and U.S., 2008–9). Christopher Nolan's *Memento* (2000) is also relevant here: Nolan's protagonist, Lennie, has no short-term memory at all; thus the crime he believes he avenges is ever-present to him.

24. Information on Stiehm's show from Saranne Miller, "Hit CBS Television Show, Based in Philadelphia, Makes Its Way to Roxborough," *Roxborough Review* (roxREVIEW.com), 19 January 2005; Rob Owen, "TV Preview: CBS's 'Cold Case' Smokes the Competition," *Pittsburgh Post-Gazette*, 22 August 2004; Susan Littwin, "In the Company of Women: Five Who Run Hit Shows at CBS," *Written By*, November 2004, http://www.wga.org/writtenby/writtenbysub.aspx?id=831 (accessed 2 January 2010); Malcolm Knox, "Chill Factor: *Cold Case* Creator Meredith Stiehm Speaks Through Her Drama," *The Age*, 9 September 2004, http://www.theage.com.au/articles/2004/09/08/1094530677311.html (accessed 2 January 2010).

25. For examples of local coverage of these squads, see Oscar Corral, "Heat on Cold Case," *Newsday* (New York), 20 September 1999; Gary Oakes and Cal Millar, "'Cold Case' Detectives Investigate 3rd Slaying," *Toronto Star*, 19 May 1997; Brent LaLonde, "Special Homicide Squad Is Revived," *Columbus Dispatch*, 21 November 1996; S. K. Bardwell, "Incidence of Homicide Continues to Fall Off; Decline Allows Police to Redirect Resources," *Houston Chronicle*, 1 January 2000; S. K. Bardwell, "Arrest Comes 20 Years after Woman Found Dead," *Houston Chronicle*, 30 June 2001.

26. Letter from James J. Green, "Not Much Pressure in Chasing Cold Cases," *New York Times*, 5 December 1999. This artisanal ethos is famously discussed in Jerome Skolnick, *Justice Without Trial: Law Enforcement in Democratic Society* (New York: John Wiley & Sons, 1966).

27. For example, see Tatsha Robertson, "Cold Case Turns Up Suspect in '76 Murder," *Boston Globe*, 7 January 2000.

28. Mike Barnicle, "The Cracking of a Cold Case," *Boston Globe*, 19 March 1992.
29. Ellement, "Unsolved Crimes Get a Fresh Look."
30. The crime wave at the heart of 1960s affluence is a commonplace in neoconservative criminology: see Wilson, *Thinking about Crime*.
31. Steven Levingston, "On the Trail of a Killer," *Boston Globe Magazine*, 8 December 1996.
32. The divergent roots of the movement are well laid out in Weed, *Certainty of Justice*. See also Bruce Shapiro, "Victims and Vengeance: Why the Victims' Rights Amendment Is a Bad Idea," *The Nation*, 10 February 1997, 11–17.
33. On this effect of victimization surveys, see John Kotre, *White Gloves: How We Create Ourselves Through Memory* (New York: Free Press, 1995), 107.
34. See Weed, *Certainty of Justice*, following Lawrence Friedman, on victims and "rights consciousness," 21ff. The preference for victimization surveys (over the Uniform Crime reports) in neoconservative criminology is again relevant here; see Wilson, *Thinking about Crime*, 66–68.
35. See Weed, *Certainty of Justice*, 32, and Nils Christie, "Conflict as Property," in *Perspectives on Crime Victims*, ed. Burt Galaway and Joe Hudson (St. Louis: C. V. Mosby Co., 1981), 234–44. For Rhodes's advocacy, see *The Insoluble Problems of Crime*, 179ff.
36. Paul Gewirtz, "Victims and Voyeurs: Two Narrative Problems at the Criminal Trial," in *Law's Stories: Narrative and Rhetoric in the Law*, ed. Paul Gewirtz and Peter Brooks (New Haven, CT: Yale University Press, 1996), 135–64; quote from 142.
37. In Levingston's story, for instance, the cold case squad in fact refuses to say how it broke the case (on the grounds it doesn't want to show its methods to other fugitives).
38. See Kopenec, "High-Tech Heats Up Cold Case Trails."
39. Regini, "The Cold Case Concept," emphasis mine; Simon, *Homicide*, 70.
40. This reversal was underscored by the Boston detective Richard Nagle, quoted in MacQuarrie, "4 Years After Murder, Squad Makes a Cold Case Hot": "We had to go out and re-interview a lot of people, some of whom weren't as reticent as they once were."
41. As quoted in Ain, "Nassau's Cold Case Squad Picks Up Chase."
42. This is certainly the casting in Ellement, "Unsolved Crimes Get a Fresh Look."
43. Regini, "The Cold Case Concept," emphasis mine. This point was reaffirmed in the Bureau of Justice Assistance pamphlet, *Cold Case Squads: Leaving No Stone Unturned* (Washington, DC: BJA, 2003), 5. This pamphlet also makes clear that administrative "vetting" of resource management was central to the strategy, and that, as of 2003 the BJA no longer "helped police departments form Cold Case squads," but directed its assistance to "cases that involve gangs and drugs" (4).
44. See Curriden, "Making Crime Pay," 42; Lehr, "The Information Underworld"; and the PBS *Frontline* report "Snitch."
45. I am thinking here of the patterns in the drug war described in Michael Massing's *The Fix* (New York: Simon & Schuster, 1996). And it should be added that, as Barnicle's rendering shows, a racial subtext often present in the idea of a cold case squad "freed" from local political pressure.
46. On these conventions in True Crime, see *Cop Knowledge*, esp. 130–68. In one interview Gourevitch confesses to this parallel. Asked whether he identified with Detective Rosenzweig, he said that for all their differences, "there was a great deal in common in the sort of obsessive, investigative, needling, relentless nature of the work that we do . . ."; the author also compared *A Cold Case* to his own investigative work in Rwanda, resulting in the harrowing *We Wish to Inform You That Tomorrow We Will Be Killed with Our Families* (New York: Farrar, Straus and Giroux, 1998). The comparison is made in Sage Stossel, "A Tale of Two Murders," *Atlantic Unbound*, 1 August 2001.

47. For these tastes on Serpico's part, see Maas, *Serpico*, 22.
48. See esp. Jerry Knight, "The Gumshoe Gets Wiingtips: Private-Investigator Business Takes on a Corporate Identity," *Washington Post*, 21 Aug. 1997; The screenwriter for *The Naked City*, Malvin Wald, had himself apprenticed under Robert Flaherty, writing World War II training documentaries. See his afterword to *The Naked City*, ed. Matthew Bruccoli (Carbondale: Southern Illinois University Press, 1979), 136–37.
49. On this lament, see esp. Skolnick, *Justice Without Trial*.
50. I refer here to the no-doubt unintentional—unless the name is a fiction—allusion to Dan Cody in Fitzgerald's novel. On the disruptions in police authority in the 1960s, and their mythologizing in recent criminology, see Samuel Walker, "'Broken Windows' and Fractured History: The Use and Misuse of History in Recent Police Patrol Analysis," *Justice Quarterly* 1 (1984): 75–90.
51. We might call this a "disarticulated" reference to racial tension. On articulation in cultural discourse—as a matter of stressing discursive or ideological correspondences—see Jennifer Daryl Slack, "The Theory and Method of Articulation in Cultural Studies," in *Stuart Hall: Critical Dialogues in Cultural Studies*, ed. David Morley and Kuan-Hsing Chen (London: Routledge, 1996), 112–30.
52. See Kotre, *White Gloves*, 36.
53. Lauren Berlant, *The Queen of America Goes to Washington City: Essays on Sex and Citizenship* (Durham, NC: Duke University Press, 1997), esp. 25–53.
54. Dennis McAuliffe, *Bloodland: A Family Story of Oil, Greed and Murder on the Osage Reservation* (San Francisco: Council Oaks Books, 1999); originally published as *The Death of Sylvia Bolton* (1994).
55. However, as Ochoa and Wistrich write in comparing civil to criminal case remedies, "evidence regarding remedies sometimes improves as time passes. It is generally more difficult to predict the future than to reconstruct the past. In a personal injury case, the extent of the plaintiff's impairment will be an important question." Tyler T. Ochoa and Andrew J. Wistrich, "The Puzzling Purposes of Statutes of Limitation," *Pace Law Journal* 28 (Spring 1997): 453–514; quote from 477. For the place of precisely this kind of reasoning in the victims' rights movement, see Shapiro's account of MADD proponent Janice Harris Lord's testimony at a crime victims' conference in 1996.
56. For the implementation of this "rational" choice-making model into the processes of law enforcement, see esp. Wilson, *Thinking about Crime*, 128–46; contrast *Cop Knowledge*, 179–81.
57. See Ochoa and Wistrich, 471, 464, and passim. Cf. Amy Dunn, "Statutes of Limitation on Sexual Assault Crimes: Has the Availability of DNA Evidence Rendered Them Obsolete?" *University of Arkansas at Little Rock Law Review* 23 (Spring 2001): 839–68; Walter Olson, "Stale Claims," *Reason* 32 (November 2000), http://reason.com/0011/co.wo.stale.shtml (accessed 2 January 2010); Suzanne M. Knight, "Rights for the Rape Victim: Lifting Statute of Limitations for Prosecution of Violent Crimes," *Buffalo Women's Law Journal* 8 (1999/2000): 11–12.
58. J. Anthony Chavez, "Statutes of Limitations and the Right to a Fair Trial: When Is a Crime Complete," *Criminal Justice* 10 (Summer 1995): 2–6, 48–51. On these "Son of Sam" laws, see chapter 1, note 67.
59. See, for instance, the cases discussed in Bai, "Cold Case Confidential." And while Gourevitch ends by showing us the gratitude of Glennon's daughter (173), a rumination of Officer Rosenzweig's own seems to cut in a different direction. "What's funny is I got into [this case]" the cop says, "because . . . I was thinking especially that I wanted to put it to rest for the victims' families and survivors. The thing I didn't think about was that many of them had long ago found their own ways of dealing with it. So while I was going

for closure, I was just re-opening it for these people. My idea of laying it to rest was their idea of an upheaval" (174).

60. On changes in the urban landscape, see David Harvey, *Spaces of Hope* (Berkeley: University of California Press, 2000). On "vigil," see *A New English Dictionary of Historical Principles* (Oxford: Clarendon Press, 1928), Vol. X , Part II, 197, definitions 4 and 5.

Chapter 4

1. I refer here to the Vidocq Society organized in Philadelphia in 1990. See Lewis Beale, "To Catch a Killer," *Los Angeles Times*, 13 May 1992; David Kinney, "Sleuth Society Helps Crack Unsolved Cases," *Ottawa Citizen*, 29 May 1998; Ronald Smothers, "The Heirs of Holmes, Hot on the Trail," *New York Times*, 2 December 1997; and Alison Motluk, "Shallow Grave," *New Scientist*, 29 April 2000, 26.

2. See esp. Michel Foucault, *Discipline and Punish: The Birth of the Prison*, trans. Alan Sheridan (New York: Vintage Books, 1979), 283ff.

3. Typical examples: the ways that we see J. Edgar Hoover's use of criminal informants as fully compatible with the style of the national security state, and the prison-industrial complex as akin to the military. On Hoover and mid-century national security, including COINTELPRO, see Powers, *Secrecy and Power*, 228–74. Potter is especially insightful on Hoover's use of the New Deal's ethos of centralized authority; see *War on Crime*, 118ff.

4. Paul Magnusson, "Your Jitters Are Their Lifeblood: Corporate Security Advisers Are in Demand," *Business Week*, 14 April 2003: 41. See also Ann Brown, "Security Sweep," *Black Enterprise* 27 (1997): 33.

5. On these developments, see Jerry Knight, "The Gumshoe Gets Wingtips: Private-Investigator Business Takes on a Corporate Identity," *Washington Post*, 12 August 1997; Steve Lohr, "In New Era, Corporate Security Goes beyond Guns and Badges," *New York Times*, 27 May 2002.

6. Invaluable efforts to rethink the family tree of detective genres include Marcus Klein, *Easterns, Westerns, and Private Eyes: American Matters 1870–1900* (Madison: University of Wisconsin Press, 1994; Michael Denning, *Mechanic Accents: Dime Novels and Working-Class Culture* (New York: Verso, 1998); and Richard Slotkin, *Gunfighter Nation: The Myth of the Frontier in Twentieth-Century America* (Norman: University of Oklahoma Press, 1998). I attempt to rethink these origins myself in "Rough Justice: Crime, Corruption, and Urban Governance," in *U.S. Popular Print Culture 1860–1920*, ed. Christine Bold (Oxford: Oxford University Press, forthcoming).

7. Frank W. Abagnale Jr. with Stan Redding, *Catch Me If You Can: The Amazing True Story of the Youngest and Most Daring Con Man in the History of Fun and Profit* (1980; rpt. New York: Broadway Books, 2000). I will also quote from Frank W. Abagnale Jr., *The Art of the Steal* (New York: Broadway Books, 2001); my chapter epigraph from 16.

8. Abagnale later admitted that key elements of the book were embellished, overdramatized, and simply invented. Jeff Nathanson's movie script apparently took even more liberties. See Andy Seiler, "Here's the Catch: True Tale Isn't," *USA Today*, 23 December 2002; Stephen Schaefer, "Former Con Man Catches a Few Fallacies in Film Bio," *Boston Herald*, 24 December 2001.

9. On Abagnale's career, see Ken Clark, "Preventive Medicine: Can Corporations Find a Hollywood Ending for Fraud?" *Chain Store Age* 79 (2003): 74; and Kathleen Sampey, "Former Thief Helps Retailer Build Trust," *Adweek*, 23 October 2006, 9.

10. This dimension—that Hanratty was a surrogate father for Abagnale—runs through Spielberg's comments in the filmbook of *Catch Me If You Can*, ed. Linda Sunshine (New York: Newmarket Press, 2002).

11. The problem in part is definitional: see Sean Patrick Griffin, "Actors or Activities? On the Social Construction of 'White-Collar Crime' in the United States," *Crime, Law and Social Change* 37 (April 2002): 245–76. For a review of the scholarship, see Michael Levi, "The Media Construction of Financial White-Collar Crimes," *British Journal of Criminology* 46 (2006): 1037–57. For a very comprehensive reading of *Catch Me If You Can* that deals with this traditional complaint in a different way, see Rodanthi Tzanelli, Majid Yar, and Martin O'Brien, "'Con Me If You Can': Exploring Crime in the American Cinematic Imagination," *Theoretical Criminology* 9 (February 2005): 97–117.

12. This was a story of an "innocent," director Spielberg repeatedly said, in an "innocent" decade. See Spielberg's comments in the filmbook of *Catch Me If You Can*.

13. On this reciprocity, I am indebted to Ian Loader, "Thinking Normatively about Private Security," *Journal of Law and Society* 24 (September 1997): 377–94; see also Loader's "Consumer Culture and the Commodification of Policing and Security."

14. Vidocq's evolution from informant to detective was built around a realization much like Abagnale's: that, as the Frenchman put it in his memoir, "the future was too dependent on the past"—that he must use his criminal associations as a police asset. Qtd. (in translation) in James Morton, *The First Detective: The Life and Revolutionary Times of Vidocq* (London: Ebury Press, 2004), 107. In *The Art of the Steal*, Abagnale writes, "In a certain sense, I'm still a con artist. I'm just putting down a positive con these days. . . . I've merely redirected the talents I've always possessed" (17).

15. Shearing and Stenning have been especially effective in showing how private security is focused upon "breaches" in existing security, and upon sustaining profit margins or competitive edges, rather than catching criminals in or after the act; moreover, this means preemptively sifting out employees that might contribute to such "breaches." Cf. Shearing and Stenning, "Modern Private Security"; Stanko, "Victims R Us," also credits the LEAA (15) for purveying a similar ethos.

16. For useful descriptions of the literary con man, see Gary H. Lindberg, *The Confidence Man in American Literature* (New York: Oxford University Press, 1982); and William E. Lenz, *Fast Talk and Flush Times: The Confidence Man as a Literary Convention* (Columbia: University of Missouri Press, 1985), esp. 75, 95.

17. Karen Haltunnen, *Confidence Men and Painted Women* (New Haven, CT: Yale University Press, 1982); see also Larry Cebula, "A Counterfeit Identity: The Notorious Life of Stephen Burroughs," *The Historian* 64 (Winter 2002): 317–33.

18. Demara was also the subject of an "as told to" biography by Robert Crichton, *The Great Imposter* (New York: Random House, 1959). See also his obituary, "Ferdinand Waldo Demara, 60, An Imposter in Varied Fields," *New York Times,* 9 June 1982, or "Fake Surgeon a Success," *New York Times,* 21 November 1951.

19. I discuss this reciprocity between professional policing and con men in relation to Ed McBain's *Con Man* (1956) in *Cop Knowledge*, 57–93.

20. Past generations of scholarship polished Flynt's contradictions or "dual existence" into an image of the "first muckraker": see, for example, Louis Filler, *The Muckrakers* (University Park: Pennsylvania State University Press, 1976), 71. More recently he has been analyzed as a forerunner of participant-observer sociology and even "immersion" journalism: see esp. Rolf Lindner, *The Reportage of Urban Culture: Robert Park and the Chicago School,* trans. Adrian Morris (New York: Cambridge University Press, 1996), and Jeremy Schocket, "Undercover Explorations of the 'Other Half'; or, The Writer as Class Transvestite," *Representations* 64 (Fall 1998): 109–33. My primary sources here

are Josiah Flynt, *My Life* (New York: Outing Publishing Co., 1908), hereafter as *ML*; and Josiah Flynt, *Tramping with Tramps: Studies and Sketches of Vagabond Life* (New York: The Century Co., 1899), hereafter as *TWT*.

21. Steven Mailloux, "The Rhetorical Use and Abuse of Fiction: Eating Books in Late Nineteenth-Century America," *boundary 2* 17 (1990): 133–57.

22. On this context, see Andrew T. Scull and Steven Spitzer, "Privatization and Capitalist Development: The Case of Private Police," *Social Problems* 21 (1977): 18–29.

23. Allan Pinkerton, *The Expressman and the Detective* (1875; rpt. New York: Arno Press, 1976), 26. Subsequent citation in text.

24. In Hammett's *Red Harvest*, for instance, the "op" carries a sheaf of cards that testify to a range of false identities. See Dashiell Hammett, *Red Harvest* (New York: Vintage Books, 1972), 7.

25. On Siringo, see Howard R. Lamar, *Charlie Siringo's West* (Albuquerque: University of New Mexico Press, 2005), esp. 135ff. Cf. Denning, *Mechanic Accents*, and Slotkin, *Gunfighter Nation*.

26. The centrality of contract relations to this era has been emphasized by Amy Dru Stanley, *From Bondage to Contract: Wage Labor, Marriage, and the Market in the Age of Slave Emancipation* (Cambridge: Cambridge University Press, 1998).

27. For useful discussions of the cultural image of criminality in this era, see esp. David Ray Papke, *Framing the Criminal: Crime, Cultural Work, and the Loss of Critical Perspective, 1830–1900* (Hamden, CT.: Archon Books, 1987), and Larry K. Hartsfield, *The American Response to Professional Crime, 1870–1917* (Westport, CT: Greenwood Press, 1985).

28. For all his romanticizing of the hobo life, Flynt's identifications were squarely with the business classes. Indeed, Flynt agreed with his employers that "the public is really the railroad company, and thus the sufferer" from tramp riders (*TWT* 308); compare *TWT*, 290.

29. On recent declarations, see Heather Howard, "The Negligent Enablement of Imposter Fraud: A Common-Sense Law Claim," *Duke Law Journal* 54 (March 2005): 1294n4; Kurt M. Saunders and Bruce Zucker, "Counteracting Identity Fraud in the Information Age: The Identity Theft and Assumption Deterrence Act," *Cornell Journal of Law and Public Policy* 8 (Spring 1999): 663; and "New Plan to Combat False-Identity Frauds," *U.S. News and World Report*, 28 June 1976, 63.

30. The federal Identity Theft and Assumption Deterrence Act was enacted in 1998. For a helpful discussion of this law, and state regulations passed in California and Arizona, see Catherine Pastrikos, "Comment: Identity Theft Statutes: Which Will Protect Americans the Most?" *Albany Law Review* 67 (2004): 1137–57.

31. On these statutes, see the discussion in Pastrikos, "Comment: Identity Theft Statutes," and in Saunders and Zucker, "Counteracting Identity Fraud in the Information Age."

32. On the early regulation of fraud, see Paula J. Dalley, "The Law of Deceit, 1790–1860: Continuity Amidst Change," *American Journal of Legal History* 39 (October 1995): 405–42.

33. Jennifer Harmon, "Speaker Puts Focus on Fraud Prevention," *National Mortgage News*, 9 February 2004, 13; "Progeny to Market AIG Identity Policies," *American Banker*, 19 June 2003, 11.

34. Quoted in Michael Grebb, "Crime: Forgotten Fraud: Counterfeit Checks," *Bank Technology News* 17 (April 2004): 1.

35. See, for instance, the working assumptions in Graeme R. Newman and Megan M. McNally's federally funded "Identity Theft Literature Review" (2005), http://www.ncjrs.

gov/pdffiles1/nij/grants/210459.pdf (accessed 4 January 2010), esp. 38–39. By "opportunity crime," the authors mean crimes where the "opportunity" presents itself—as when a credit card is left at a restaurant.

36. See Marx's discussion in his "Soft Surveillance," 37–56, and Simon A. Cole and Henry N. Pontell, "'Don't Be Low Hanging Fruit': Identity Theft as Moral Panic," in *Surveillance and Security: Technological Politics and Power in Everyday Life*, ed. Torin Monahan (New York: Routledge: 2006), 125–47.

37. This redefinition was central, of course, to the neoconservative claim that American affluence and permissiveness had exacted a "cost" in greater crime and disorder; see Wilson, *Thinking about Crime*, 234–49.

38. See, for instance, Henry Pontell, "'Pleased to Meet You . . . Won't You Guess My Name?' Identity Fraud, Cyber-Crime, and White-Collar Delinquency," *Adelaide Law Review* 23 (2002): 305–28.

39. See Loader, "Thinking Normatively about Private Security," esp. 377.

40. Lardner, "CEO Cop," 53

41. On Business Improvement Districts, see Kelling and Coles, *Fixing Broken Windows*, 112. On insurance feedback and public policing, see Ericson and Haggerty, *Policing the Risk Society*, 23–24, 108–10.

42. See, for instance, Edwin Meese III and Bob Carrico, "'Taking Back the Streets': Police Methods That Work," *Policy Review* 54 (Autumn 1990): 22–32.

43. See the frank acknowledgment in Wilson, *Thinking about Crime*, 77ff.

44. On this point, see esp. Lucia Zedner, "The Pursuit of Security."

45. Rhodes, *The Insoluble Problems of Crime*, 175.

46. Stanko, "Victims R Us," 19

47. Scheingold makes a similar point about "the adjustments" urban dwellers make; see *The Politics of Street Crime*, 19.

48. In the film, emphasizing the central theme of Jeff Nathanson's script, Abagnale (Leonardo DiCaprio) tells his dispossessed father (Christopher Walken) that he is going to get back everything the IRS had taken from the family. Abagnale's father, however, was never in tax trouble; nor was Frank Jr. an only child; nor did his mother immediately remarry (see Schaefer, "Former Con Man Catches a Few Fallacies in Film Bio").

49. As I write in chapter 1, in crime narratives like William Wellman's *The Public Enemy* or Nicholas Pileggi's *Wiseguy*, the child apprentice's exemption from adult criminal justice is tied to his mobility, his nimble elusiveness as a go-between and errand boy. And Hill's apprenticeship to the mob ethos of "getting over" on workaday stiffs begins with escaping his father's own blue-collar world; see Pileggi, *Wiseguy*, 25–31.

50. Tzanelli, Yar, and O'Brien, in "'Con Me If You Can,'" are especially incisive on this point.

51. Abagnale's story seems almost weightless, free even of the guilt that actually haunted Demara. See David W. Maurer, *The Big Con: The Story of the Confidence Man* (1940; rpt. New York: Anchor Books, 1999), 103–33.Contrast, as well, the decidedly more "ward-centered" narrative of J. R. "Yellow Kid" Weil, coauthored with W. T. Brannon, *Con Man: A Master Swindler's Own Story* (1948; rpt. New York: Broadway Books, 2004).

52. In one instance in the book version, Abagnale cons citizens trying to make late-night bank deposits. He dresses up in a uniform and puts an "out of order" sign on the night deposit box (recounted in *Art of the Steal*, 118–19). On "low hanging fruit," see Cole and Pontell, "'Don't Be Low Hanging Fruit.'"

53. Abagnale has admitted to practicing law in the Louisiana courts for about a year; see the interview on the DVD of *Catch Me if You Can* (Dreamworks SKG 2002).

Chapter 5

1. Ted Conover, *Newjack: Guarding Sing Sing* (2000; rpt. New York: Vintage, 2001), 171–209. All further citations in text. The *Oxford English Dictionary* tells us that "keep" has referred both to the care or responsibility over someone, and to an inner tower or stronghold. See also the meditation on "jail" and "cage" in John Edgar Wideman, *Brothers and Keepers* (1984; rpt. New York: Penguin, 1985), 34; all further citations in text.

2. See Joseph T. Hallinan, *Going Up the River: Travels in a Prison Nation* (New York: Random House, 2001), xiv.

3. See Gore Vidal, *Perpetual War for Perpetual Peace* (New York: Thunder's Mouth Press/Nation Books, 2002).

4. And dismal they are. In 2009, the Sentencing Project reported that one out of five prisoners in California, and one in ten nationally, was serving a life sentence. Solomon Moore, "Study Finds Record Number of Inmates Serving Life Terms," *New York Times*, 23 July 2009. This included 6,807 juveniles, 1,755 serving without the possibility of parole. For an overview of the literature on incapacitation as crime control, see Franklin E. Zimring and Gordon Hawkins, *Incapacitation: Penal Confinement and the Restraint of Crime* (New York: Oxford University Press, 1995).

5. Jonathan Simon's point about the recent reciprocity of back to basics traditionalism and new strategies of control is thus, again, very much on point. See "Governing Through Crime," 177. And Simon and Feeley themselves attach incapacitation to actuarialism; see "Actuarial Justice," 174ff.

6. Susan Sheehan, *A Prison and a Prisoner* (Boston: Houghton Mifflin, 1978). Subsequent quotations in text. For my understanding of the context from the 1970s forward, I am indebted to the texts discussed in following: Eric Schlosser, "The Prison-Industrial Complex," *Atlantic Monthly*, December 1998; Hallinan, *Going Up the River*; Cristina Rathbone, *A World Apart: Women, Prison, and the Life Behind Bars* (New York: Random House, 2005); Andi Rierden, *The Farm: Life Inside a Women's Prison* (Amherst: University of Massachusetts Press, 19970); and Parenti, *Lockdown America*.

7. The idea of a "prison-industrial" or "corrections-industrial" complex was well in circulation before Schlosser's essay; see, for example, the activists quoted in Fox Butterfield, "Political Gains by Prison Guards," *New York Times*, 7 November 1995. See also *The Celling of America: An Inside Look at the U.S. Prison Industry*, ed. Daniel Burton-Rose, Dan Pens, and Paul Wright (Monroe, ME: Common Courage Press, 1998); the many publications of Human Rights Watch; and David Ladipo, "The Rise of America's Prison-Industrial Complex," *New Left Review* 7 (January./February 2001): 109–23. Other important nonfiction texts on prison's effects on families and communities include Adrian Nicole LeBlanc, *Random Family* (New York: Scribner, 2003), and Jennifer Gonnerman, *Life on the Outside* (New York: Picador, 2004).

8. The best summary of these practices by the late 1990s is Charles N. Davis, "Access to Prisons," *Quill* 86 (May 1998): 19–29. See also William Glaberson, "Irked by Focus on Inmates, California Bans Interviews," *New York Times*, 29 December 1995.

9. Rathbone, *A World Apart*, 262–68.

10. See Conover's interview in *The New New Journalism*, ed. Robert S. Boynton (New York: Vintage, 2005), 17, and his comments in *Newjack*, 17ff.

11. Since prison officials were often given the right to determine who was an "official" press representative, these practices often fell with particular force upon freelance journalists, who were often forced to invent ingenious counter-tactics. Rathbone, for instance, is often forced to broach her principal subject, guard-inmate sexual abuse, through the testi-

mony of third parties; see, for example, Rathbone, *A World Apart,* 44. For his part, Hallinan combines his talks with prison officials, inmates, guards, and town residents with visits to inmate families outside jail; testimony from trials; talks with prisoners transferred out of maximum security, or those prisoners rewarded for good behavior by expanded visitation options. Or, witness *Albany Times-Union* reporter Paul Grondahl's tactics as recounted in Michelle Girardi, "Locked Out," *The News Media and the Law* 28 (Spring 2004): 25–26. See also Peg Tyre's interview with Rhonda Cook, "Inside Stories: Life on the Prison Beat," *Columbia Journalism Review* 38 (May/June 1999): 16; and Susan Burgess, "The First Amendment Behind Bars," *The News Media and the Law* 30 (Winter 2006): 27.

12. On "economism" in cultural studies, see Stuart Hall, "Gramsci's Relevance for the Study of Race and Ethnicity," in *Stuart Hall: Critical Dialogues in Cultural Studies,* ed. David Mulvey and Kuan-Hsing Chen (New York: Routledge, 1996), 417–89.

13. On budgets, see Hallinan, *Going Up the River,* 104–5; on families, see Rathbone, *A World Apart,* 107; and on Colgate's tube, see Rathbone, 195.

14. Schlosser, "The Prison-Industrial Complex," 51–58, 62–66, 68–70, 72–77.

15. This similarity has been recently noticed by Cecelia Tichi; see her *Exposés and Excess: Muckraking in America 1900/2000* (Philadelphia: University of Pennsylvania Press, 2004).

16. See also Lincoln Steffens's famous formulations in his *Autobiography* (New York: Harcourt, 1931), as well as those in Lippmann's "The Underworld: Our Secret Servant."

17. Parenti describes a darker version of this cycle, where overcrowding produces more violence, and thus the requests for more funding (*Lockdown America,* 173). He also provides a useful left-critique of the "Prison-Industrial Complex" paradigm (213ff.).

18. Schlosser does point out the beginnings of a backlash, as has the Sentencing Project; see also Pam Belluck, "As Prisons Go Private, States Seek Tighter Controls," *New York Times,* 15 April 1999. According to the Bureau of Justice Statistics, although the percentage of private facilities has been rising at an alarming rate, they still constituted only about 23 percent of all U.S. institutions as of 2005, and some states (notably California itself) reported *declines* in inmates housed in private facilities. Most private facilities were also small (about two in three housed fewer than than 100 inmates). "Census of State and Federal Correctional Facilities, 2005" http://bjs.ojp.usdoj.gov/content/pub/pdf/csfcf05.pdf (accessed 7 January 2010).

Timothy Gilfoyle's recent account of Sing Sing in *A Pickpocket's Tale: The Underworld of Nineteenth-Century New York* (New York: Norton, 2006) makes clear that the isolation of the prison from the outside world was a byproduct of historical change in the 1870s, not something (as earlier accounts assumed) intrinsic to its design. See Gilfoyle, 160–61, 173ff. Meanwhile, the early-twentieth-century reforms experimented with integrating private capital and mass media, notably at Sing Sing itself: see Rebecca McLennan, "Punishment's 'Square Deal': Prisoners and Their Keepers in 1920s New York," *Journal of Urban History* 29 (July 2003): 597–619. Malcolm W. Feeley has also explored the history of entrepreneurial connections to Anglo-American prisons, notably transporting of prisoners, experiments with private prisons for convict-lease in the early nineteenth century, and "training" schools for juveniles and "community corrections" programs. See his "Entrepreneurs of Punishment: The Legacy of Privatization," *Punishment and Society* 4 (2002): 321–44.

19. This is a point that DeParle himself discusses. But as he shows, recent studies have challenged this crime-control hypothesis. See Jason DeParle, "The American Prison Nightmare," *New York Review of Books,* 12 April 2007, 33–36. On union resistance in the New York State context, see Monte Williams, "Down-and-Out-Town Sees Survival in

a Private Prison," *New York Times,* 24 March 1997. Parenti's point about social services on 216.

20. See Harcourt, "Reflecting on the Subject"; Wilson, *Cop Knowledge,* 177ff.

21. For one of the grimmer ways punishment was interpreted, see the discussion of LAPD Chief Darryl Gates, in John Gregory Dunne, "Law and Disorder in Los Angeles," *New York Review of Books,* 10 October 1991 and 24 October 1991; see esp. the second installment, 65.

22. Cf. van den Haag, *Punishing Criminals,* 243ff.

23. See the discussion by Thomas G. Blomberg and Karol Lucken, *American Penology: A History of Control* (New York: Aldine de Gruyter, 2000), which declares for similar reasons that incapacitation's "effectiveness was guaranteed" (175). Ruth Wilson Gilmore makes a wonderful turn on claims like these when she writes, if "incapacitation . . . is not ambitious in a behavioral or psychological sense, it is, ironically, the theory that undergirds the most ambitious prison-building project in the history of the world. Incapacitation doesn't pretend to change anything about people except where they are" (14). See also the discussion of sentencing grids in Hallinan, *Going Up the River,* 42–43; and Zimring and Hawkins, *Incapacitation,* 72ff.

24. Conover refers to Schlosser's account implicitly; see *Newjack,* 232.

25. See Barbara Ehrenreich's reluctance to adopt the "undercover" label, in her *Nickel and Dimed: On (Not) Getting By in America* (New York: Henry Holt, 2001), 6. On material bodies in sensational fiction, compare Peter Brooks, *The Melodramatic Imagination: Balzac, Henry James, Melodrama, and the Mode of Excess* (New York: Columbia University Press, 1985).

26. Conover's first memoir, *Rolling Nowhere* (New York: Viking Press, 1984), presents itself as an ethnographic "adventure narrative" in the hobo underworld, very much akin to Josiah Flynt's. Compare *Newjack*'s discussion of this method (18). In his interview with Boynton, Conover admits that his assignment to Sing Sing was accidental (13).

27. In my understanding of this *New Yorker* style, I have been influenced by the comments of Dwight MacDonald and Mary McCarthy on "naturalism" in John Hersey's *Hiroshima;* see Michael J. Yavenditti, "John Hersey and the American Conscience: The Reception of 'Hiroshima,'" *Pacific Historical Review* 43 (February 1974): 40–41.

28. Here, Conover's reading (207) of *Soul on Ice* (New York: McGraw-Hill, 1968), Eldridge Cleaver's famous rendering of black prisoners' view of incarceration, is also relevant.

29. Conover, *Rolling Nowhere,* 274.

30. Barbara Ehrenreich makes a similar point at the start of *Nickel and Dimed:* "There's no way," she writes, ". . . to pretend to be a waitress: the food either gets to the table or not" (9).

31. James Clifford, "On Ethnographic Authority," in *The Predicament of Culture,* 21–54.

32. Recent attention to undercover reporting has focused on its performative dimensions. See, for example, Jean Marie Lutes, "Into the Madhouse with Nellie Bly: Girl Stunt Reporting in Late Nineteenth-Century America," *American Quarterly* 54 (2002): 217–53; Eric Schockett, "Undercover Explorations of the 'Other Half,' or the Writer as Class Transvestite, *Representations* 64 (Autumn 1998) 109–33; and Kate Baldwin, "Black Like Who? Cross-Testing the 'Real' Lines of John Howard Griffin's *Black Like Me,*" *Cultural Critique* 40 (Autumn 1998): 103–43.

33. Conover, for instance, invokes the trope of domestic return at the end of his book—as in Victorian travelogue, lamenting that he can go "home" when prisoners themselves cannot. And he compares his return to that of a foreign exchange student (317–18).

34. See Baldwin, "Black Like Who?" 118. Lutes's incisive reading of Nellie Bly, likewise, argues that it was ultimately Bly's resistance to inhabiting the identity of immigrant working girls—pointedly, the incompleteness of her transformation—that protected her readers from the dangers of over-identification with the urban underworld (232).

35. This is my point about Flynt; see pages 103–4 in chapter 4.

36. Conover's follow-up to this quizzical moment is an attempt at sympathy. Extrapolating from the film of *The Bird Man of Alcatraz*, Conover speculates that visitors come to see prisoners because they are the "only life" they have (156). This view, however, needs to be contrasted with the Widemans' reflections, discussed in following.

37. Part of the sensational idiom is a fear of being overwhelmed by what one sees: see, for example, Bly's uncovering of the asylum's practice of shocking cold baths in *Ten Days in a Mad-House* (New York: Ian L. Munro, Publisher, n.d.), http://digital.library.upenn.edu/women/bly/madhouse/madhouse.html (accessed 8 January 2010). Compare the similar fears in Ray Sprigle, *In the Land of Jim Crow* (New York: Simon & Schuster, 1949), 274, or John Howard Griffin, *Black Like Me* (New York: New American Library, 1962), 35, 138. I have written about a similar association of prison with the loss of identity, in Mark Twain's imagination: see "'The Mulatto in the Iron Mask': Mark Twain and Alexandre Dumas," in *Reading without Maps: Cultural Landmarks in a Post-Canonical Age*, ed. Christophe Den Tandt (Brussels: PEI, 2005), 319–36.

38. In my judgment, "passing" narratives of the mid-twentieth century often run this risk: in *Black Like Me* or Sprigle's memoir, the unconscious mimicry of a "model minority," the "Negro" who avoids trouble, clearly informs the experiment at hand.

39. Cf. Sheehan, *A Prison and a Prisoner:* on corruption following prison "frisks," 72–73; on what she calls the "'lumps and bumps' school of behavior modification," 74; on guards' racism and nostalgia for the pre-Attica era, 134–40, 144–45.

40. In the novels of Joseph Wambaugh, street cops refer to the downtown office building of the LAPD as the "glass house." See my discussion in *Cop Knowledge,* 110–23.

41. Skolnick's work on the artisanal outlook of police officers is again quite relevant here: see his *Justice Without Trial.*

42. See, for example, the emphasis on manipulative "eloquence" in the beat officer, in William Ker Muir Jr., *Police: Streetcorner Politicians* (Chicago: University of Chicago Press, 1977), 227ff.

43. Local prison unions, which have grown in political strength in the prison boom, tend to focus on bread-and-butter issues. And in the case of California's guard union, it supported prison expansion, "three strikes" legislation, and victims' rights. See Butterfield, "Political Gains by Prison Guards." But this focus has sometimes also included advocacy for disability coverage following job-related stress or injury. Requesting improved training and greater psychiatric resources, especially in the face of cutbacks, is also not unknown: see, for example, "Connecticut Prison Union Asks Help to Handle Suicidal Inmates," *New York Times,* 3 April 1999.

44. The quite sensational appeals process, which partly revolved around whether Robby could have murdered a crime victim whose family would successfully sue the responding hospital for malpractice, ran on for some two and a half decades. See Jim McKinnon, "Court Pulls Plug on Wideman Retrial," *Pittsburgh Post-Gazette,* 23 May 2000. Though I have taken the Widemans at their word about prison experience, I have tried to make no judgment on the matter of Robby's original guilt.

45. For the most pertinent of recent readings, see Michael P. Moreno, "The Last Iron Gate: Negotiating the Incarceral Spaces of John Edgar Wideman's *Brothers and Keepers,*" *University of Mississippi Studies in English* 9 (2004): 54–70; Heather Andrade, "'Mosaic Memory': Auto/biographical Context(s) in John Edgar Wideman's *Brothers and Keep-*

ers," *Massachusetts Review* 40 (Autumn 1999): 342–67; and Michael Feith, "'The Benefit of the Doubt': Openness and Closure in *Brothers and Keepers*," *Callaloo* 22 (1999): 665–75.

46. This view of an inward-turning, recursive history is also brilliantly rendered in the film by two brothers, Albert and Allen Hughes, *Menace II Society* (1993). In this movie we see a similar kind of doubling: to a brother named "Cain," a name played off sugar cane, candy cane, "K-nine" dogs, cocaine—and, of course, the biblical killer. The film's signature becomes the spiraling exit ramp from a parking garage, an image that calls up the historical re-visitations of the 1960s, and Watts history, throughout the film.

47. William Julius Wilson, *The Truly Disadvantaged: The Inner City, the Underclass, and Public Policy* (Chicago: University of Chicago Press, 1990).

48. I discuss the Broken Windows theory above (5, 57–58) and in *Cop Knowledge*, 177–84; see also Harcourt, "Reflecting on the Subject."

49. See John Edgar Wideman's interview with Jessica Lustig in *African American Review* 26 (1992): 454.

50. Compare the Widemans' discussion of the undercover officers in Homewood, 101–2, with Michael Patrick MacDonald, *All Souls: A Family Story from Southie* (Boston: Beacon Press, 1999), esp. 176, 190–91, 194.

51. Compare Feith, "'The Benefit of the Doubt,'" 673–74. The "longer look" is described in an interview with Wilfred D. Samuels, "Going Home: A Conversation with John Edgar Wideman," *Callaloo* 6 (February 1983): 49–59, in reference to his maternal grandfather.

52. Airport profiling, of course, was central to the emergence of risk management tactics; see Cloud, "Search and Seizure by the Numbers."

53. James Clifford and George E. Marcus, introduction to *Writing Culture: The Poetics and Politics of Ethnography* (Berkeley: University of California Press, 1986), 7.

54. Peter Caster's discussion of a similar motif in prison films is right on point. As Caster writes, "[t]he fundamental problem with the logic of the redemption narratives of these films is that they largely endorse the use value of the same judicial system they at least in part describe as unjust. These films largely posit prison as man-making, as a setting for personal transformation." *Prisons, Race, and Masculinity in Twentieth-Century U.S. Literature and Film* (Columbus: The Ohio State University Press, 2008), 165.

Epilogue

1. Peter Høeg, *Smilla's Sense of Snow*, trans. Tiina Nunnally (New York: Farrar, Straus and Giroux, 1993), 207. Emphasis mine.

2. In *A Cold Case*, Rosenzweig refers to this phrase as a personal truth; see 27.

3. This substitution is commonplace among the rhetorical and material practices described in this book—and not only by neoconservatives. While this might seem a claim reminiscent of Nixon's "silent majority" rationale, in fact it was evident, just as forcefully, in the Clinton Justice Department's support of community policing, what it called "democracy in action." See, for instance, Bureau of Justice Assistance, *Understanding Community Policing* (Washington, DC: Department of Justice, 1995), 7.

4. I have discussed another instance of this reshuffling of community memory in "Lost Boys and Recovered Classics."

5. Nicole Rafter calls this balancing motif a "double movement": see her *Shots in the Mirror: Crime Films and Society* (New York: Oxford University Press, 2006), 3 and *passim*.

6. See my discussion of Stanko's work, 114–15 above. Sebold's character is cited in the epigraph to my Introduction.

7. On the mythic role of the "permissive" 1960s in neoconservative thought, see George Lipsitz, *American Studies in a Moment of Danger* (Minneapolis: University of Minnesota Press, 2001).

8. See my discussion in chapter 5 for the byplay between Conover's "participant observation" and these sensational inheritances (135–37), or the discussion concerning Pileggi's notion of working on "wiseguys in Samoa," 173n54. For the broader reservoir of literary antecedents, see Christopher Herbert, *Culture and Anomie: Ethnographic Imagination in the Nineteenth Century* (Chicago: University of Chicago Press, 1991).

9. Again, on these problems in realist ethnography generally, see George E. Marcus and Michael M. J. Fischer, *Anthropology as Cultural Critique*.

10. One of the ironies of the Whitey Bulger case—and the continuing prosecution of FBI agent John Connelly—is that many of these cases are built around other informants: a corrupt former agent and Whitey's own partner. See my "'Where's Whitey?'" The best-known treatment of some of these crosscurrents is Janet Malcolm, *The Journalist and the Murderer* (New York: Knopf, 1980).

11. On undercover work, see esp. Gary T. Marx, "The Interweaving of Public and Private Police in Undercover Work," in *Private Policing*, ed. Clifford D. Shearing and Philip C. Stenning (Newbury Park, CA: Sage Publications, 1987), 172–93, and my "Undercover: White Ethnicity and Police Exposé in the 1970s." On surveillance, see esp. Monahan's *Surveillance and Security*. On the integration of immigration, crime, and welfare, see esp. Daniel Kanstroom, *Deportation Nation* (Cambridge, MA: Harvard University Press, 2007).

12. On these fronts, see Sebastian Rotella, *Twilight on the Line: Underworlds and Politics at the U.S.–Mexico Border* (New York: W. W. Norton, 1998).

13. Lincoln Steffens, *The Shame of the Cities* (1902–1903; rpt. New York: Hill & Wang, 1957), 101.

14. It is sometimes said, for instance, that the recent movement to require videotaping of interrogations has limited police coercion and brutality. Assuming that some independent oversight of its use is in place, I am in favor of videotaping. But if the courts and prime-time TV sanction police deception, videotaping might soon seem superfluous. I make a parallel argument about federal guidelines on informants that attempt to regulate practices that intrinsically mimic criminal deception (45–46 above).

15. The tension was made evident to me in the spring of 2001, at a Boston College conference hosted by Families of Murder Victims Opposed to the Death Penalty. Here victims' families spoke of often being pitted against prosecutors who sought the death penalty. See also Frank Rich's "It's Closure-Mongering Time," *New York Times*, 28 April 1001, and his "Rush to Closure," *New York Times*, 5 June 1997.

16. For awareness of this continuing debate—and of community resistance to prison expansion—I am indebted to Jason DeParle, "The American Prison Nightmare," available at http:///www.nybooks.com.proxy.bc.edu/articles/20056 (accesssed 19 January 2010).

17. The neoconservative trek from rejecting "root causes" in crime theory to supporting the invasion of Iraq (because one feels democracy is a root cause) is not necessarily a logical one. On the genealogy of neoconservatism by a thinker recanting its influence, see Francis Fukuyama, "After Neoconservatism," *New York Times*, 19 February 2006.

18. "Transcript: Charlie Rose Interviews CIA Chief Gen. Michael Hayden," at the Talking Points Memo Web site, http://talkingpointsmemo.com/news/2007/10/transcript_charlie_rose_interv_1.php (accessed 10 January 2010).

19. After 9/11, congressional debates on these seemingly distinct fronts sometimes overlapped chronologically. For a fuller discussion, see Dan Kennedy, "O Brother, Where Art Thou," *Boston Phoenix*, 27 June–3 July 2003; and Hayden's own confirmation statement, available at the Central Intelligence Agency Web site, https://www.cia.gov/news-information/speeches-testimony/2006/d-cia-nominee-haydens-confirmation-statement.html (accessed 10 January 2010).

20. See, for example, Fox Butterfield, "Justice Dept. Report Shows Trouble in U.S. Jails Preceded Job Fixing Iraq's," *New York Times*, 6 June 2004.

Index

Abagnale, Frank W., Jr. 98, 109–10, 111, 112, 116, 124, 156, 157, 162. See also *Art of the Steal; Catch Me if You Can*
actuarialism, 8, 13, 15, 101, 113, 133, 178n33; bail reform and, 14; prisons and, 13, 125, 133, 139, 167n14. See also risk and risk management
airport security, 4, 10, 120, 147, 192n52
Alger, Horatio. See *Ragged Dick*
American Family Association, 61
American Society for Industrial Security, 99
Analyze This (Ramis), 40
Apalachin Conference, 25, 44
Army Field Manual, 162
Art of the Steal (Abagnale), 98, 102, 109–10, 118
Atlantic Monthly, 17, 103, 159
Attica Correctional Facility, 123, 134–42

bail reform, 14
Baldwin, Kate, 136
Barnicle, Mike, 84, 86
Bass, Timothy, 83
Beaumont, Gustave de, 138, 140
Bell, Daniel, 27
Berlant, Lauren, 93
Bernstein, Lee, 25, 28

Black Mass: The Irish Mob, the FBI, and a Devil's Deal (Lehr and O'Neill), 21
Block, Alan A., 31, 171n16
Bly, Nellie, 134
Bochco, Steven, 49, 52, 73; *Hill Street Blues,* 49, 54
Bonnano, Bill, 28
Bonnano, Joseph, 33
Bonnie and Clyde, 26
Boston College Point-Shaving Scandal, 37, 44–45
Boston Globe, 23, 84
Boston Police Department, 23, 82, 84–85
Bourdieu, Pierre, 61
Boynton, Robert. See *New New Journalism, The*
Bratton, William, 58, 59, 62, 72, 82, 113, 178n33
Brauer, Stephen, 7
Breslin, Jimmy, 61
Broken Windows Philosophy, 15, 23, 58, 145, 152, 159, 160, 166n8; essay by James Q. Wilson and George L. Kelling, 5, 132. See also Wilson, James Q.
Brooks, Peter, 51
Brothers and Keepers (Wideman and Wideman), 12, 19, 124, 19, 137; Broken Windows references in, 145, 149; corrections officers in, 147,

195

149; form and style of, 143, 144–45; incapacitation in, 147, 148, 151; macroeconomic forces in, 142–43, 146; neighborhood ethos re-created by, 145, 146, 149–50; time in, 143–44, 145, 148; Robert Wideman's survival depicted in, 151–52; slavery in, 148–49; visiting rooms in, 146–47, 147–48, 151; war on crime in, 142–43, 149
Bulger, James ("Whitey"), 21–22, 26, 45, 162, 193n10
Burke, Jimmy, 44
Burnham, David, 56
Bush, George W., 120
Business Improvement Districts, 113–14
Byrnes, Thomas. See *Professional Criminals of America*

Cagney, James, 41, 90. See also *Public Enemy, The*
California State Prison (at Sacramento), 129
Carroll, Dan, 26
Caruso, David, 59, 64, 65
Castellammarese War, 27, 31–32
Catch Me If You Can (Abagnale with Redding), 11, 99–100, 101–2, 116–22; Alger template in, 117; confidence man genre conventions in, 117, 118; FBI in, 100, 116, 121–22; form and style of, 101, 116–17, 120; ghostwritten by Stan Redding, 99; masculinity in, 117–18, 119; nostalgia and retro diction in, 117, 120–21; prison depicted in, 121; white-collar ethos in, 100, 118, 119; film version (Spielberg), 99, 100, 117, 120, 121, 187n48
Central Intelligence Agency (CIA), 161
Century, The, 103
Charlie Rose (TV series), 161–62, 163
Chavez, J. Anthony, 96
Clancy, Tom, 78
Clapp, Gordon, 68
Clark, Bill, 11, 51, 53, 54, 136, 157, 178n42, 179n48; background and outlook, 61–62, 63–64, 65–76; Irish ethnicity and, 64, 69; Vietnam ethos and, 65, 73, 140, 157. See also *True Blue*
Clark, Ramsey, 14
Clifford, James, 135, 150
Clinton, Bill, 4
Closer, The (TV series), 49, 74
cold case (criminal justice approach), 14; DNA testing and, 81–82; FBI sponsorship of, 82; "foreseeable harm" argument and, 80, 86, 95, 96; "meaningless" criminal motive depicted in, 55, 85, 86–87, 93, 95, 156; media portrayals of, 83–86, 181n23; police officers depicted in, 80–81, 84, 85, 86, 178n47; police tactics and self-image in, 14, 83–84, 86–89; scientific policing advances and, 81–82; sensational cases involving, 81; statutes of limitation affected, 11, 12, 79; victim's rights dimension, 78–79, 80, 84, 86; wartime ethos in, 182n46
Cold Case (cable TV series), 78
Cold Case (CBS TV series), 78, 157
Cold Case, A (Gourevitch), 11, 77–78, 81, 89, 116, 136, 153, 154; ethnicity depicted in, 90, 92; form and style of, 89, 90, 93, 182n46; nostalgia and retro effects in, 91, 92–93, 94, 95; racial conflict depicted in, 92; time in, 89–90, 93, 94, 95; victims depicted in, 92, 93, 94, 183n59; vigilance depicted in, 91, 96–97
Cold Case Files (A&E TV series), 83
Coleridge, Samuel, 53, 75
community policing, 5, 57, 192n3. See also Broken Windows Philosophy
CompStat, 5, 12, 13, 58, 82, 113
confidence men: history of, 101–2
Connolly, John J., Jr., 21–22
Conover, Ted, 19, 156. See *Newjack*
Conroy, John, 51
conservatism. See neoconservative turn
"Crown of Feathers, A" (Singer), 77, 90, 97
cryptomnesia, 92
CSI Crime Scene Investigation (TV series), 49, 50, 80, 180n12
"CSI" effect, 7, 51, 59, 180n12
Cuomo, Mario, 4, 127
Curriden, Mark, 22

Daly, Michael, 61
De La Beckwith, Byron, 81
Demara, Ferdinand, 102
Denny, Reginald, 141
DeParle, Jason, 131
Dewey, Thomas, 28
Diary of Ann Frank (Frank), 137
Dick, Philip K. See "Minority Report, The"
Dickens, Charles, 78, 123
Didion, Joan, 14
Dillinger, John, 26
Dinkins, David, 57
Disneyland, 10, 120
DNA testing, 80, 81
Dred Scott v. Sanford, 148
Drug Enforcement Agency (DEA), 22

Eisenhower, Dwight, 130
Ellroy, James. See *My Dark Places*
Emmy Awards, 51, 63
Ericson, Richard, 8
Evers, Medgar, 81

Farm, The (Rierden), 127
Feder, Sid, 21, 27, 34
Federal Bureau of Investigation (FBI), 21, 22, 38, 44, 54, 96, 99–109; cold case sponsorship, 82; *FBI Bulletin*, 87–88; Frank Abagnale relationship, 99, 100, 110, 116, 121–22; organized crime crusade, 22, 25, 26–27; "top echelon" informant program of, 171n20; Whitey Bulger and, 21–22. See also Hoover, J. Edgar
Federal Trade Commission (FTC), 109
Federal Victims of Crime Act (1984), 4
Feeley, Malcolm, 5, 18, 14
Fitzgerald, F. Scott. See *Great Gatsby, The*
Flamm, Michael, 4, 13
Flemmi, Stephen, 21
Flynt, Josiah (alias of Josiah Flynt Willard), 101, 102–9, 113, 116, 126, 134, 186n28; detective work and, 104–8; vigilance and, 108; youth of, 103–4. See also *My Life; Notes of an Itinerant Policeman; Tramping with Tramps*

Fontaine, Tom, 49
foreseeable harm, 80, 86, 95. See also victims and victim's rights
Forum, The, 103
Foucault, Michel, 17, 101; micropolitics and, 9; on "delinquents," 106; on Vidocq, 98, 106
Frank, Anne, 137
Franz, Dennis, 63
French Connection, The (Friedkin), 49
Friedkin, William. See *French Connection, The*

"Gangster as Tragic Hero, The" (Warshow), 24, 31–32, 35, 41, 44
Garland, David, 8, 10, 110. See also responsibilization
Geary, William, 29
Genovese, Vito, 31, 32–33, 36
Gewirtz, Paul, 86, 95
Giuliani, Rudolph, 23–25, 58, 113, 162
Glennon, Richie, 89, 90, 92. See also *Cold Case, A*
Godfather, The (Puzo), 24, 31, 37, 39, 40, 37, 39, 40, 42
Going Up the River (Hallinan), 124, 127, 128, 130
Goldfarb, Ronald, 22, 29, 30; idea of Witness Protection as intelligence gathering, 30
GoodFellas (Scorsese), 11, 37, 93
Gourevitch, Philip. See *Cold Case, A*
Great Imposter, The (Crichton), 102
Great Gatsby, The (Fitzgerald), 39–40, 92
Green Haven Correctional Facility, 126–27
Gutman, Herbert, 42

Haggerty, Kevin, 8
Hallinan, Joseph. See *Going Up the River*
Hammett, Dashiell, 108
Handt, Robert, 52
Hawthorne, Nathaniel, 78. See also "Wakefield"
Hayden, Gen. Michael, 160–62
Hearst, Patricia, 81
High Noon (Zinnermann), 54, 90, 92

Hill, Henry, 28, 37–48, 93, 102, 157.
    See also *Wise Guy: Life in a Mafia Family*
Hill, Karen, 41, 45
Hill Street Blues (TV series), 49
Hodder, Alfred, 103, 107
Høeg, Peter. See *Smilla's Sense of Snow*
Hoffa, Jimmy, 30, 44
Holmes, Sherlock, 83
Homicide (TV series), 50
Homicide: A Year on the Killing Streets (Simon), 49, 87, 88; on interrogation, 49, 59, 175n9; on motiveless murders, 87; Hoover, J. Edgar, 14, 22, 25, 54, 168n29, 184n3; informant use by, 25, 26
Houchins v. KQED, Inc., 128
Houston Chronicle, 99
Hugo, Victor, 78
HUMANITAS Prize, 52, 63, 65, 73, 175n9; controversy surrounding, 73–74

identity theft, 109, 110; identity fraud and, 109, 111, 119; street disorder and, 112–16
Illinois v. Gates, 4
incapacitation (neoconservative theory), 13, 14, 15–16, 129, 151, 160, 163, 190n23; James Q. Wilson on, 15–16
informants, criminal, 11; 2001 Justice Department Guidelines on, 21, 46–47, 169n2, 174n69; anthropological informants, compared to, 36, 173n54, 193n8; as "intelligence gathering," 59; Bulger case and, 21; corporate model of organized crime and, 25, 28–31; growth during the neoconservative turn, 22–23; Henry Hill as, 37, 41, 43–44, 45–46, 48; J. Edgar Hoover and, 25, 26; Joseph Valachi as, 31, 33–34; prison expansion and, 33, 170n11; Rudolph Giuliani on, 23, 25; scandals involving, 11, 23–24, 174n70. See also Witness Protection Program
interrogation: deception by police in, 14, 53; Miranda rights and, 14, 58–59; narrative possibilities of, 59; *NYPD Blue* episodes depicting, 68, 69, 69–72, 73; physical coercion and, 67–69, 71; recent prime time police melodrama and, 49; recent scholarship on, 51–52; third degree and, 176n32. See also *Miranda v. Arizona*

James, Henry, 66, 76
Johnson, Lyndon, 30

Kefauver Committee, 25, 169n39, 172n31
Kelling, George L., 5, 8, 132. See also Broken Windows Philosophy
Kelly, Ray, 61
Kennedy, Robert F., 11, 13–14, 22, 24, 33, 36, 42, 43, 45, 47; crusade against organized crime, 24, 25, 28–31; *Valachi Papers* legal agreement with, 31, 173n50
King, Martin Luther, 145
King, Rodney, 91, 92, 141
Knapp Commission Report, 55, 56–57, 61, 177n30
Koehler, Frank, 89–94, 97
Kojak (TV series), 14, 49
"*Kojak* Liberals," 14
Kroll Inc., 99, 121

Landrum, Larry, 73
Lansky, Meyer, 62
Law & Order (TV series), 49
Law & Order: Criminal Intent (TV series), 49
Law Enforcement Assistance Administration (LEAA), 14, 56, 178n33, 183n15
Lawes, Lewis, 123
Lehr, Dick, 21
Leo, Richard A., 8, 59; on interrogation, 59
Lesser, Wendy, 17
Leuci, Robert, 54, 56, 58. See also *Prince of the City*
Levingston, Steven, 84, 85–86, 95
Levinson, Barry. See *Homicide* (TV series)

Lindberg, Gary, 102
Lindner, Rolf, 103, 107
Lippmann, Walter, 34, 130
Little Caesar (LeRoy), 37
Lloyd, David, 75
Loader, Ian, 8, 13, 19, 112; on private security and consumerism, 112, 119–20; on crime and public discourse, 8
Lockdown America (Parenti), 127, 131
Louima, Abner, 91, 92
Lovely Bones, The (Sebold), 1, 157
Lufthansa Theft, 28, 37
Lumet, Sydney. See *Serpico*, film (Lumet)

Maas, Peter, 31, 173n50. See also *Serpico*, book (Maas); *The Valachi Papers*
Mafia, 11, 21–22, 23, 24, 27–28, 31, 35–45, 157. See also organized crime
Mailloux, Steven, 103
Mann, Abby, 49
Mann, Michael, 49
Maple, Jack, 82
Marx, Gary T., 8, 13, 110; on the "only you" refrain in neoconservatism, 110
Maurer, David, 118
McAuliffe, Dennis Jr., 94
McClellan Committee, 24, 25, 31–32
McDaniel, James, 74, 75. See also *NYPD Blue*
McDonald, Edward, 37, 38, 44–45
McGinn, Pete, 89
McParlan, James, 105–6
Miami Vice (TV series), 49
micropolitical, 2, 24, 167n19; Foucault on, 8–9; Jonathan Simon on, 9; macropolitical contrasted to, 8; Witness Protection narrative and, 42, 47; prison labor and, 131–32, 136, 139
Milch, David, 11, 19, 51–76, 79, 92, 136, 157, 175n9; background, 53, 62–63; creative philosophy of, 63, 75; race and, 73–74, 179n56. See also *NYPD Blue*; *True Blue: The True Stories Behind* NYPD Blue
Miller, William Ian, 76
Mills, David, 74
Minority Report (Spielberg), 120
"Minority Report, The" (Dick), 120

minorityism in police culture, 55
Miranda v. Arizona, 11, 14, 51, 52, 55, 56, 59–60, 66, 68, 70, 71, 72, 74, 175n9. See also interrogation
Morris, John, 21
Morris, Kathryn, 83
Moxley, Martha, 81, 83
Muir, William Ker, Jr., 8
Murder, Inc. (Burkus and Feder), 21, 27, 34
Murphy, Patrick, 56, 57
My Dark Places (Ellroy), 81, 94
My Life (Flynt), 103, 106, 107, 108

Naked City: film (Dassin), 54, 90; two TV series, 49, 53, 54, 92
neoconservative turn, 8–9, 19–20, 100, 113, 167n16; "conservative" values and, 13–14, 75–76, 133, 167n16, 168n26; crime control and, 5–6, 178n46, 182,n30, 193n17; emulation of criminality in, 16–17, 25, 30, 75, 101; Great Society disenchantment and, 4, 13, 52, 165n5, 187n37, 193 n7; nostalgia in, 79, 84–86, 90–91, 116–17, 120–21; prisons role in, 133; utilitarianism in, 14–15
New New Journalism, The (Boynton), 135
New York Police Department (NYPD), 77; Knapp Commission Report effects on, 55–57, 177n30; management philosophy in, 57–59, 177n30; retrenchment in the 1970s and 1980s, 54–59
New York magazine, 2, 17, 37
New York Times, 56
New Yorker, The, 2, 17, 89, 90, 91, 93, 126, 135
Newjack: Guarding Sing Sing (Conover), 11, 12, 19, 134–42, 160; connections to community policing in, 141; corrections officer culture in, 137, 139–40, 141–42; form and style of, 134, 135, 136, 137–38; incapacitation in, 127, 138, 139, 140; participant observation and undercover strategy in, 135, 136–37, 138, 157–58; race in, 140–41; sensational conventions in,

134–35; time in, 123–24, 134, 138; visitor's rooms in, 137
Niederhoffer, Albert, 57
Nixon, Richard, 14, 22, 85
no-knock warrants, 58, 170n10
Notes of an Itinerant Policeman (Flynt), 103
NYPD Blue (TV series), 3, 11, 51–53, 58–59, 60–76; American Family Association conflict, 61, 62; audience demographic and, 51; constitutional violations shown on, 176n17; creative partnership behind, 52, 61–66; Emmys and, 51, 63; form and style of, 54–55, 56, 58–59, 72; HUMANITAS prizes and, 52, 65, 73–74; Miranda warnings and interrogation in, 51, 66–72, 76; pluralism and post-liberalism in, 52–53, 73–74, 76; police minorityism in, 55; "Prostrate Before the Law" (episode), 69–80; public controversies surrounding interrogation scenes, 51, 175n8; racial conflicts around, 73–75; terrorism depicted in, 70–73

Ochoa, Tyler T., 96
Ofshe, Richard J., 59
Olson, Sarah Jane, 81
O'Neill, Gerard. See *Black Mass*
order-maintenance policing. See Broken Windows Philosophy; community policing
organized crime, 11, 12, 14; anti-Communist hysteria and, 28–29; "Americanization" thesis and, 27, 42, 46–47; corporate organization and, 27, 47, 80, 159, 171n22; David Milch's family history and, 62; ethnicity in, 29, 36; "Fordist" conceptions of, 27, 34; historiography on, 22, 25–27, 171n16; police corruption and, 55, 58; RICO and, 25, 29–30; romantic images of, 26–27; suburbanization and, 41. See also Kennedy, Robert F.; Mafia; *Valachi Papers, The*; *Wise Guy: Life in a Mafia Family*; Witness Protection Program

Osborne, Thomas Mott, 123

Parenti, Christian, 127, 131
Pell v. Procunier, 128
Peress, Gilles, 93
Pileggi, Nicholas, 2, 11, 37. See also *Wise Guy: Life in a Mafia Family*
Pinkerton, Allan, 104–5, 106. See also Pinkerton Detective Agency
Pinkerton Detective Agency, 99, 105
Police Story (TV series), 49
Potter, Claire Bond, 22; on celebrity bandits, 26
pre-political attitudes, 13, 79, 116, 168n25
Prince of the City (Daley), 55
Prison and a Prisoner, A (Sheehan), 126, 128, 135, 137–38
prisons: conditions, 127–31, 188n4; corrections officers and, 131–32; neoconservative idea of incapacitation in, 124–25, 132–34; privatization, 127–28, 129–31,189n19; public views of, 124; restrictions on journalistic access, 128–29, 188n11; visitors rooms in, 127, 129–30, 130–31, 192n54; women in, 128. See also Attica; California State Prison; Green Haven; prison exposés; prison-industrial complex; Western Penitentiary
prison exposés: conventions of, 129–30, 130–31, 192n54; muckraking tradition in, 129–30; restrictions on journalists affecting, 128–29; views of labor in, 131–32. See also *Newjack*; prison-industrial complex
prison-industrial complex, 124, 129–30, 131, 150–51; Eric Schlosser essay, 127, 130, 132–34, 160
private security and private detective work: Allan Pinkerton on, 104–5; Frank Abagnale's practice of, 98, 102, 109–10, 118; in studies of crime narrative, 98–99; Josiah Flynt on, 104–8; Pinkerton Agency and, 99, 104–5; public-private partnerships and, 11, 15, 98–99, 110, 111, 112–16; recent growth in, 5, 109; shadow

narrative tradition and, 101, 104–7; war on crime role in, 98, 110, 112–16. *See also* identity theft
Professional Criminals of America (Byrnes), 26
profiling, 4, 10, 147, 192n52. *See also* actuarialism; airport security
Prohibition (19th Amendment), 26, 62; effect on organized crime, 26, 171n16
Public Enemy (Wellman), 37, 41
Puzo, Mario. See *Godfather, The*

Racketeer Influenced and Corrupt Organizations Act of 1970 (RICO), 13, 25, 29–30, 47, 88, 171n17, 174n70, 177n29. *See also* Kennedy, Robert F.; Shur, Gerald; Witness Protection Program
Ragged Dick (Alger), 39–40, 41, 102, 117
Ranalli, Ralph, 22
RAND Corporation, 56–57, 132, 133, 177n29; Habitual Criminals Program, 14
Rapping, Elayne, 7
Rathbone, Cristina. See *World Apart, A*
Reagan, Ronald, 120
Redding, Stan, 11, 99, 116
Reiner, Robert, 6
responsibilization, 9, 110, 113, 115–16; and "only you" refrain, 110
Rhodes, Robert P., 1, 8, 9, 86, 114; on victimization surveys, 115
Rich, Frank, 160
Richardson, Elliott, 85
Rierden, Andi. See *The Farm*
Riis, Jacob, 134
risk and risk management, 8, 9, 15, 16, 19, 56, 76, 80, 86, 113, 114–16, 118, 133, 167n15; CompStat and, 58; incapacitation and, 15–16; private security and, 101, 109–12, 114–16, 118, 119–20
Rose, Charlie, 161–62, 163
Rosenzweig, Andy, 89–97, 136, 154, 162. See also *Cold Case, A*
Ruggierio, Vincenzo, 27
Runyon, Damon, 117

Santayana, George, 63
Saxbe v. Washington Post Co., 120
Scarry, Elaine, 51, 58, 76
Scheingold, Stuart, 4, 8, 13
Schlosser, Eric. *See* prison-industrial complex
Scorsese, Martin. See *GoodFellas*
Sebold, Alice. See *Lovely Bones, The*
Seltzer, Mark, 49
Serpico: book (Maas), 55; film (Lumet), 56
Serpico, Frank, 54, 55, 56, 90
shadowing and shadow narratives, 101, 104–7
Shame of the Cities, The (Steffens), 159, 164
Shearing, Clifford, 15
Sheehan, Susan. See *Prison and a Prisoner, A*
Shur, Gerald, 22, 30
Simon & Schuster, 37
Simon, David. See *Homicide: A Year on the Killing Streets*
Simon, Jonathan, 3, 5, 8, 14, 57; on micropolitical steering mechanisms, 9, 79
Singer, Isaac Bashevis. See "Crown of Feathers, A"
Sing Sing Correctional Facility at Ossining, New York, 123, 129, 134–42, 189n18
Siringo, Charlie, 105–6
Skakel, Michael, 81, 85
Skolnick, Jerome, 8, 51
Smilla's Sense of Snow (Høeg), 153–54, 160, 161
Smits, Jimmy, 59, 61
Soliah, Kathleen. *See* Olsen, Sarah Jane
"Son of Sam" Legislation, 46, 62, 96
Sopranos, The (TV series), 40, 41
Spielberg, Stephen, 120. See also *Catch Me If You Can; Minority Report*
Stanko, Elizabeth, 8, 13, 114, 157
Steffens, Lincoln, 26, 34, 164. See also *The Shame of the Cities*
Stenning, Philip C., 15
Stiehm, Meredith, 78, 83, 92, 94, 157. See also *Cold Case* (CBS TV series)
Stone, Albert, 31
Supreme Judicial Court of Massachusetts, 23

Talese, Gay, 28
terrorism, war on: cross-currents with domestic war on crime, 161–64
Thinking about Crime (Wilson), 15–16, 19, 80; on incapacitation, 132–33, 141
Thomas, Paul, 75
Tocqueville, Alexis de, 123, 138, 140
Tom Sawyer (Clemens), 103, 118
Tramping with Tramps (Flynt), 103, 104, 107, 108
True Blue: The True Stories Behind NYPD Blue (Clark and Milch), 60–76
Trump, Donald, 102
Turkus, Burton B. See *Murder, Inc.*

Uniform Crime Reports, 54; compared to victimization surveys, 114

Valachi, Joseph, 11. See also *Valachi Papers, The*
Valachi Papers, The (Maas), 24, 27, 31–36, 56; Castellammarese War in, 31; class outlook of Valachi in, 33–34; corporate theme in, 34, 35; ethnicity in, 32, 34; form and style of, 34–36; informant situation in, 31, 33–34; legal situation surrounding, 32; Valachi's own manuscript and, 32–34; Valachi Senate testimony and, 31–32; *Wise Guy* compared to, 38, 39, 42
Van den Haag, Ernest, 133
Vario, Paul, 39, 40, 44
victimization surveys, 12, 86, 114–15; contrasted to Uniform Crime Reports, 114, 182n34
victims and victim's rights, 4, 7, 8, 9, 11, 46, 65, 66, 80, 86, 93–95; identity theft and, 111; legislation on, 4; statutes of limitations and, 12, 14–15, 79, 95–96; victim circle, 78, 83, 86, 95, 183n59, 193n15
Vidocq, Eugène François, 98, 101, 106, 185n14
Vidocq Society (Philadelphia), 98
Violence Crime Control and Law Enforcement Act (1994), 4–5

"Wakefield" (Hawthorne), 108
Walker, Samuel, 5
Wambaugh, Joseph, 49, 191n40
Ward, Benjamin, 57, 127
Warren, Robert Penn, 53, 63, 75
Warshow, Robert. *See* "Gangster as Tragic Hero, The"
Weed, Frank, 4
Western Penitentiary (PA), 142, 147–50, 151–52
Wideman, John Edgar and Robert. See *Brothers and Keepers*
Wild, Jonathan, 102
Willard, Frances, 103
Willard, Josiah Flynt. *See* Flynt, Josiah
Wilson, James Q., 5, 8, 76, 114; on incapacitation, 15–16, 132–33; on prison sentencing and "human nature," 133. *See also* Broken Windows Philosophy; *Thinking about Crime* (Wilson)
Wilson, Pete, 128
Wilson, William Julius, 145
Wise Guy: Life in a Mafia Family (Pileggi), 11, 24, 36–45, 47–48, 156; Alger template in, 39–40; anthropological rationale of, 37; Boston College point-shaving scandal in, 37, 44–45; class outlook of Henry Hill in, 40–41, 42, 47; ethnicity and, 39, 40, 42, 47–48; *Godfather* repudiations in, 37, 39, 40; informant situation in, 41, 43–44, 45–46, 48; Supreme Court case involving, 46
Wistrich, Andrew J., 96
Witness Protection Program (WITSEC), 11, 13, 25, 30; as intelligence gathering, 30; differences from earlier witness protection practices, 29–30; Henry Hill in, 37, 41, 44, 45–46, 47; scandals involving, 30
Wolf, Dick, 49, 52
Wolin, Sheldon, 13
World Apart, A (Rathbone), 127, 128–29, 134

Young, Deborah, 59

zero tolerance, 2, 4, 16, 80, 150

www.ingramcontent.com/pod-product-compliance
Lightning Source LLC
Chambersburg PA
CBHW020947230426
43666CB00005B/205